AUTHORSHIP ROLES IN POPULAR MUSIC

Authorship Roles in Popular Music applies the critical concept of auteur theory to popular music via different aspects of production and creativity. Through critical analysis of the music itself, this book contextualizes key concepts of authorship relating to gender, race, technology, originality, uniqueness, and genius and raises important questions about the cultural constructions of authenticity, value, class, nationality, and genre. It visits areas as diverse as studio production, composition, DJing, collaboration, performance and audience using a range of case studies such as:

- Tamla Motown, PWL/Stock, Aitken and Waterman, and the idea of the music studio as auteur
- Procol Harum's "A Whiter Shade of Pale" court ruling and how performers assume authorship
- Gender, genre, critical status, degrees of autonomy and the careers of Kate Bush, Madonna, Bjork, and Beyoncé
- Phil Spector, George Martin, Daft Punk and how record producers assume authorial status
- Popular music consumption, appreciation, and how scenes and communities help shape creative and authorial choices

Authorship in Popular Music is an essential introduction to the critical issues and debates surrounding authorship in popular music. It is an ideal resource for students, researchers, and scholars in popular musicology and cultural studies.

Ron Moy is Lecturer in the School of Media, Critical and Creative Arts at Liverpool John Moores University, UK.

AUTHORSHIP ROLES IN POPULAR MUSIC

Issues and Debates

Ron Moy
Liverpool John Moores University

Routledge
Taylor & Francis Group

NEW YORK AND LONDON

First published 2015
by Routledge
711 Third Avenue, New York, NY 10017

and by Routledge
2 Park Square, Milton Park, Abingdon, Oxon, OX14 4RN

Routledge is an imprint of the Taylor & Francis Group, an informa business

Library of Congress Cataloging-in-Publication Data
Moy, Ron, 1956– author.
  Authorship roles in popular music : issues and debates / Ron Moy,
Liverpool John Moores University.
    pages cm
  Includes index.
 1. Popular music—Writing and publishing. 2. Authorship—
Philosophy. 3. Popular music—History and criticism. I. Title.
  ML3800.M788 2016
  781.64—dc23
  2014048202

ISBN: 978-1-138-78067-5 (hbk)
ISBN: 978-1-138-78068-2 (pbk)
ISBN: 978-1-315-77055-0 (ebk)

Typeset in Bembo
by Apex CoVantage, LLC

Printed and bound in Great Britain by
TJ International Ltd, Padstow, Cornwall

CONTENTS

ACKNOWLEDGEMENTS

I would like to thank many work colleagues, past and present at Liverpool John Moores University who have provided me with so much companionship and support since 1992: Danijela Bogdanovic, Stuart Borthwick, Mike Brocken, Alex Germains, Ned Hassan, Simone Krüger (and thanks for her great help in writing the book proposal), Nickianne Moody and Julie Sheldon.

The scholarly work of many outside of my own institution has been of enormous benefit to my work, in particular I must mention (and recommend) the writings of: Philip Auslander, Hugh Barker & Yuval Taylor, Roland Barthes, Richard James Burgess, Judith Butler, Evan Eisenberg, Michel Foucault, Simon Frith, Kevin Holm-Hudson, Shane Homan, Carys Wyn Jones, Emma Mayhew, Allan Moore, Keith Negus and Michael Pickering, Simon Reynolds and Joy Press, Roy Shuker, Will Straw, Jason Toynbee, Virginia Wexman and Sheila Whiteley. My biggest thanks go to Laura Ahonen, whose pioneering work on authorship I discovered in the very earliest days of researching this subject. It has proven invaluable to me on so many occasions. Richard James Burgess also read a draft chapter and added much-needed technological and critical criticism. Kevin Holm-Hudson's comments on an early draft chapter and the final manuscript were very valuable and I would like to thank him for all his efforts, which have improved the book in many ways.

Many friends outside of academia have also helped me with informal discussions of music including: David Buckley, Brian and Rosemary Dunne, Ian and Jane Mills, Steve and Ruth Morley, Ian Runeckles and Brian Sharp.

This book would not have been possible without the inspiration of teaching so many lovely students far too numerous to name (or remember!). In particular Chris Cawthorne and Tony Turrell have provided me with material that I have included in this book.

Tony Turrell, Mike Brocken and Alex Germains have also been interviewed as part of this project and provided valuable insights from the industry and musician's perspective. Thank you all.

Three critical reviewers provided valuable advice during the planning stages of this book: one remains unknown, but my thanks to all of them, including Kevin Holm-Hudson and Nicola Spelman. Esperanza Miyake has my gratitude in correcting an early draft of one section. I would also like to thank all those at Routledge/Taylor & Francis for having faith in this project. Particular mention should go to Denny Tek, in the early stages and Denise File, who in the later stages was always so helpful in times of stress and confusion.

I would like to pay tribute to the many musicians whose work has provided me with both source material and boundless pleasure for the whole of my life. Particularly important in terms of this book has been the music of: Tori Amos, Ian Anderson/Jethro Tull, the Beatles, Björk, Black Sabbath, Kate Bush, Genesis, Goldfrapp, Liam Howlett/the Prodigy, Joni Mitchell, Janelle Monáe, Laura Mvula, Opeth, Nerina Pallot, Dawn Richard and Roy Wood. In addition, I would like to give collective thanks to the numerous musicians who worked on Motown, Philadelphia International and Invictus/Hot Wax recordings. I loved this music in my teens and I love it still.

My ageing body has benefitted from the devoted care of many staff working for the National Health Service. In particular, Dr Lucy Black and all those based in the Dermatology department at Leighton Hospital, Crewe deserve my boundless thanks.

Finally, I would like to thank my family, the thought of whom always gives me a warm glow: Anne, Byron and Elena; particularly Elena for her proof-reading and helpful suggestions. Prior to publication, she is the only person, apart from the author, to have read every word. I'll work on those excessive commas, my dear.

INTRODUCTION

> The search for an author, like any other quest for parentage, reveals more about the searcher than the sought.
>
> (Garber, 2008: 28)

We live in an age of biography. We live in the age of the Rowling (or Galbraith) novel, the Hirst artwork, the Gehry building, the Coen Brothers production, the Westwood collection, the Gucci handbag and the One Direction fragrance. The ghostwritten memoir or work of fiction is a long-established phenomenon, but in the contemporary era, certain titular authors are shameless in admitting to having no real creative input into the work that bears their name. It is almost as if their own star/celebrity status is considered totally separate from their assumed literary persona—authorship has many levels.

Within popular music, we have authorship that stretches from the traditional Bowie composition to the contemporary Dangermouse "mash-up", Stuart Price remix and Pharrell Williams' production. For the last few years, I have been based in a building formerly known as the Art and Design Academy; it has now been renamed the John Lennon Art and Design Academy. John Lennon already has an airport named after him (and all four members of the Beatles have streets named after them in Liverpool, including, more recently, early drummer Pete Best), but the reasons for not naming this building after the other members of the band are obvious when considering Lennon's global, authorial status. We have to accept that part of his legacy rests on his premature death. As opposed to Paul McCartney, Lennon's authorship has "closure". Unlike living authors, his status cannot be tainted by supposedly inferior works as he ages and his talent "declines".

The assignation of auteur status is not fair, logical or the result of a unified narrative. In addition, we have to consider what Laura Ahonen terms the "author image" (2008). This aspect has always been hugely significant for popular music. As an example, in 2013 more than half of the top 40 selling singles in the UK included a featured guest vocalist (Cragg, 2014: 4–6). The reasons for this are varied, but do indicate how widely the tentacles of iconic authorship reach.

On March 21, 2014, Kate Bush announced that she would be doing her first live dates for over three decades later in the year. This was a global news media story. On the following day, the *Guardian*, admittedly a liberal/left-leaning organization with a readership sympathetic to artists such as Bush, featured the news and a large colour photo of the artist on their print cover page (author and photographer uncredited). Page three was devoted to old and newer images of Bush, plus a feature story (Petridis) and a reprint of a review from a previous concert in 1979. On page nine, a full-page colour advertisement for Bush's upcoming concerts encourages us to view the news announcement as part of a media "tie-in", while on page thirty-one, a regular columnist devotes most of her space to an ecstatic response to the news (Orr, 2014). Even Bush's stated wish for attendees not to use camera phones at the concerts received wide publicity. Clearly done with the best intentions, issues of control and authorship are raised by such pronouncements.

As a long-standing admirer of Kate Bush, my surprise at her announcement to play live was probably superseded only by my surprise at the sheer amount of coverage. Part of the reason for this outpouring of publicity may lie in her accrued status and the chronological distance between the previous and forthcoming concerts. But part of it lies in the simple fact that, as many previously noted with regard to David Bowie's reemergence in 2013, *authorship really matters*. On the day following the first of her concerts, four UK national newspapers (*Daily Mail, Daily Telegraph*, the *Guardian* and the *Times*) featured a large photograph of Kate Bush from the previous night's stage show. It was the principal pictorial news story on all of the front covers. It is interesting to note that even the nature of the live events encourages a focus upon authorship. Rather than touring, Bush played multiple dates in the same venue. This was thus akin to notions of the "artist in residence", encouraging fans to embark on a romantic pilgrimage. Connotations of Wagner's productions at Bayreuth might be considered in this context (Holm-Hudson, 2014).

As a final aside on Bush's reemergence, if this amount of coverage is considered to be an example of hype, it works. After devouring all of the articles, I played her first album from start to finish for the first time in years, as well as ordered a DVD of her original concert tour. I also made a mental note that this development would provide me with more teaching material, and I would need to mention it in this book. Here it is.

Within what is now termed the "heritage industry", locations and cities (Abbey Road, New Orleans, Nashville, Tamla Motown Studios, etc.) promote heritage tourism based around mythical connections between location and musical creativity. According to Rebecca Sanders, in 2011 international star Rihanna was appointed as "Barbados Tourism Ambassador" for three years and her author images became an integral part of the promotional materials for the island (cited in Krüger and Moy, 2014: 59–86). Much of Liverpool's bid for European Capital of Culture status in 2008 was predicated on the city's authorship of a certain brand of popular music. For many years, it has been possible to tour specific sites relating to individual members of the Beatles' pasts (see Krüger and Trandafoiu, 2013). The city has made millions from global tourists seeking to make personal and authored connections between a place, an epoch and a series of popular music-based narratives. Mike Brocken has run a master's programme entitled *The Beatles: Popular Music and Society* at Liverpool Hope University for several years, as well as published widely in the field (Brocken, 2010; Brocken and Davis, 2012). This course recruits postgraduate researchers from all over the world. In an interview, Mike claimed that the Beatles, as both an authorial phenomenon and a prime example of popular music heritage, have helped to transform Liverpool, culturally and economically, over the past few decades (Brocken, personal interview, 2014). We should never overlook notions of base and superstructure when exploring the wider implications of authorship and heritage.

The author has become both a logo and a celebrity, stalked by paparazzi, feted with attention, awards, prizes and, in some cases, huge riches. In broad historical terms, we have moved through successive epochs that have seen the figure of the author (and the connected concept of authorship) slowly penetrate the mainstream of everyday culture. In the process, the figure of the author has moved from states of anonymity to those of vague, often esoteric, status and recognition, and from periods (such as the Romantic) that have lauded the author only then to see authorial status challenged or partially discounted (the Modern). During the course of this research, the notion of the world of popular music as essentially still romantic will be referenced. This book is not here to dismiss a romantic approach (centred on the transcendent powers of the individual) in totality, but rather to problematize many aspects of a romantic discourse relating to and built upon notions and myths of authorship.

In an increasingly fragmented and pluralistic era (what some might refer to as the contemporary and others as the postmodern), all unifying theories relating to authorship can be said to be, at the very least, open to challenge. Yet despite the lack of solid foundations on which to base any critical or philosophical treatise on the subject, authorship—sometimes explicitly, perhaps more often implicitly—remains a key signifier. In part, this comes about through its broad applications. Equally, its close connection to other weighty concepts such as creativity, value, culture, status, convention, individuality, uniqueness and genius accounts for its continuing presence within the worlds of criticism, analysis and appreciation.

Michel Foucault's theories relating to discourses surrounding areas such as sexuality, deviance and, indeed, authorship are equally applicable to the specific referent of popular music. Foucault's observation in *The History of Sexuality* that "we are dealing less with *a* [his emphasis] discourse on sex than with a multiplicity of discourses produced by a whole series of mechanisms operating in different institutions" (1978: 33) is equally relevant to discursive discussions surrounding popular music authorship and its issues and debates. Foucault's explorations illuminate contexts of philology, ethics, morality, jurisprudence and culture in addition to the core topics under scrutiny. He argues that so much comes back to the overarching concept of power: "It is in discourse that power and knowledge are joined together" (Ibid: 100). Therefore, the discourse(s) of authorship and mythical and actual power structures will be central to the discussions in subsequent chapters.

In his essay "What Is an Author?" (1977), Foucault states that he "wanted to locate the rules that formed a certain number of concepts and theoretical relationships in their works" (1977: 114) rather than mentioning authors' names. His explorations largely eschew notions of biography and causation, but he also recognizes the implicit contradictions in pursuing such a position: "If an individual is not an author, what are we to make of those things he has written or said?" (Ibid: 118). Writings are authored; Foucault authored; this book is authored. But "problems arise in the use of an author's name. What is the name of an author? How does it function" (Ibid: 121)? Foucault argues that we can use the metaphorical disappearance of the author and exploit the "gaps and fault lines" (Ibid). This is classic deconstruction, reveling and exploiting inconsistencies in order to advance our understanding of the discourses at play within the authorship debate. "The proper name and the name of the author oscillate between the poles of description and designation" (Ibid), or as it could be termed, *assumed* and *assigned* roles. These roles are not singular. One of Foucault's principal author functions "does not refer, purely and simply, to an actual individual insofar as it simultaneously gives rise to a variety of egos and to a series of subjective positions that individuals of any class may come to occupy" (Ibid: 130–131). This notion of subjective positions can be applied not only to musicians, performers and technicians but also to audiences, scenes and "mere listeners".

The contemporary era has witnessed the development and growth in status of new art forms: electronically mediated modes of communication such as cinema, popular music and recent innovations such as those made possible by digital micro-technologies. All of these new developments reflect upon the concept of authorship and ask us to reappraise our own individual value systems. To take one example, during the latter part of the twentieth century, the world of conventional cinema criticism was shaken by the writings of a small group of film critics, many based in France, who formulated a new way of approaching cinema through a position variously known as *la politique des auteurs*, or rendered in English as auteur theory or auteurism. In a sense, film criticism was only engaging in similar debates as those that had already taken place within the worlds of literature or painting. Auteur theory soon splintered and fragmented, as all theories do. Indeed, a whole body of recent film criticism has expressly opposed the theory. Its great legacy was both to broaden the critical terrain upon which film could be judged and also to galvanize the world of criticism itself.

Existing Sources: Popular Music Authors on Authorship

Popular music theory, as an even younger discipline than film theory, has become a remarkably broad school of criticism, teaching and analysis, particularly over the past forty years. Having said that, I speak as someone who has spent this entire period as a fan of the form, over twenty years as a student and then as an academic in the subject field. The *relative* absence of the *explicit* issue of authorship within popular music studies has long been perplexing. As Laura Ahonen notes, "Until recently, popular music studies have typically treated authorship as just that: authorship is something that exists, but it receives no special attention, at least not from a theoretical or philosophical point of view" (2008: 13).

Of course, biographical accounts of popular music figures, particularly those of so-called "iconic" status (for example, Dylan, Springsteen, Madonna), have concentrated on notions of authorship or rather the star/image dimensions of what Michel Foucault called "the author function" (1991). However, both biographies and less artist-centred critical accounts have partially avoided engaging with the deeper critical and aesthetic implications raised by the paradigm.

There is little place for explicit authorship debates in compilations such as *The Popular Music Studies Reader* (Bennett, Shank and Toynbee, 2006), with the notable exception of Toynbee's own essay (Ibid: 71–77). In overall terms, the same is true of Christoph Cox and Daniel Warner's collection of essays dealing with modern music (2004) and Karen Kelly and Evelyn McDonnell's edited collection of papers entitled *Stars Don't Stand Still in the Sky: Music and Myth* (1999). This is despite the fact that this wide-ranging collection consistently engages with a deconstruction of romantic mythologies of authenticity held by diverse groups such as audiences, critics and the industry. Nevertheless, the concept of authorship is not broached as part of this exploration of myth. Authorship is more typically discussed within individual essays or sections within edited collections (see section III within Washburne and Derno, 2004, by way of example).

It is my contention that authorship demands and deserves a more comprehensive focus.

Equally, in a wide-ranging collection of essays entitled *Expression in Pop/Rock: Critical and Analytical Essays* (2008), Walter Everett mainly concentrates upon formal musicology. In addition, attempts by single scholars to offer a summary of the critical field, such as Tim Wall's *Studying Popular Music Culture* (2003), chose not to foreground authorship as a cultural concept despite dealing with areas as broad as history, industry, form, meaning and audiences. However, for the most part, I do not intend to take an oppositional approach to others' work, although there will inevitably be moments when strong differences do emerge in this study. It is not a matter of apportioning blame if others choose not to focus on authorship. Rather, I simply refer back to authorship's puzzling absence as an explicit concept.

Mention should be made of the work of Roy Shuker at this point. Across several texts (for instance, 2008 and 2012) primarily concerned with a holistic analysis of popular music, Shuker returns to the concept of authorship and associated fields such as genre and the "canon" on a number of occasions. Although his focus is too broad to devote much space to the specifics of the authorship discussion, his work is an excellent overview of some of the more salient issues and debates. Shuker often talks explicitly about authorship, but usually within one section that is part of a more comprehensive analysis of popular music texts and culture. His focus upon "the dynamic interrelationship of the production context, the texts and their creators, and the audience for the music" (2008: 47) indicates a desire to move beyond outdated notions of the auteur. In particular, his writings on authorship and stardom (Ibid: 68–71) and genre and the canon (Ibid: 119–135) in *Understanding Popular Music Culture, Third Edition* (2008) establish this critical terrain very economically. In addition, it would be remiss not to mention Simon Frith's work, in particular *Performing Rites: Evaluating Popular Music* (1998). In this text, Frith deals principally with aesthetics but does engage with authorship implicitly and sometimes explicitly. His work is a valuable source for many that follow, including Ahonen.

In the aforementioned texts, authorship is, in fact, an often ghostly presence, subsumed beneath signifiers such as "authenticity", "agency" or "identity" (see Ahonen, 2008: 13). Authenticity and authorship, in particular, are closely linked. However, authenticity paradigms are ultimately connected to notions of assumed worth. Conversely, authorship is less concerned with worth; an authored work is no guarantor of intrinsic value. Authorship is more concerned with individual and social roles and with the *perception* of those roles. Admittedly, this will often return us to constructions of value, but these may well be predicated on different discourses from those attached to notions of authenticity. Thus, while authenticity, agency and identity are all key concepts, I would argue that they are also all authoring processes because they are *transformational*. Rather than being stable, they are all both "written" by individuals and also written about, and as a consequence, the discourse of authorship is a foundation or a touchstone for so much in popular music.

Keith Negus and Dave Hesmondhalgh talk of the participants in popular music debates seeking to "address the relationships between musical meaning, social power and cultural value" (2002: 7). This is a fair summary of the central concerns of the critical field. Authorship can be said to intercede into all these areas, but its importance is not often made manifest: "authorship is something that exists, but it receives no special attention" (Ahonen, 2008: 13). The reasons for this are doubtlessly complex and will be explored in depth throughout this book. What must be the first task, however, is to acknowledge those existing principal writers' sources whose pioneering work has helped inform my own research. The second task will be to trace the historical development of the authorship debate itself before returning to explore its partial absence from the world of popular music studies.

Several works, in particular the investigations of Laura Ahonen (2008), Paul Auslander (2006, 2008), Keith Negus and Michael Pickering (2004), Will Straw (2000) and Jason Toynbee (2000), have proven a provocative and educational influence during the research for this book. Although, as the title *Creativity, Communication and Cultural Value* suggests, the concept of authorship is neither fundamental nor the central conceptual concern for Negus and Pickering; what they do promote is both a holistic and philosophical questioning of the authorship issue in its broadest sense, while also providing a mechanism and structure that allows for this debate to take place. By giving chapters metaphysical titles such as "Creation", "Experience", "Industry", "Convention", "Tradition", "Division" and "Genius", investigations can range widely across historical periods, texts and social contexts. Their central thesis seems to lie within the questioning and critical deconstruction of dichotomies, such as seeing innovation and tradition, exceptionality and the everyday, individuality and collectivism, or commerce and creativity as necessarily in opposition. When they state that "the label creativity provides a means of according value and establishing a cultural hierarchy" (2004: 48), I see their work, if I may be presumptuous, as running in parallel to my own, albeit operating in a more sociological and widely focused terrain. What they have tried to do in exploring concepts of creativity, I am trying to do in the field of authorship in popular music.

As well as being grounded in the sociological work of major figures such as Pierre Bourdieu, the authors are also vehement that what they term "spirituality" (Ibid: viii) remains an important dimension within both creativity and its cultural appreciation. Although I prefer terms such as "transformative" to spirituality (to escape the religious connotations), all authors must recognize (using whatever term they see fit) the importance and centrality of transcendental moments when processes of creativity result in the feeling that time has stood still or the writer/reader has entered a state of "dreamtime" or epiphany—what Roland Barthes would perhaps refer to as "jouissance" (1977). Nonetheless, at the same time, such moments can only be realized by building upon more prosaic elements such as structured and logical thought, accurate memory and biographical general knowledge. In this manner, Negus and Pickering's questioning (yet acknowledgement) of dichotomies can be brought to bear on all of our creative experiences. Thus, critically loaded terms such as genius are shown to be potentially divisive and elitist, yet still capable of rehabilitation within their rationale:

> Our preference is for an understanding of creativity which embraces both the ordinary and exceptional in terms of their productive tension. This is as true of works and performances to which genius is attributed as it is of those which are evaluated as relatively minor.
>
> (2004: 159)

Such a position, expressed as a way beyond traditional (and counter-traditional) values, is articulated in many different contexts throughout this book. The notion of popular music as both ordinary and exceptional is one that the authorship debate can fruitfully explore. In the process, Negus and Pickering's sociological theories can be adapted to the more grounded terrain of specific case studies and the semiotics of popular music authorship.

Toynbee has conducted valuable research in the field that does incorporate musical case studies. His investigations into the working methods of jazz musician Charles Mingus show that dialogue between the singular author and the collective/collaborative notion of what he calls "social" (Toynbee, 2000: 73) authorship is an important precursor for subsequent debates within rock and pop. However, his work has still been primarily concerned with the workings of the industry, and his focus upon "a radius of creativity" surrounding areas of political economy, commercial institutions and the market for music moves it into a more sociological terrain than one I intend to adopt. His chapter on dance music is very valuable, not least for indicating how much the critical terrain within the field of authorship has shifted in the several years since he researched the genre.

Will Straw's brief overview of authorship in a collection of essays dealing with key terms within the field successfully summarizes many of the most pertinent elements of the issue. As he states, it is important not to overlook the more prosaic dimensions of authorship. It is as much about an industrial process built upon "protected investments" (2000: 201), "order" and "predictability" (Ibid: 203) as upon artistic values of aesthetics and creativity. Timothy Corrigan talks about "the commerce of auteurism" and its links to stardom and celebrity (cited in Wexman, 2003: 96–111). In addition, the profit motive should also never be overlooked. Statistics indicate that in 2006, shortly before downloading and streaming really made inroads into physical sales, one hit single would earn a writer, in one year, between \$200,000 and \$500,000, which doubled if the writer owned the publishing rights in the US alone (cited in Plasketes, 2010: 223–224). Thus, in crude terms, an authored pop song makes the writer a millionaire and guarantees an ongoing income. Whether the paltry income that accrues from downloading and streaming renders this traditional source of income less relevant in the future is a moot point at present (Holm-Hudson, 2014).

Straw also articulates many of the challenges to orthodox auteur theory, as it developed in France in the 1950s, by drawing upon the work of post-structuralists such as Roland Barthes and Michel Foucault (already referenced). In short, such writers challenged the hegemony of the "Author-God" (Barthes, 1977), although Foucault's notion of the author function is a more nuanced stance than Barthes' admittedly influential author "assassination". Foucault recognized the limitations of the auteur, but also acknowledged the social need for such a construct and such a discourse. Perhaps my own stance is closest to this, the position of a dissident akin to those critics who Straw showed had countered the myth of the director as sole auteur in film discourse to suggest "that actors, cinematographers or producers might be equally entitled to stand there" (2000: 199). If we substitute the cinematic role with musical roles hitherto thought subservient to the author such as session players, remixers and social authors, the audience notions of the "Author-God" can be challenged by more collective and less hierarchical authorial roles in popular music.

As a final observation, Straw indicates that authorship is about process and change, with certain musical developments such as disco and subsequent electronic dance genres posing a challenge to rock authorship: "The history of popular music is marked by movement back and forth between collective tradition and moments of individual transformation of that tradition" (Ibid: 201). Thus, debates and issues are central to the question of authorship, as the title of my book makes clear.

One more recent writer who has conducted empirical analyses of authorship and made case studies fundamental to her thesis has been Ahonen (2008). Ahonen's research into the area has set the standard for work to follow. As an ethnographer, she is interested in areas such as *author image* and its public perception, particularly in the new realms of internet chat rooms and blogs. In her own words, "the focus of the study [lies] . . . in the ways in which these images are produced, distributed and consumed" (Ibid: 17). Although visual dimensions are particularly important, Ahonen does also pay close attention to musical aspects in certain chapters. As well as acknowledging (and being puzzled by) the absence of authorship from popular music discourses (Ibid: 13), Ahonen is quick to acknowledge that different criteria apply in music as distinct from literary criticism. She recognizes the essentially mediated world in which pop operates and divides her analysis of author image into three areas: *presented author image* (image constructed by the artist and/or the marketing industry), *mediated author image* (image constructed by the media) and *compiled author image* (image constructed by the audience members) (Ibid: 18–22).

Ahonen's valuable and painstaking work is the single most comprehensive overview of the authorship question yet published within popular music studies. This book is indebted to her research. However, as an ethnographer most concerned with placing authorship in its social context, her approach differs from my own author-based exploration of roles and its more text-based slant. I am less concerned with mediated image and interviews with music-makers (although they do feature when appropriate), and more concerned with the music itself and how authorship debates and issues influence our own aesthetics. My explorations will be as much about how roles within music-making and music consumption help articulate the concept of authorship as about the authors themselves. The core of my research lies in the investigation of *assumed* and *assigned* roles. In addition, within Ahonen's study, while the notion of gendered authorship is a topic of exploration in several sections, gender itself is deliberately overlooked as a "stand-alone section", with Ahonen seeing it as an area "for future studies" (Ibid: 198). It will be noted that the structure of this book sets aside its focus upon a specific authorial role in each chapter only once, in order to explore the overarching area of gender. As a linked topic, gender and authorship is too important to be situated within discussions of technology, marketing or audiences, for instance. In arguing that constructions of authorship have been fundamentally hierarchical and patriarchal, the gender issue demands its own chapter, partly to build more comprehensively upon the work of others in the field.

My approach will reflect closely upon the teaching and research that I have carried out for many years. Among my most valuable critical touchstones have always been Roland Barthes' explorations of myth (1977: 165–169). Myth functions to naturalize a historical process, such as that surrounding authorship. This often results in a hierarchical and self-fulfilling set of assumptions that become inscribed canonically in culture and aesthetics. Myths must be deconstructed, but not obliterated, and this applies equally to myths surrounding authorship. They have important roles to play, not least because mythic constructions of authorship give people *pleasure*. As I always say to students, like what you want to like, admire or love who you want to admire or love, but be self-aware of the processes at play; this will then help deconstruct the canon of worth and value, but not the individual experiences themselves. This sounds incredibly pompous, but as a result, we will like what we like for the right reasons—ones that validate our own critical constructions—and not be merely in the thrall of others.

When focusing upon authorship, one must always be aware that the search for self-identity (or the *authoring* of the self) runs alongside the larger investigation into identity itself; as the quotation that prefaces this section suggests, it can be more about the searcher rather than the sought (Garber, 2008: 28). Outdated distinctions relating to the active creator and the passive consumer must be challenged. As John Fiske noted, there are no consumers, only "circulators of meaning" (1989: 27).

Despite my desire to at least attempt to break new ground, albeit by building upon the work of others, there are areas within the authorship debate that I do not have the space (not the knowledge) to cover. In particular, formal explorations of technology, political economy and the workings of the music industry will only be covered in passing rather than being granted discrete sections. However, Toynbee has already covered these dimensions in some detail (2000). In addition, Ahonen's work (2008) within areas such as video and author image provides a very good overview of these aspects. While not ignoring music and musicians, Auslander's work (2008) focuses more extensively upon performance, performing personae and the processes of what he terms "mediatization". In addition, he concentrates upon live settings. Thus, there is a small but crucial distinction between his interpretation of authorship roles and my own. While I am not rejecting the constructed nature of roles in popular music, my focus upon specific jobs (player, writer, producer, etc.) does place authorship in a different terrain than the more image-based *projections* of authorship found in the work of both Ahonen and Auslander.

Any other major omissions will need to be broached by those scholars who, in turn, will build upon existing research in the future. As John Berger concluded in his groundbreaking semiotic analysis of art and interpretation, all research must ultimately "be continued by the reader" (1972: 166).

All research into authorship is essentially philosophical and autobiographical. This factor alone differentiates and personalizes our work. There is much fresh research to be done within popular music studies and the study of authorship, but before beginning this task, authorship's more traditional, historical terrain must be sketched out.

A (Very) Brief History of the Authorship Question

This section cannot hope to provide the space (or, indeed, employ the expertise) needed to adequately cover a major philosophical debate that has flowed for over 2,000 years. All it can do is to illuminate some of the most salient issues pertinent to the debate, map some of the broad changes that have occurred, and then signal some of the ways that the debate can both shed light on its partial absence from popular music studies and on the reasons and ways in which it should assume a more prominent presence in the future. For more specialist or complex investigations of the authorship debate, readers are advised to explore the works of many of the writers whose work I can only summarize below (Ahonen, 2008; Bennett, 2004; Bourdieu, 1984; Burke, 1995 and 2008; Caughie et al., 1981; Kimmelman, 1999; Negus and Pickering, 2004).

In the mainly preliterate world, the author was often anonymous or merely the performer of works of poetry, lyrics or tales. What we call the oral tradition has rendered problematic the notion of authorship, with Andrew Bennett (2004: 28–38) suggesting that some authorial names may merely stand as singular symbols of a more collective compositional process. However, evidence certainly points to the assignable authorship of philosophers such as Plato and Socrates, who saw "the poet" (a kind of collective term for the author in ancient times) as one apart and through whom the gods speak. This position of seeing an author as a channel through which divine pronouncements merely pass is one that has continued to resonate through the ages, and it has only been comprehensively challenged over the past few centuries. The Greeks and Romans called the poet a diviner, seer or prophet (again, another critical stance that continues to hold much resonance for all students of authorship). Eammon Dunphy quoted John Lennon's quasi-mystical approach to authorship: "The real music comes to me, the music of the spheres, the music that passes understanding. . . . I'm just a channel. . . . I transcribe it like a medium" (Lennon, cited in Dunphy, 1987: 86). This position is symbolic of numerous neoclassical stances on authorship and creativity, and ones that still hold sway today in both contemporary criticism and art values and aesthetics.

The impact of organized religious systems upon aesthetics and philosophy was immense in the period following the fall of the Roman Empire, through the so-called "Dark Ages" (itself now proven a myth constructed by writers validating other eras of authorship) and the Medieval world. This vast tract of time is extremely difficult to summarize, but for the most part, scholars agree that the author in this period is still a largely anonymous or disregarded figure, taking (largely *his*) authority from a deity. There was also little practical advantage to knowing the identity of an author, with works mainly passed on verbally and within small, mostly oral circles.

The impact of printing was rapid by the standards of the time. In Britain, named authors such as Langland and Chaucer emerged by the late-fourteenth century. Despite Chaucer's modest self-assessment of his role as "compiler" of the *Canterbury Tales*, writers such as Burt Kimmelman have claimed that this early period of printed works allowed writers to "create opportunities for self-advancement, for recognition as individuals, through the very craft of authorship" (1999: 7). Interestingly, the linking of the terms author and authority is also said to date from this period, but for many writers, their authority was conferred posthumously. Over the next few hundred years, a widespread "culture of books" emerged, with the relative explosion of titles allowing for the construction of the individual authorial voice. By the seventeenth century, we can talk of the establishment of a form of canon as well as critical distinctions between the perceived vulgarities of commercial or professional writings and the mythological "purity" of the amateur at work (Bennett, 2004: 46–48). What is interesting is the extent to which many of the critical poetics of authorship continue to make an impact in the contemporary world, albeit in an often amended form. Commercialism can still be used as a negative signifier, while the elevated notion of art for art's sake has never been totally distinguished. Courtly patronage declined in the period following the Renaissance, to be partly replaced by the emergence of the more market-oriented publishing industry during the seventeenth and eighteenth centuries.

The emergence of copyright laws (for instance, the British Copyright Act of 1710), with its implications for "intellectual property", encouraged the transformation of nations into consumer societies and strengthened distinctions between works of marketable and intrinsic value. Bennett argued that such developments did much to remove the stigma from the writing profession (Ibid: 49). In addition, notions of remuneration and royalties were also drivers in the steady path toward the establishment of the cult of the autonomous, creative author.

Academics such as Seán Burke (1995) have signaled the Romantic period as one crucial to understanding the establishment of the modern notion of authorship and the author. Not only did romantic concepts of originality, genius and the sublime challenge the primacy of God the creator over the individual author, but also the cult of celebrity, so central to twenty-first century ideas of authorship, became more pronounced. This move has often been referred to using the metaphorical shift from that of the mirror to that of the lamp. Some of the more extreme manifestations of romantic authorship also allowed for the inevitable reassessments that followed in the Modernist interpretations of authorship that proceeded into the twentieth century. Although Modernist representations of authorship were far from consistent, there was certainly a tendency for the personalized author to be denied (or to be rendered irrelevant or incoherent for the likes of Joyce and Yeats). Conversely, the growth of the authorial memoir or autobiography was another feature of this epoch.

For Bennett, "professional academic criticism emerged in the late nineteenth and twentieth centuries" (2004: 73). This establishment of institutionalized criticism and literary analysis was built partly upon rejecting many Romantic tenets in favour of a more scientific rigour. Subsequently, a fragmentation and proliferation of critical stances relating to authorship issues was engendered, leading to formalism, feminism, New Historicism, New Criticism, structuralism, post-structuralism and postmodernism, which have all, to a certain extent, held some sway over the past century.

Various important developments relating to positions such as the "death of the author" (Barthes, 1977), the "intentional fallacy" (Wimsatt and Beardsley, originally published in 1946) and "écriture feminine" have possessed a radical dimension, while others can be seen merely to re-inscribe or amend established historical positions as the ebb and flow of the perceived status of author(s), work(s), individual readers and the reading community has made its mark upon the critical climate.

What must be emphasized is that almost all historical theories of authorship have either implicitly or explicitly focused upon individual acts of literary composition. For the most part, literary criticism has also heavily favoured text over context or artistic biography over political economy. It is not within the remit of this work to delve deeply into such debates. In particular, arguments relating to Barthes' polemic have raged in academic circles for decades (see Burke, 2008). But perhaps his most important contribution has been to problematize *authority* itself. Many have not appreciated the implicit mischief in Barthes' work (how can this author really subscribe to anything more than a symbolic or metaphorical death?). The author figure is not dead, or even terminally ill, but certainly the patient is under close observation.

"Everywhere, under the auspices of its absence, the concept of the author remains active" (Ibid: 165), but its claims to primary agency have been rendered unstable. Burke talks of the "need to arrive at a model of situated subjectivity" (Ibid: x) and that is indeed one of the principal goals in my subsequent investigations.

Contemporary technological and academic developments force us to challenge the primacy of any one element within such constructed dichotomies or binary oppositions (see Negus and Pickering, 2004). Many underlying concepts of authorship, some dating back hundreds or thousands of years, remain important, but the development of new fields of creativity and communication demand the establishment of new debates using innovative critical tools. In particular, the concept of authorship within popular music cannot be solely based upon prior models; its relationship to technology, collaboration and the market demands that new critical criteria are applied in addition to some long-established ones.

Before the concept of authorship within popular music is explored within a series of linked case studies, it is necessary to investigate how theories of authorship in another modern, collaborative field of communication, that of cinema, have developed over the past few decades. In a sense, these theories act as a valuable microcosm of the historical debates that took place prior to the form's emergence. Therefore, they can act to assuage, in part, the lack of space that I am able to devote to historical authorship discussions. In addition, they can also shed valuable light on popular music and its own authorship debates.

Authorship and Auteur Theory

As was the case when exploring the broad literary field of authorship analysis, this section cannot hope to do more than skim the surface when investigating film criticism's relationship to the same issue. Much of the criticism was originally published in French, but has recently been translated, deconstructed and become part of the critical canon. Edited collections such as Caughie (1981) and Wexman (2003) give a comprehensive overview of auteur theory and more recent critical developments (for example, psychoanalysis, feminism, discourse analysis, queer theory, minority cinema and questions of ownership and rights). Ahonen has also offered a brief overview (2008: 78–85). All of which I can only attempt to summarize.

Film and popular music share many characteristics, which will be mapped out below, but the first task is to historicize film theory and authorship. The early days of cinema saw very little accompanying criticism beyond fan-based accounts and star-system publicity. From around the 1930s, the impact of the growing canon, the development of what much later came to be termed art house, and the establishment of analytical journals (for instance, *Sight and Sound*, which was first published in 1932) all contributed to the validation process, which sought to present cinema as a serious art form worthy of intellectual scrutiny. Much the same process happened within popular music in later decades. Claims for the scriptwriter, the producer, or the studio to be assigned the chief authorial role had all been made in the cinema's early period. Andrew Sarris quotes novelist Gore Vidal, who, doubtless as a consequence of his profession, disparaged the director-as-auteur position: "Movies are stories; only writers can tell stories. So the wrong people are making the movies. . . . We do need the cameraman, the editor. But above all we need the script" (Sarris quoting Vidal, cited in Wexman, 2003: 23). However, such positions became increasingly eccentric in the years following World War II, when the widespread assignation of authorship to the director became the orthodox critical stance. This position is still maintained: "the assumption that directors hold the keys to a film's quality is accepted as a given in most movie reviews" (Wexman, 2003: 1).

A prime mover in the elevation of the role of the director was the work of a group of mostly French critics working on the journal *Cahiers du Cinema* in the 1950s. Writers such as François Truffaut, Eric Rohmer and Claude Chabrol helped formulate the position summarized as *La Politique des Auteurs* or the *Cinéma des Auteurs*. This position, although never unified or without schisms, proved hugely influential upon both British and American film criticism, with later critics such as Peter Bogdanovitch (also a director, it should be noted), Pam Cook, Colin McCabe, Andrew Sarris and journals such as *Movie, Screen* and *Film*

Culture all actively drawing upon auteur theory in order to discuss film, challenge its tenets and adapt new positions (Wexman, 2003: 1–18).

French auteur theory did operate using some basic assumptions, which can be broadly paraphrased in these terms:

1. Film is a collective medium, but is critically considered to possess more value if it can be essentially assigned to an individual director's will or style.
2. If the director is seen to be an artist, the film will be an expression of an individual personality.
3. This artistic personality can be traced through a thematic and/or stylistic consistency over all, or most, of the director's films.
4. There are clear distinctions between artistic auteurs and uncreative, "journeyman" directors or *metteurs-en-scène*.

It can be said that early auteur theory attempted to reconnect the director with the figure of the romantic artist and was, in a sense, going against the grain of "new" literary criticism at the time through the notion of attributing value in this fixing of meaning (Ahonen, 2008: 78–80). In its attempt to valorize commercial cinema (sometimes above art cinema in seeing true artistry as coming about through working against [or in spite of] industry-based commercial constraints), early auteur theory was also countering the traditional literary critical dichotomies relating to genre, art and mass culture. Thus, Wexman can talk of Hollywood "marketing directors as saleable commodities" (2003: 1). Auteur theory was more in step with many twentieth century critical developments in its insistence on detailed close analysis of deep structures and *mise-en-scène*. Film was fun, but it was also art and needed to be taken seriously despite being largely driven by economic narratives, as was the star system (see Goodwin, 1993: 32). Auteurism was thus rigorous, yet openly valued enthusiasm and emotions in its criticism; it was romantic yet progressive in essence. Later developments of auteur theory, particularly in the liberal atmosphere of 1960s criticism, resulted in a more nuanced form of analysis that became more of an attitude than a theory and that recognized contradictions, looked more closely at the industry and genre, and saw auteur theory as merely one facet capable of generating meaning. Post-structuralist theories of authorship "present their makers not as originary artists but as transmitters of cultural knowledge" (Wexman, 2003: 12).

Contemporary director Jim Jarmusch largely dismisses auteur theory, claiming to solely use the term "*a film by*, [his emphasis] as a protection of my rights" (cited in Ehrlich, 2014: 11). Conversely, some critics took auteur theory in a more semiotic direction or moved into psychoanalytical or feminist areas of scrutiny (see Silverman, cited in Wexman, 2003: 50–75).

It is clear that there are many connections between film and popular music. The breadth of these connections is worth further exploration at this point, in order to illuminate how both forms have been and can be connected to the issue of authorship:

> Many of the most widely recognized approaches to authorship have been developed with traditional forms in mind. When confronted with filmic or televisual works, critics are faced with special difficulties. Such texts are typically produced by groups, not individuals. Many are generated as part of gargantuan business enterprises in which the value of financial as well as aesthetic contributions must be weighed. Further, the technological resources that are mobilized in movie production raise the problem of distinguishing artists from technicians. In addition, films readily lend themselves to conceptualizations casting them as mechanical reproductions of a pre-existing reality rather than as humanly crafted expressions of the imagination. Moreover . . . a film . . . exists not as a unique original object, but as a series of copies created from a negative functioning as a matrix. Finally, in contrast to high art forms such as poetry and painting, most films and television productions are intended to appeal to mass audiences who may lack the specialized educational backgrounds that could enable them to appreciate subtleties of style and imagery.
>
> (Wexman, 2003: 7–8)

Barring the fact that, unlike film, music in its purest form has no external referent, in essence, all of Wexman's other points can be seamlessly applied to popular music. Equally, *Cahiers'* four tenets have also all been applied in examples of popular music criticism, but being essentially evaluative and ideological, such applications are more open to challenge. Bennett accounts for the contradiction between authorship as singular and unique and its wide adoption in the collaborative world of film by stating, "In retrospect, the whole project of *auteur* theory and *auteurist* film analysis . . . suggests above all the seemingly ineluctable cultural desire for the author" (2004: 107). Bearing in mind that authorship theories and film have, as a result of this cultural imperative, been closely linked for over fifty years, one could therefore logically assume that the same connection would be true for authorship and popular music, but this is just not so. It is the complex reasons for this to which I must now turn.

As previously established, the similarities between film and popular music are many and wide-ranging. We can also make some homological connections between the constituent roles in the two forms. For the actors, we can talk of the musicians or singers; for the technical staff, the studio employees; for location staff, the road crew; for the script or screenplay writer(s), we can forward the equivalent of the songwriters (formerly often separate from the players but increasingly since the 1960s performing dual roles); and for the film director, we can substitute the record producer. There are, of course, differences across these linked roles, but there are also parallels. However, in response to Wexman's widely held conclusion that the director holds the key to the film's quality (and this is open to dispute), who would be the equivalent figure in popular music? There is no obvious candidate. No single role or position possesses the same status or has been critically invested with the same degree of authorship as that of the director. The reasons for this are varied and will be explored in the chapters ahead. But if authorship is assigned to one figure (or, to a lesser extent, a group of figures or an organization) in popular music theory, it is, more often than not, assigned on the basis of pop's equivalent signifiers to authorship, drawing upon key terms such as creativity and authenticity.

The exciting thing about popular music and authorship is that there still seems more work to be done. This book seeks to build upon the works of many authors who have set out the appropriate critical terrain, many of whom have explored authorship in passing, essays or have explored the concept in a "parallel fashion".

Key terms such as authenticity, authorship and creativity all prompt parallel critical discourses, yet there remain important distinctions. Authorship analysis is as much about identification and assignation as it is about simple adjectival value. Although the term can never be totally value-free, it comes with less critical baggage than parallel terms. I would argue that this gives the critic more space for application, particularly through and with the assistance of what we can refer to as musicultural analysis. This dimension is one frequently overlooked in popular music studies. It is one that in my own untutored manner, I have been seeking to redress in all my research over the course of my academic career. Popular music studies, as a critical canon, lacks a sufficiently holistic analysis of questions of authorship that is grounded in examples, case studies and accessible close analyses of musical roles, texts and practices. This book is my attempt to cover such terrain.

Authorship: The Key Concepts

Below are summarized the principal critical concepts that I will be employing and exploring within this authorship debate. Some will be investigated further in the chapters ahead, but what they do in this brief form is answer the fundamental question that all researchers must initially ask of themselves—why bother?

1. Authorship has been seen as a symbol of our "developed society" that moves us beyond notions of the "primitive" or "oral-based". An exploration of this concept sheds valuable light on issues of race, ethnicity and "Eurocentrism".

2. Authorship's rise can be said to parallel the rise of the cult of the bourgeois individual, thus further informing discussions about the Western system of values and creativity. For Burke, "the figures of the author and the human subject are said to fill the theological void, to take up the role of ensuring meaning in the absence of metaphysical certainties" (2008: 21).

3. Authorship allows for the creation of hierarchies and distinctions. It allows us to explore the hugely important concept of myth and to problematize binary modes of thinking. In a similar vein to Negus and Pickering, my use of examples and case studies intend to draw upon authorship debates to show how they "bring high and low culture together in disqualification of the divide between them" (2004: 18).

4. Authorship has become intrinsically connected to the culture industry and the political economy of the creative world. It helps illuminate the creative tensions between different fields and ideologies. For Ahonen, "author images serve as a means of uniting and classifying everything an artist does into a coherent body of works" (2008: 54).

5. Authorship helps account for the growing cult of celebrity that many have seen as fundamental to the experience of the postmodern condition.

6. Authorship debates help dismantle the myth of the history of the "great white man" by making gender and class discussions central to our understanding.

7. Authorship encourages the illumination and problematizing of value-based systems of analysis and appreciation.

8. Authorship sheds light on the importance of etymology, philology and epistemology. The fact that my son is named Byron and my daughter is named Elena (and not the more usual [British] Eleanor) is not the result of a random choice but a symbolic representation of the authorship debate—as are many naming processes.

9. Authorship exposes and reflects upon the fundamental human need to identify, elevate and celebrate the sublime, transcendent or the spiritual dimensions of existence.

10. Notions of authorship give *pleasure*. It is fun to have author-figures and author-functions. Authorship fulfils a fundamental need. It allows "the products (to) appear unique and original and, thus, desirable" (Ahonen, 2008: 54).

This very brief summary has set out to establish some salient points relating to the development of theories of authorship. Perhaps the most important element to accommodate is the total lack of a unified or stable position. At its core, the authorship debate is essentially ideological and philosophical. In its pure, formalist state, the debate matters little to those outside of the academy or the critical journal. However, in its more applied and grounded manifestations, it matters a great deal to us all. Here are two empirical, "trivial" examples to help make this point and conclude this section.

Author! (ship) Author! (ship)

In 2008, during the period that may eventually prove to constitute the death throes of the CD, I was scanning the increasingly marginalized music shelves (much more space is now given over to "specular" media such as computer games, mobile phones and DVDs) in a local Woolworth store (talking of death throes . . .). CD prices had recently declined, with many bargains to be had, and my eye was attracted by a double CD compilation of ELO priced at only £2. I am not a huge fan of the band, but the price proved irresistible (raising notions of financial versus intrinsic "worth"). When I subsequently first listened to the recording, an experience doubtlessly familiar to many of us occurred: crowd noise indicated that this was a live performance. There is a long history of substandard CD recordings, many live, being sold to consumers under "false pretences", and I felt "had".

After my initial annoyance, I consulted the CD sleeve only to discover that in small, poor visibility print was the legend, "All tracks on this album are live recordings". So, it was my own fault for not wearing my glasses, although, implicitly, one might argue there was still an attempt to deceive (why not entitle the CD *ELO Live?*). Nonetheless, proceeding on the premise that I'd paid for it so I might as well listen to it, I sat down to do just that. The recording was very good quality, and the playing and vocal harmonies were particularly impressive. The lead vocals did sound different from the studio recordings, but bearing in mind the difficulty of singing live in front of an amplified band, and the fact that the recordings may well have occurred more than twenty years after the originals, I thought that leader Jeff Lynne didn't do a bad job. And yet, after a few tracks, I began to wonder if this was indeed Lynne. The sleeve notes seemed to offer no indication. However, as well as most of ELO's Lynne hit compositions, there were a number of, to me, unknown group compositions. They were clearly inferior in quality to Lynne's songs. Why were they there? Just to bulk out the double CD? Even the title of the CD was a mystery—*ELO II*. And then the penny dropped, not only was that the title of the album but also the name of the band. This was clearly the post-Lynne manifestation of ELO, renamed. I was now feeling doubly ripped off.

However, whoever was handling lead vocals was doing a pretty good job. He sounded pretty close to Lynne at times, and I began to reappraise the experience in light of my new conclusions. I ceased to feel exploited and foolish and started to appreciate the music for its own merits, no doubt still bolstered by the cheap price of my purchase (on one level, no longer quite the bargain, but on the other hand, still not a bad deal).

This experience raises many pertinent issues that are actually quite profound; it relates to notions of worth, economics, authenticity, authorship, marketing and aesthetic appreciation. Ultimately, it absolutely affirms Garber's conclusion that prefaces this whole introduction. Questions of authorship matter because they speak *us*, in helping to manifest all of our identity projections, self-perceptions and value systems. We author ourselves. The music is both the artistic text and the provider of a symbolic social and philosophical context. It provides aesthetic pleasure and furnishes us all with the means to reflect upon ourselves as individuals, as members of a society and upon that society itself. Not bad for £2.

From 1998 to 2001, the comedy series *Goodness Gracious Me* ran on British television. It featured Anglo-Asian actors and writers often parodying assumptions and mythologies based on ethnic stereotypes. Thus, a group of Asian actors would go out to a restaurant for "an English" and demand the blandest dish, to deconstruct the existing norm of a group of English people going to an Indian restaurant and ordering the hottest curry available. In another running sketch, a young anglicized man is confronted by his traditional father claiming almost everything and everyone is really "Indian!" I can identify with this as I have spent many a long hour reading scholarly texts dealing with a wide variety of topics, only to think or, on occasion, shout out my leitmotif—"Authorship!"

To end this introduction, I can only echo the process of illumination within *Goodness Gracious Me*, whereas in the past, theatre audiences might end the successful debut performance of a play with cries of "Author!", I can only commence my research by summoning the "absent episteme"—"Authorship!" As for the success of the project that follows, it can only be for others to judge, as authors of the reading experience.

Bibliography

Ahonen, Laura (2008) *Constructing Authorship in Popular Music: Artists, Media and Stardom*, Milton Keynes: VDM Verlag.

Auslander, Philip (2006) *Performing Glam Rock: Gender and Theatricality in Popular Music*, Ann Arbor: University of Michigan Press.

Auslander, Philip (2008) *Liveness: Performance in a Mediatized Culture*, London: Routledge.

Barthes, Roland (1977) "The Death of the Author", in *Image, Music, Text*, London: Fontana, pp 142–148.

Bennett, Andrew (2004) *The Author*, London: Routledge.

Bennett, Andrew, Barry Shank & Jason Toynbee (eds.) (2006) *The Popular Music Studies Reader*, Abingdon: Routledge.

Berger, John (1972) *Ways of Seeing*. London: BBC & Penguin.

Bourdieu, Pierre (1984) *Distinction: A Social Critique of the Judgement of Taste*, Cambridge: Harvard University Press.

Brocken, Mike (2010) *Other Voices: Hidden Histories of Liverpool's Popular Music Scenes, 1930s-1970s*, Farnham: Ashgate.

Brocken, Mike (2014) Personal interview, Comberbach, Cheshire, August 13.

Brocken, Mike & Melissa Davis (2012) *The Beatles Bibliography: A New Guide to the Literature*, Manitou Springs: The Beatles Works Ltd.

Burke, Seán (1995) *Authorship: From Plato to the Postmodern*, Edinburgh: Edinburgh University Press.

Burke, Seán (2008) *The Death and Return of the Author: Criticism and Subjectivity in Barthes, Foucault and Derrida*, Third Edition, Edinburgh: Edinburgh University Press.

Caughie, John, et al. (1981) *Theories of Authorship: A Reader*, London: Routledge.

Corrigan, Timothy (2003) "The Commerce of Auteurism", in Wexman, Virginia (ed.), *Film and Authorship*, New York: Rutgers University Press, pp 96–111.

Cox, Christoph & Daniel Warner (eds.) (2004) *Audio Culture: Readings in Modern Music*, New York: Continuum.

Cragg, John (2014) "Young Guns for Hire", *the Guardian G2*, 10 January, pp 4–6.

Dunphy, Eammon (1987) *Unforgettable Fire: The Story of U2*, London: Viking.

Ehrlich, David (2014) "Fangs for the Memories", *the Guardian Review*, 21 February, pp 10–11.

Everett, Walter (2008) *Expression in Pop-Rock: Critical and Analytical Essays*, Abingdon: Routledge.

Fiske, John (1989) *Understanding Popular Culture*, London: Unwin.

Foucault, Michel (1977) *Language, Counter-Memory, Practice: Selected Essays and Interviews by Michel Foucault*, Donald Bouchard (ed.), Ithaca: Cornell University Press.

Foucault, Michel (1978) *The History of Sexuality, Volume 1: An Introduction*, London: Allen Lane.

Foucault, Michel (1991) "What is an Author", in Rabinow, Paul (ed.), *The Foucault Reader*, London: Penguin.

Frith, Simon (1998) *Performing Rites: Evaluating Popular Music*, Oxford: Oxford University Press.

Garber, Marjorie (2008) *Profiling Shakespeare*, Abingdon: Routledge.

Goodwin, Andrew (1993) *Dancing in the Distraction Factory*, London: Routledge.

Holm-Hudson, Kevin (2014) Personal correspondence, December 1.

Horner, Bruce & Thomas Swiss (eds.) (2000) *Key Terms in Popular Music and Culture*, Oxford: Blackwell.

Kelly, Karen & Evelyn McDonnell (eds.) (1999) *Stars Don't Stand Still in the Sky: Music and Myth*, London: Routledge.

Kimmelman, Burt (1999) *The Poetics of Authorship in the Late Middle Ages: The Emergence of the Modern Literary Persona*, New York: Peter Lang.

Krüger, Simone & Ruxandra Trandafoiu (eds.) (2013) *The Globalization of Musics in Transit: Music Migration and Tourism*, London: Routledge.

Mayhew, Emma (2004) "Positioning the Producer: Gender Divisions in Creative Labour and Value", in Whiteley, Sheila, Andy Bennett & Stan Hawkins (eds.), *Music, Space and Place: Popular Music and Cultural Identity*, Aldershot: Ashgate, pp 149–162.

Negus, Keith & Dave Hesmondhalgh (eds.) (2002) *Popular Music Studies*, London: Arnold.

Negus, Keith & Michael Pickering (2004) *Creativity, Communication and Cultural Value*, London: Sage.

Orr, Deborah (2014) "One of My Best Parenting Achievements? I've Raised a Son Who Is a Kate Bush Fan", *the Guardian*, 22 March, p 31.

Osborne, Richard (2012) *Vinyl: A History of the Analogue Record*, Aldershot: Ashgate.

Petridis, Alexis (2014) "I've Come Home: 35 Years After She Last Toured, Bush to Play Live Again", *the Guardian*, 22 March, p 3.

Plasketes, George (ed.) (2010) *Play It Again: Cover Songs in Popular Music*, Farnham: Ashgate.

Sanders, Rebecca (2014) "Issues with Culture: Rihanna as the Tourism Ambassador for Barbados", in Krüger, Simone & Ron Moy (eds.), *Popscript: Graduate Research in Popular Music Studies*, Raleigh: Lulu Press, pp 59–86.

Sarris, Andrew (2003) "The Auteur Theory Revisited", in Wexman, Virginia (ed.), *Film and Authorship*, New York: Rutgers University Press, pp 21–29.

Shuker, Roy (2008) *Understanding Popular Music Culture*, Third Edition, Abingdon: Routledge.

Shuker, Roy (2012) *Popular Music Culture: The Key Concepts*, Abingdon: Routledge.

Silverman, Kaja (2003) "The Female Authorial Voice", in Wexman, Virginia (ed.), *Film and Authorship*, New York: Rutgers University Press, pp 50–75.

Straw, Will (2000) "Authorship", in Horner, Bruce & Thomas Swiss (eds.), *Key Terms in Popular Music and Culture*, Oxford: Blackwell, pp 199–208.

Toynbee, Jason (2000) *Making Popular Music: Musicians, Creativity and Institutions*, London: Arnold.

Toynbee, Jason (2003) "Making Up and Showing Off", in Bennett, Andy, Barry Shank & Jason Toynbee (eds.), *The Popular Music Studies Reader*, Abingdon: Routledge, pp 71–77.

Wall, Tim (2003) *Studying Popular Music Culture*, London: Arnold.

Washburne, Christopher & Maiken Derno (eds.) (2004) *Bad Music: The Music We Love to Hate*, New York: Routledge.

Wexman, Virginia (ed.) (2003) *Film and Authorship*, New York: Rutgers University Press.

Wimsatt, William & Monroe Beardsley (1946) "The Intentional Fallacy", *The Sewanee Review* 54(3), Baltimore, John Hopkins University Press, pp 468–488.

Audio-Visual Source

Goodness Gracious Me (1998–2001), Gareth Carrivick, Nick Wood & Christine Gernon (directors), television series, BBC.

1

THE STUDIO/LABEL AS AUTEUR

To begin the investigation into the concept of authorship, this chapter will initially explore some of the most nebulous areas related to the topic, such as time, space and place. These aspects will be critically grounded through an in-depth exploration of the output of the Tamla Motown record label (and associated contributors) during the period of its greatest critical and commercial impact (around 1964–1972). In addition, a comparative analysis of the work of the Invictus/Hot Wax studio (a contemporary and rival of Motown) and of the later British label PWL (itself evidently closely modeled on the Motown modus operandi) will further the debates into authorship and aesthetics.

Over the past couple of decades, Tamla Motown has been a fertile field of study for both popular music fans and academic researchers. Existing written sources range from the biographical and the hagiographic through the technological and musicological (by way of overview, see Early, 2004; George, 2003; Licks, 1989; Lodder, 2005; Posner, 2002; Smith, 1999; Werner, 1999). Such texts give the reader a comprehensive historical overview of the label, and that story does not need repeating here. What most accounts also share is an interest in what is generally referred to as the "Motown Sound". A mythology has been established that states that a relatively small family of musicians, writers, producers and business staff overseen by Berry Gordy Jr. all contributed to the construction of a recognizable and unique style or subgenre of music. This was integrally linked to a modest recording studio situated at 2648 West Grand Boulevard in Detroit known as "Hitsville U.S.A." (Licks, 1989: 13). In a sense, this studio and its label are granted authorial status. Indeed, in broader terms, Richard James Burgess notes that "some contracts refer to the label as the record producer or the producer" (2013: 1), so our first area of research must explore the process whereby a specific location and business organization can be vouchsafed a status granted to very few others in the field of popular music.

The Space and the Place

The Russian literary critic Mikhail Bakhtin popularized two concepts applicable to the explorations of this chapter. Bakhtin helped popularize the terms "chronotope" and "dialogic" (see Morris, 1994). While predating Motown (and not relating to popular music), the critical application of these concepts helps to account for, and also problematize, the authorial specificity of Motown. In short, a chronotope is a connection between time and space or "the intrinsic connectedness of temporal and spatial relationships that are artistically expressed" (Bakhtin, cited in Morris, 1994: 184). These two elements of time and space do not exist in isolation, but for Bakhtin, every utterance or act of creativity must exhibit interconnectedness between time and space.

We must be careful to acknowledge the constructed nature of the chronotope and briefly to note some of its exceptions. Holm-Hudson has talked about chronotopes that effectively "reach forward" in some knowingly "retro" recordings when he refers to the work of Todd Rundgren, who can "invoke the authorial qualities of another time or space", whether it be simulations of the Motown Sound or the Beatles (2014). Another musical polymath, Roy Wood, painstakingly evoked a large number of past eras on his recordings with the Move, Electric Light Orchestra, Wizzard and on solo recordings. This historical challenge to the linear chronotope could also be seen as a factor in the tribute band phenomenon, which will be referred to in another chapter.

Although Bakhtin developed the theory of the chronotope to help explain generic developments in epic literary forms, his claims that no one factor can be isolated from another and that creative agency cannot be removed from social contexts provides us with a pluralistic model that allows for scholars to move beyond an overreliance upon strictly textual or contextual constraints. The chronotope model encourages an exploration of genre, which, in popular music, is another concept that pushes us to bridge the gap between text and context. Bakhtin's notions of the importance of the reader in determining meaning also predate the postwar critical developments exploring the role of the author, already outlined in the Introduction.

How far can Bakhtin's theories of time and space go in helping us comprehend constructions such as the Motown Sound?

Gerald Early (2004) documents the importance of Detroit in the section of his book entitled "The Midwest as Musical Mecca and the Rise of Rhythm and Blues". In terms of geography, as one of the principal destinations for African

Americans escaping the poverty and racism of the Deep South, Detroit is clearly very important, but then so is Chicago and, to an extent, St. Louis, Kansas City or any other large conurbation that is situated near the Great Lakes or on the banks of rivers such as the Missouri and the Mississippi. Detroit, it is said, was "a real music town" (Williams, cited in Early, 2004: 67). However, we must ask, what major North American city was not? Detroit had blues, jazz, gospel, R&B, classical, pop and opera—but so did many others. Early is correct in situating Detroit in the vast region of the Midwest; one that, at least in broad terms, was less racist, less racially segregated and less conservative than the Deep South (however, this is all relative; see Early, 2004: 14–16, George, 2003: 8–16 and Posner, 2002: 6 for accounts of Detroit's history of segregation, race riots, etc.). In other words, ethnomusical crossovers may have been more achievable, allowing for jazz, in particular, to blossom in a sometimes interracial manner; although, more rigid, regional racial segregation did not preclude the success of FAME Studios in Muscle Shoals, Alabama, to give just one example. However, there is little that is specific to Detroit that allows for Motown to come into being. Notwithstanding this conclusion, Gordy himself claimed to have adapted automobile assembly line techniques to his own company, in terms of standardization and quality control. Also, in the years before the remix became central to dance culture, the quality control process at Motown was already often rejecting mixes on the basis of unsuitability (Posner, 2002: 83).

Certainly, Detroit's connection to huge companies such as Ford and General Motors does set it apart from other cities in the US, but only to a limited extent. This process raises "the apparent dichotomy of commerce versus creativity" (Negus and Pickering, 2004: 46). However, for these two authors, drawing upon sources and arguments that move beyond the somewhat simplistic positions constructed by many, including Theodor Adorno, commerce and creativity are not only "indistinguishable . . . in the modern economy" (Ibid: 47), but the commercial imperative actually encourages, or even inspires, creativity. We will return to the importance of Gordy ahead.

Let us now turn our attention to the space rather than the place. As well as anecdotal accounts of the actual recording space in Detroit, we must consider other contributory elements such as technology, in addition to aspects of musicianship, composition and arrangement, and ethnicity. First, all accounts reference the relatively cramped size of the two acoustic spaces, leading perhaps to its nickname, the Snakepit—alluding to the serpent-like trail of leads and wires that the players had to accommodate. In addition, the limited space encouraged the direct input of the bass guitar into the mixing desk and the small number of microphones employed to record the drum kit. Licks stated that until about 1963, "a used vintage 1939 Western Electric recording console" was the only mixing desk available to the studio (1989: 16). According to Lodder

(2005), most Motown recordings from around 1964 included a string section, or small orchestra, in the backing track, which would have been overdubbed at another time, in another space. However, there is nothing unique to Motown in any of these practices. Thus, if we are looking for authorial input from the studio space, we are entering territory that is, at best, unpersuasive and, at worst, mythological or deluding. This is not to say that certain studio spaces cannot contain a degree of sonic individuality—certainly no British attempts to create a soul sound close to Motown existed in the mid-1960s, and none of Al Green's soul tracks recorded by Hi Records in Memphis can be mistaken for Detroit's Motown Sound—but rather that the degree itself is difficult to quantify. Thus, the chronotope can provide us with a critical framework but not in any defini-tive sense. This authorial dilemma will be investigated further when we consider the actual recordings below. In addition, studio sounds can be copied, which means that we can only confer authorial status upon a space if we base our argument upon notions of originality or historical precedent—rather restricted parameters, some would say.

Before turning to these actual recordings, it may be beneficial to map out, at least in broad terms, the assumed or assigned mythical unique characteristics of the most archetypical Motown recordings of its golden age. However, the gener-alized nature of these characteristics must always be recognized. Many Motown tracks fulfill all the criteria listed below, but others far fewer (see also Borthwick and Moy, 2004: 12–14).

1. An overall paucity of blues-based progressions such as the standard tonic-dominant-subdominant model employed in the twelve-bar blues progression or song structure.
2. The relative lack of slow (i.e., below 80 bpm) tempo. Even Motown bal-lads tended to include an implicit rhythmic danceable component that sepa-rated them from mainstream pop ballads (listen, for instance, to songs such as "Tracks of My Tears" [1965] or "My Girl" [1964]).
3. Song structures often favoured the Tin Pan Alley style of composition featur-ing middle-eights, key changes and structural development over and above the simple verse/refrain pattern of traditional blues or gospel.
4. The vast majority of Motown singles from 1964 feature at least a string sec-tion, if not a small orchestra.
5. Singles tended to be deliberately mixed for transistor radio reception. This involved the incorporation and prominent mixing of treble elements such as tambourines, glockenspiel/xylophones and hi-hats, with playback on small speakers at a certain point in the postproduction process.
6. Bass lines rarely employ the blues' "walking bass style" (moving from and returning to chordal root notes via crochet intervals, or what Licks refers

to as the "two beat, root-fifth patterns" [1989: 12]). Instead, bass lines are often freer, employing jazz style embellishments; the incorporation of fourth, eighth and sixteenth interval notes; and the adoption of chromatic spacing and runs.

7. The drumbeat would often invert the standard pop kick/snare pattern, with the snare operating a metronomic crochet beat rather than only emphasizing two points in the bar. This then left the kick to be more syncopated than in standard pop or R&B styles.

8. Instrumental solos tended to be short and economic, and often employed the tenor or baritone saxophone as the instrument of choice.

9. The rhythm guitar would often emphasize alternate snare beats by utilizing the simple damped, chop stroke, resulting in the instrument being essentially percussive rather than melodic.

10. Most Motown session musicians came from a jazz, or even a classical (see Lodder, 2005: 22), rather than a blues/R&B background. Certainly, in comparison to most African American musicians working on commercial recordings in the period, this made them unusual.

11. The quality control process, culminating in Friday meetings where mixes and releases were discussed, accepted or dismissed, was certainly an unusual, if not a unique, facet of Motown's staff.

12. The widespread, if inconsistent, adoption of unusual instruments, many from the classical world, such as piccolo, celeste, theremin, flute and harpsichord, set the Motown subgenre apart from many of its rivals.

All of these criteria, or musical tendencies, do bolster claims for an identifiable, distinct, authored sound. Allan Moore termed Motown recordings "an identifiable sound world . . . instruments migrating from one layer to another . . . notable for the absence of a prominent electric guitar" (Moore, 2012: 27). In addition, we might note the importance of the wide sound spectrum. With guitars often inhabiting the percussive treble register, the midrange was often filled by organ, piano and orchestration. Furthermore, the often intensely "brittle", "sizzling" (I am adopting Virgil Moorefield's terms here, 2010: 22), "tinny" top-end qualities imbued with reverberation, echo and highly mixed vibraphones and tambourines were well balanced by a prominent bass guitar and baritone saxophone. Roland Barthes spoke of the inadequacy of the adjective as a tool for musical analysis (Roland Barthes, 1977), and certainly, as listeners or analysts, we must never preclude the possible clouding of the issues by subjective, assumed notions of authenticity, mythology and ideology. However, there does come a point where the use of symbolic signifiers seems unavoidable. Music is not brittle or tinny in a formal sense, but such terms do communicate meaning to a reading community. Motown's productions, certainly in the mid-1960s, evoke (or encourage) a real sense of drama and tension, at least in this reader, but also for countless others. But in a sense, Motown's authorial status remains negotiated, and thus hegemonic, rather than immanent or "given".

The Musicians and the Controversies

In addition to the importance stressed by many commentators upon place and space, perhaps even more fundamental to the construction of the Motown Sound has been the significance placed upon a small group of session musicians generally now known as the Funk Brothers, who for Edmonds are "the studio band who were the bedrock of every Motown recording" (2001: 59). Were this to have been the case, bearing in mind the huge volume of releases, let alone recordings undertaken by Motown, it is likely that at least a few of the musicians listed below went without any sleep for periods of at least weeks, if not months. In addition, despite several commentators' claim that the studio operated more or less around the clock in its prime, even jobbing musicians have to take a break. Licks only slightly modifies this exaggeration by commenting that the bassist James Jamerson "during the heyday of Motown . . . played on almost every record" (1989: 78). Even given the production-line professionalism and long hours regularly undertaken in the studio, this statement is again open to challenge. What is more important is what such claims tell us about the mythmaking process and its relationship to authorship. In the period 1964–1972, the most prominent of Motown's session players were said to be:

> Keyboards: Ivy Joe Hunter (and increasingly Earl van Dyke).
> Drums: Benny Benjamin (and increasingly Uriel Jones), Richard "Pistol" Allen.
> Guitar: Joe Messina, Eddie Willis, Robert White.
> Bass: James Jamerson (later Bob Babbitt and Michael Henderson).
> Percussion: Jack Ashford, Eddie 'Bongo' Brown.
> Reeds: Dan Turner, Hank Cosby, Mike Terry.

In addition, and even more anonymous in terms of wide recognition, Howard Priestley claimed that the female backing singers known as the Andantes may have made a contribution to up to twenty thousand sessions (2012). As with other contributing musicians, the Andantes had to wait until 1971 to receive a credit on a Motown album, Marvin Gaye's *What's Going On*.

In particular, the rhythm section of Benjamin and Jamerson was said to provide the unique bedrock of the Motown Sound, particularly between about 1964–1967, after which the increasingly unreliable behaviour of Benjamin led to Jones taking a more prominent role. Unlike within the authorial model developed by (and about) the meta genre of (white) rock, which placed great emphasis upon the band as the mythical construction unit (see Negus, 1992), within "black" soul, the emphasis rested far more upon producers and house session musicians; additional examples such as the Stax/Volt sound and the Hi Records sound bear out this distinction. Keyboard player Earl van Dyke shed significant light on the role of the Funk Brothers when he stated, "it was just a gig to us; all we wanted to do was play jazz" (Licks, 1989: 29). This suggests a journeyman approach by musicians more concerned about making a living than creating art—even though they (inadvertently?) managed to do both. Certainly, if one explores the role of the session musician throughout popular music, it is difficult to escape the conclusion that the status of art and authorship is almost totally displaced in favour of notions of financial stability, a sense of detached craft and a certain cavalier, if not downright mercenary, approach to the end product. When escaping the constraints of Gordy's assembly line, most of the Motown session musicians found their true creative role lay in "moonlighting" in jazz clubs. Authorship and the session musician is a topic that will be returned to in Chapter Three.

Accounts such as Licks' *Standing in the Shadows of Motown* (1989) do a valuable job in giving due credit to the musicians who remained unsung and largely anonymous during Motown's golden age. This was a time when anonymity was the norm: "The role of the studio musician as a star in their own right is a seventies and eighties concept" (Licks, 1989: 63). This notion suited Gordy's modus operandi. Early's overview of Motown's role in American culture stated:

> At Motown during the sixties, producers could also write songs and songwriters could produce, but artists—either singers or session musicians—were not permitted to do either . . . It was in the 1970s when the artist became both producer and writer—in short, when the album became a "work" in black music and the artist became an *auteur*—that Motown faltered, as Gordy was uncomfortable with that trend.
>
> (Early, 2004: 53–54)

This statement is largely true, with some exceptions found in the broad-based authorship of the young Stevie Wonder, from about 1966, or Marvin Gaye's later work, for instance. But authorship has still been assigned to musicianship. Constant reference is paid to the creative and unique authorial centrality of the Funk Brothers and "all the individual elements that went into Motown's famed rhythm section sound" (Licks, 1989: 32). However, this raises a problem. To the untrained ear, hundreds of Motown recordings do sound unique—albeit within a standardized set of musical parameters. It is easy to be persuaded or to believe that certain musicians have made a unique, authorial contribution. I can still remember, as a teenage fan of Motown, noting the presence of "unique" drum fills or track arrangements. However, for a variety of reasons, it is possible that we have been fooled at least to the extent of the significance of the Funk Brothers. As a final caveat, Brian Ward is also correct when he refers to Motown's early output as being about "not its homogeneity, but its diversity" (Ward, cited in Abbott, 2001a: 44–45) before proceeding to list the breadth of Motown recordings, stretching from hard-driving R&B, gospel and funk to sweet pop sounds to Broadway and Tin Pan Alley show tunes and standards.

The first problem with the issue of identification rests with the lack of hard evidence relating to who played on which track and where. Gordy kept his session musicians' identities anonymous for reasonable (and doubtless unreasonable) business concerns. These were probably related to issues such as the role of celebrity leading to star status and financial implications—in essence, connections to constructions of authorship. In addition, when you have groups of musicians working up to eighteen hour days on multiple, even overlapping sessions, and being paid below union rates (i.e., illegally), it makes sense not to document the process. Posner stated that at a time when union rates for a three hour session were between $47–60, Motown session players were paid "as little as five dollars per side" (Posner, 2002: 50). Anecdotal evidence also indicates that at least some of the musicians were high on more than just the creative process, for at least some of the time. In addition, the passage of time plays its part. Martha Reeves claims that on "Jimmy Mack", Earl van Dyke, James Jamerson and Benny Benjamin all play (cited in Mayo, 2008), but this is a recollection of a transient event forty years gone. In addition, the song has a shuffle rhythm, which often meant that Uriel Jones was preferred to Benjamin in that era. In short, how much trust can be placed upon participants?

Licks claimed, doubtless correctly, that Jamerson "never kept accurate records of his session work" (1989: 88). To these elements, we can add the evidence, again mostly anecdotal, that from around 1964 (the date varies according to the source), the prolific success of Motown meant that recording sessions were farmed out, in particular to a group of session musicians based in California known later to some as the Wrecking Crew. Brenda Holloway's hit "Every Little Bit Hurts" is documented as having been recorded on the West Coast, and produced by Marc Gordon and Hal Davis in 1964 (George, 2003: 178, 238). In fact, George claimed that "by 1965, Motown was recording in New York and Los Angeles with regularity" (Ibid: 119). In that same year, Posner claimed that Motown had under contract "175 artists" (2002: 150). Bearing in mind the huge volume of work undertaken by the likes of Jamerson and Benjamin in Detroit, it is highly unlikely that they would have been commuting thousands of miles to do sessions on the West Coast with any regularity. Drummer Hal Blaine claimed to have played on the Supremes' hit "The Happening" (1967) (2003: xvii). This raises the questions: If this recording took place in Detroit, why use Blaine and not a Motown session player? Yet, if it took place in California, where Blaine was based at the time, were other non-Motown session players employed? If Motown backing tracks were indeed recorded in a different place and a different space by a different group of mostly white musicians, then the whole edifice of the constructed Motown Sound begins to crumble.

At this point, the specific evidence relating to examples of bass playing on Motown tracks needs to be considered. Even if the recordings did take place in Detroit, not other cities, the Temptations' Otis Williams claimed that once many business operations moved from West Grand Boulevard to the Donovan Building in 1966 that "the recording began taking place in other studios" (Williams, in Posner, 2002: 179). When we consider that at one point in 1968, Motown had five out of the ten top-selling singles in the US (Posner, 2002: 226), we can further doubt the specificities of the unique chronotope.

Motown and Fragmentation

In referring back to the admittedly mechanistic twelve criteria outlined earlier, what does become clear to any avid student of Motown's recordings is that the writing and production team of Eddie Holland, Lamont Dozier and Brian Holland (henceforth, H-D-H) is perhaps the label's quintessential partnership. The justification for this statement lies in the extent to which the majority of their recordings measure up to most of the determining criteria. Of course, whether they themselves subscribe to such criteria, or rather help establish them, is a moot point. Certainly, in historical terms, their successes with Martha Reeves & the Vandellas and the Supremes happened early in Motown's ascent to commercial, global success, with the breakthrough hit "Where Did Our Love Go" entering the UK charts in September 1964 just a few months after what was probably the first major international Motown hit, Mary Wells' "My Guy" dating from May 1964.

As was customary with Motown, writing teams formed strong relationships with specific acts for as long as their success was ongoing. The Supremes waited a long time for their first hit, but once it was achieved, they stayed with H-D-H until the team left Motown in 1967. Similarly, the Four Tops was essentially another vehicle for H-D-H from 1965 until 1967. According to Dean Rudland, the team left Motown in 1967, as they "felt they were undervalued and underpaid. . . . Motown supremo Berry Gordy sued, H-D-H countersued, and at least as far as song writing and producing were concerned, the team were unable to work for three years" (Rudland, 1998).

What is more accurate, and particularly pertinent for the authorship issue, is that, in fact, the team did continue to work, both in setting up two labels—Invictus and Hot Wax—and, more interestingly, in continuing to produce (see more on H-D-H ahead).

In 1967, a period begins that marks the fragmentation of every aspect of Motown. The Supremes were renamed "Diana Ross & the Supremes" (a clear authorship issue), and after Motown's supply of H-D-H material was exhausted in 1968, they filled the void with various alternative writing and production teams. In 1970, Diana Ross left to pursue a very successful solo career, and the Supremes, with Ross replaced by Jean Terrell, reverted to their former title and also enjoyed continuing success, particularly from 1970 to 1973. A brief analysis of Ross and of the Supremes' hits during the period 1970 to 1973 does provide yet more evidence of a fragmentation of the Motown Sound. In overall terms, the brittle, tinny sound of the mid-1960s was superseded by a drier, less claustrophobic mix that moved away from the rigid divisions of instruments into wide-panning arrangements. "Love Child" (1968) and "I'm Livin' in Shame" (1969), both composed and produced by multiple writers, shifted the lyrical concerns from conventional romance narratives to the realms of social commentary. While "Floy Joy" (1972) harked back (knowingly?) to the mid-1960s' mould in its use of highly mixed vibraphone and crochet-beat handclaps to introduce the track (showing strong echoes of the Supremes' breakthrough hits from 1964), with "Bad Weather" (1973), Stevie Wonder's chromatic jazz melodies and the doubling of tom and snare (reminiscent of Al Green's recordings in Memphis) effectively remove the act from the Motown template. Interestingly, "Floy Joy" was written and produced by Smokey Robinson, whose work, even by this late period, was still redolent of the more conservative Motown blueprint of the mid-1960s. By this period, Wonder and others such as Marvin Gaye had moved beyond this standardized terrain into a more auteurist manifestation of their individual careers.

Diana Ross's solo career in the 1970s, as with that of the Supremes in the same period, also symbolizes shifts from the Motown standard. Although documentation does not allow for definitive answers to questions of personnel or locations, it is more than likely that the Funk Brothers would not have been heavily involved at this time, as few of the surviving members had made the move to California with the label. In particular, the drum rolls on tracks such as "I'm Still Waiting" (1970) and "Doobedood'ndoobe, Doobedood'ndoobe, Doobedood'ndoo" (1970) are slower and have a distinctive and frequently employed rhythm of a single floor (or deep) tom stroke followed by three beats on a snare that was never found on "classic" Motown tracks. On each of these tracks, this signature roll is employed on multiple occasions. Where the links with the past are still evident, as with the Supremes, are on tracks such as "Remember Me" (1971), written and produced by Nickolas Ashford and Valerie Simpson—a stalwart team whose work was central to 1960s' acts such as Marvin Gaye and Tammi Terrell and who were well steeped in the Motown ways.

Seemingly from nowhere in the summer of 1970, Invictus artists such as Freda Payne and Chairmen of the Board emerged with global hits ("Band of Gold" and "Give Me Just a Little More Time", respectively). For the next few years, these acts, along with others such as the Flaming Ember and the Honey Cone, gained appreciable success, certainly rivaling Motown in terms of quality, if not quantity. Despite no longer having exclusive access to the same musicians or the same studios, many H-D-H releases sound uncannily close to their own and others' Motown releases. Not only are stereo mixes and instrumental sounds a near duplication of Motown examples, but whole songs or acts seemed influenced by Motown developments of the era. As well as closely duplicating classic Motown, H-D-H also traced their former label's stylistic developments. For example, the Honey Cone's "Want Ads" and "Stick Up" (both 1971) seemed to adopt the late-Motown model of the Jackson 5's "I Want You Back" and "ABC" (both 1970) as their rhythmic and vocal template. Equally, the use of multiple clavinets to drive the funk rhythm track of Chairmen of the Board's "Finders Keepers" (1973) would seem to have been influenced by Stevie Wonder's work on songs such as "Superstition" (1972).

My reading of the career of H-D-H post-Motown would be that their early songs may have been stored up from the period following their abrupt departure and, as a consequence, carry strong echoes of their origins. Once their separation was legitimized by success, they seemed to have the authorial license to move further away from the Motown template. For instance, Chairmen of the Board were a playing-and-writing band, developing conceptual "progressive" segued tracks on their final album, *Skin I'm In* (1974), augmented by Parliament and produced by Jeffrey Bowen in a manner more akin to the rock auteur model (see Waring, 2006). Despite being a mainly H-D-H production, the band was allowed more authorial autonomy than any other in the classic Motown era. However, H-D-H's dealings seem to have duplicated some of the practices that drove the three away from Berry Gordy. Indeed, the team itself split subsequently. Of course, as previously mentioned, I may be merely (and falsely) assigning authorial influences posteriori, one of the problems being the paucity of even anecdotal evidence relating in particular to H-D-H's brief post-Motown period of success. Furthermore, the authorial wrangling responsible for H-D-H's departure from Motown was to continue, both internally, with Dozier leaving to go solo in 1973, and also within other acts on the labels themselves. These factors may influence the lack of documentation. But certainly, for a brief but fruitful period, Invictus/Hot Wax was a significant rival to Motown, both in terms of commercial success and, to a degree, creative similarity.

A final interesting point in relation to H-D-H sheds more light upon the fraught authorial process and its aesthetic assignation. In the early stages of researching their post-Motown productions, the songwriting credits for many Invictus/Hot Wax hits were noted. On several huge hit singles, compositional credits to the likes of Dunbar, Dumas and Wayne crop up repeatedly. Upon a close listen, these compositions closely resemble H-D-H songs—which, of course, further research proved them to be. An unnamed internet source claimed such names were their noms des guerre to mask the actual composers' identities during periods of litigation. However, Dozier claimed that this was not the case, that they shifted roles and "had to train the writers and show them and guide them to be a team like Motown had" (Waring, 2006). If this was the case, as tutors rather than auteurs, they did a very good job.

Of course, additional (albeit anecdotal) evidence can totally change our aesthetic response to texts. In this case, my critical scenario shifted from being amazed at how close these unknown writers came to duplicating H-D-H to then being amazed at how easily I could be fooled. (Of course, such songs *had* to be the work of H-D-H. The evidence was clear!) But we cannot trust our ears, nor, to an extent, uncorroborated personal accounts. With regards to authorship, the watchwords must always be skepticism and flexibility. H-D-H's post-Motown work further challenged any notion of the label's claims to authorship, certainly beyond specific parameters.

Whitfield and Motown: Another Ball of Confusion

A very different creative model—that centred on the figure of Norman Whit-field, a man who achieved most of his success while remaining a Motown employee—sheds yet further light upon the authorship issue.

Norman Whitfield's relationship to Motown has not been comprehensively documented, but Ben Edmonds provided us with a valuable summary (2001: 56–64). Whitfield, often in collaboration with co-writers such as Barrett Strong, became a staff writer and producer in the early and mid-1960s before wresting control of the Temptations from Smokey Robinson in 1966 following Robinson's lack of commercial success with the act (Ibid: 60). Whitfield's angle on the Motown Sound was more gospel-based and aggressive than Robinson's smoother, doo-wop-based balladry. Perhaps more significantly, Robinson was a prolific songwriter and competent musician, whereas Whitfield had almost no playing skills. Instead, he would listen, learn and appropriate from diverse sources, relying heavily on others to interpret his ideas and turn them into musical texts. This is a different form of creativity, but does indicate that the lack of concrete musical skills is not an obstacle to achieving, or being assigned, authorial status. Certainly by 1971, it is perfectly possible to talk about a recognizable Norman Whitfield sound, although perhaps his authorial status was, to an extent, titular or assumed.

In the period between 1966 and 1973, Whitfield's productions and compositions provide evidence of an author strongly influenced by prevailing trends and social conditions to the extent that such contributory factors can themselves be assigned some authorial influence (the zeitgeist as auteur, I will return to this concept in Chapter Six). From the mainly standardized, generic terrain of "Ain't

Too Proud to Beg" and "Beauty Is Only Skin Deep" (both 1966), Whitfield and his collaborators incrementally pushed the boundaries of what was acceptable on Motown singles and albums. On 1969's "Cloud Nine", the Motown Sound had been augmented (Edmonds stated that Jamerson and Jones played on the session, 2001: 62) by outside musicians from the psychedelic or rock world (guitarist Dennis Coffey, drummer Spider Webb). The resulting mix was still identifiably Motown, but with added elements that removed it from a standardized terrain. In addition, the ambiguity of the lyric, replete with drug, civil rights and racial connotations, was far removed from classic Motown romantic fare.

After a relatively long introduction of some twenty-three seconds, in structural terms, the song eschews the standard verse/chorus/bridge model of much pop and Motown in favour of a looser form wherein the chorus is actually split between two sections, the first an understated refrain (at 1.03, "I'm doin' fine", etc.) and the second a call and response vocal over a syncopated yet sparse drum, bass and conga rhythm. The complete backing track only enters at around 2.07 (with, appropriately, the phrase beginning "up, up"). "Cloud Nine" is standard pop length, at less than 3.30, but what is significant is the breaking of the temporal tension/resolution model of standard pop and soul, with over half the track being given over to tension and incremental additions to the mix before we, the listeners, are "rewarded" from 2.07 onward.

The commercial success of this track (the first Motown release to win a Grammy) gave Whitfield the authorial status to further stamp his own style upon subsequent releases. Major hits such as "Ball of Confusion" (1970) and "Papa Was a Rollin' Stone" (1973) were even more eccentric from the Motown norm. The former, replete with ironic references (to the Beatles' latest recording or to a mythical band playing), a driving rock-style bass riff and a running time of 4.05, was an even bigger hit in the UK than "Cloud Nine", whereas the latter clocked in at over eleven minutes in its unedited form. However, in the midst of such experimentation, other tracks such as "Just My Imagination" (1971) remained much closer to the template of the soul ballad, although still included a lyrical twist.

By the time of the release of the Temptations' 1973 album *Masterpiece*, Whitfield's output transcended individual authorial status, and he was being credited as the single most important presence on the album. Following his departure from Motown, he set up his own label (called, perhaps unsurprisingly, Whitfield Records). He achieved great, if short-lived, success with the act Rose Royce. Anyone familiar with the Temptations' track "Law of the Land" (1973) was given clear indication that the person at least partially responsible for the syncopated handclaps and counterpoint string arrangement may also have had a strong input into "Car Wash" (1976), such was their sonic similarity. It is almost possible to transpose elements from one track onto the other without noticing any discrepancy.

Again, the tensions between seemingly opposite concepts of standardization and individuality are brought into close contact.

What Whitfield's work indicated is that it is fully possible to forge a distinctive authorial presence within an organization or label that itself can claim (or be apportioned) a trademark sound or style. Equally, it is possible for the individual elements to partly or almost completely subsume the house style, and for distinctive elements to continue to survive in a completely different physical or organizational environment (as with H-D-H). Authorship is contingent upon a whole host of internal and external determinants.

George claimed that after 1967, Motown began to fragment: "In this period of instability old heads and youngbloods created some enduring masterpieces—but the best of it was too personal, too idiosyncratic to create and establish a 'new' Motown sound" (2003: 169). This indicates a temporal aspect may be as important to authorship as many other variables. Authorial status is never static, nor independent of circumstances, yet it, at least, partially determines how all factors and circumstances are subsequently appraised and judged.

PWL: The British Motown?

As already indicated, many labels have, either deliberately or unwittingly, duplicated some of Motown's musical and business practices (Stax/Volt, Philadelphia International, Invictus/Hot Wax, etc.). However, the company that most blatantly set out to attempt to reproduce the Motown modus operandi was PWL (Pete Waterman Ltd.), set up and run by Mike Stock, Matt Aitken and Pete Waterman (S-A-W) in 1984. Exploring aspects of this organization allows us to shed light on questions of authorship in several respects. In particular, issues of race, politics, sexuality, nationality, canonization, sound and critical reception can be brought to bear.

Pete Waterman had established a long career in the pop industry that encompassed DJing, production, songwriting and management. In the years following him linking up with Stock and Aitken, whose strengths lay in playing, composition and production, their collaborations on releases by the likes of Mel & Kim, Hazel Dean, Divine, Dead or Alive, Kylie Minogue, Bananarama, Rick Astley and Jason Donovan brought them huge—and in the UK, unrivalled—success, particularly in the singles chart. In 1985, S-A-W contributed to thirty-five top 40 UK singles. Many of these artists were signed to the trio's production and management company, and had their music released on the PWL label.

The parallels between PWL and Motown were myriad and, in many cases, quite deliberate. Waterman stated that Lamont Dozier, part of H-D-H, was "my all-time hero" (Waterman, 2001: 126), and the S-A-W credit nomenclature was structured to closely resemble that of H-D-H. Waterman "had a vision of Motown-type songs with more modern chords and techno, gay disco rhythms" (Ibid: 136). As with H-D-H, the three members of S-A-W would all focus on different areas; in the main, Stock would be the music composer, Aitken would play and program much of the music, and Waterman would produce and sometimes contribute lyrics (Ibid: 138). PWL's studio, the "Hit Factory" (echoes of "Hitsville U.S.A."), was situated in an unfashionable, somewhat rundown part of London. For Waterman, another Motown connection was made manifest: "[T]his was like Motown. The idea of having offices and studios all in the same place in this dilapidated building just brought to mind Motown's rickety old place in Detroit" (Ibid: 159). At one point, PWL acts were all sent out on a package tour in a deliberate echo of the Motown Revue (Ibid: 227). In addition, songs and backing tracks were sometimes not written with specific artists in mind, and the acts themselves had very little authorial input into the writing, production or recording processes. As with the Motown studio, the Hit Factory was just that, a factory churning out largely standardized pop songs aimed mainly at the mainstream commercial market and the dance floor. Former "tea boy" Rick Astley was (supposedly) moulded into an international star at PWL, in much the same way that typist Martha Reeves was transformed at Motown.

The comparisons between the two organizations are evidently legion, but the crucial distinction lies in the critical appreciation afforded Motown and PWL. The first point to make is that Motown has been afforded an extensive (and burgeoning) critical archive, whereas PWL has been relatively ignored or dismissed. When the status or legacy of the organizations is discussed, the disparities could not be more evident. Hicks stated that "Motown records single-handedly created a Rock and Roll revolution" (Hicks, cited in Wright et al., 2007: 78). For George, "the music of Motown Records is a challenge and an inspiration to anyone making pop records, because, quite simply, the musical achievements of Berry Gordy's company have been monumental" (George, 2003: xv). Countless quotations of a similarly laudatory nature could be referenced. In a sense, critical acclaim for Motown has become mythological and canonical. In stark contrast, the artistic achievements of PWL have been more typically overlooked or denigrated. In the television programme *The 80s on Trial*, Stuart Maconie referred to PWL's commercial practices as "exploitative and irresponsible" and their music as "disposable product" and "musical wallpaper" (Maconie, cited in Whalley, 2008). Cliff Richard, whose long and successful career has similarly not escaped critical discrimination, claimed to have encountered more problems from people in justifying his work with PWL on a single than in justifying his faith in God (Richard, cited in Waterman, 2001: 223). In short, despite the huge similarities between PWL and Motown, the one organization is critically lauded, while the other is not. The reasons for this are most illuminating when considering questions of authorship.

Selective Canonization

As with the concept of authorship (although often broached as a topic) linked to notions of worth and aesthetic value, specific academic texts on the construction of a canon in popular music are rare. Sherril Dodds' work on popular dance, while only connected to popular music, sets out the critical terrain effectively, centring on the concept of "acts of evaluation" (2011: 14). Dodds' choice of the term "acts" is a crucial signifier in symbolizing that this process of canonization is one built upon historical processes rather than being merely about common sense or a given. Traditional uses of the term often ignore questions of "whose canon" and to what ends the canon is being employed.

Carys Wyn Jones, in the most comprehensive deconstruction of the notion of a canon in popular music, notes that within academia, discussions around the canon are subsumed into "subjects with canonical implications" (2008: 110). Academia's desire to move beyond high versus low culture distinctions does result in a constructed canon being seen as a contradiction within this scenario (Ibid: 11). Even despite recognizing both the positive and negative implications of a canon, when Jones states that "a canon is now, more than ever, useful in steering our choices" (Ibid: 123), the connotations of the term "steering" suggest an outside imposition acting upon an individual aesthetics.

In the main, an imposition of a (partial) canon is based upon its broad adoption in the popular media (Ibid: 104). The popular music canon is based chiefly upon individual works in the rock meta genre, but, certainly, labels such as Motown are granted canonical status, with Marvin Gaye's *What's Going On* (1971) acting as its standard bearer, at least according to countless greatest album lists.

Despite both organizations working within a relatively standardized musical and production terrain, the archetypal 1960s' sound of Motown is critically praised and the archetypal 1980s' sound of PWL is not. In a sense, this symbolizes the critical mythologies of the two decades. In particular, the 1980s' chronotope is seen as producing synthetic, overproduced pop reliant on drum machines, synthesizers, sequencers, computers and unsympathetic production, rendering the recordings "cheesy", "clinical" and "cold". Of course, such terms are highly subjective, but 1980s' production techniques do certainly problematize the actual contributions of musicians. For Ian Trickett, the consequence of Motown songs being played rather than programmed results in unique moments, with an "organic and human sound which a three minute recording captures forever. Another recording from the same session but twenty minutes later would not sound the same—there would be subtle, almost immeasurable differences" (Trickett, 2008: 18–19).

In contrast, PWL's more synthetic sound "gives some form of entertainment, but not as far as jouissance as we find it far more difficult to relate to a programmed machine than we do other human beings" (Ibid). Despite these arguments being open to challenge, the last part of the statement does ring true for many musical critics and commentators and for constructed theories of authorship.

Another critical distinction draws upon mythologies of sexuality. Certainly, early in its history, PWL was aiming, to at least a fair degree, at the audience for high-energy, disco-style music. A large percentage of the audience for this style of music was gay, whereas the dance-floor audience for Motown soul was not. It is my contention that a degree of unacknowledged, latent homophobia exists in the negative criticism that PWL has attracted, although this is a matter of conjecture rather than vouchsafed by hard evidence. In addition, particularly in the UK, dance music (particularly homegrown) had never been afforded the same critical praise as so-called authentic genres such as rock, punk or, indeed, US dance.

Much easier to justify is a racial distinction between the two organizations. In being mainly black-owned and black-run, particularly in its classic years, Motown came to stand as a powerful symbol of black pride and black achievement. While not socialist, Motown can be seen as counter-establishment. This is particularly important in a country and an industry with a deep-seated history of racial discrimination. For Early, Motown effectively became "the voice of struggling Black America" (2004: 109). Crooke described Motown as "a soundtrack to getting our equal place in the world" (Crooke, cited in Early, 2004: 87). With regard to its more entrepreneurial impact, Smith stated that "never before had a black owned company been able to create and produce the musical artistry of its own community, and then sell it successfully to audiences across the racial boundaries" (1999: 266).

We can contrast these positive observations with those placed upon PWL, which was widely represented as the unacceptable face of capitalism. In particular, the perception of Waterman as a shameless wheeler-dealer more interested in exploiting artists and making money than in producing works of art was widespread. Even his desire to make PWL "the sound of a Bright Young Britain" (Stock, 2004: 107) only encouraged commentators to link the label with the right-wing policies of Thatcher's Conservative government. In another television documentary to critique its ideology, Franz Ferdinand's Alex Kapranos depicted PWL as "the soundtrack of that woman's cold, black heart" (Croft, 2008). Claims from Waterman decrying any constructed links between PWL and Conservatism, and merely stating that they "just wanted to create entertainment, not take away from 'real bands'" (Waterman, 2001: 167), failed to recuperate their perceived status. If we add their pigment, nationality, and perceived uncoolness to the equation, we can see that any critical acceptance would be grudging at best, with connections to auteur theory practically nonexistent.

Whether PWL will ever be critically recuperated, as has more recently been the case with acts such as Abba or Duran Duran, genres such as disco, or even eras such as "the eighties", remains to be seen. More likely, their pariah status will survive, giving auteur theory an easy target by which to create, in the main, ideo-logically subjective, selective and (partly) untenable critical positions.

Summary

This first chapter has not been narrowly focused. As is often the way with this type of research, the process has become rhizomatic rather than linear. This will prove to be a feature of all the subsequent chapters. I have sought to problematize any easy or definitive answers to the issues of authorship raised by the overarching referents of time, space and place, and the more grounded elements of production, musicianship, identifiable styles and individual musical texts. My conclusion regarding Motown and its relationship to authorship is that the period when the label did indeed rep-resent a consistently collective house style was comparatively short-lived—between about 1964 and 1967. After that point, fragmentation occurred. Paradoxically, some of the productions of H-D-H at Invictus/Hot Wax remained closer to the Motown model than other productions emanating from inside the Motown of the early 1970s. Thus, the concept of the chronotope is at least challenged.

Exploring the disparate critical reception granted to the likes of Tamla Motown and PWL has allowed for the relationship between authorship and the concept of the canon to be broached. What is clear is that popular music's own construc-tion of a canon of great works is, in many respects, nothing more than an updated romantic, hegemonic process. It is based upon values of worth that result from assumed and assigned notions of truth, virtuosity, genius and innovation. However, the canonization of popular music cannot rest solely on the values associated with the classical tradition. Philip Tagg has stated that within popular music studies, fine art aesthetics or, in his phrase, "elitist old hat", has been superseded by what he termed "elitist hip":

> We convert the "classical" concern for "real art" or the "folk" fetish for the "genuine" into "popular" equivalents like "street credibility", "intrin-sic ephemerality", "real rock", "genuine popular expression", "the latest", "youth rebellion", "anti-authoritarian", "corporal", "down-home", etc.
>
> (1989: 293)

Tagg's notion of "elitist hip" has been vouchsafed to analyses of Motown, but not to PWL, for reasons already explored in this chapter: the problem with concepts such as canonization lies within its unquestioning acceptance by an elitist hip hegemony. A more progressive application of the term canon would not seek to dispense with the term—we all construct taste hierarchies—but would rather replace a hegemonic canon with a more personalized one. Jones argues for an "inherently optional [canon that] might ultimately become a matter of individual perception" (Jones, 2008: 136, 139), and in our pluralistic, fragmented age, that seems a persuasive conclusion.

Questions of authorial value can never preclude the potential for prejudice. It is for this reason that, on an ideological level, I am prejudiced against many of the artists included in the popular music canon (by way of example, Nick Cave, Bob Dylan, Van Morrison, Bruce Springsteen). But at least these prejudices are constructed and not imposed, and are against artists in little need of further attention and hagiography. In its more holistic focus, explorations of authorship help problematize the inevitably partial nature of canonization while maintaining that, for good or ill, the self is structured through manifest inconsistencies.

In a sense, this chapter's diverse arguments become symbolic and metonymic of broader, deeply philosophical debates that underpin this whole project, including the search for our own sense of identity and worth. In answer to questions of why do issues of authorship matter, we might initially conclude that it is because people want them and need them to matter—and for a wide variety of reasons. Not only do we, as listeners, assign symbolic value to musical texts, but those figures that help produce these texts assume value as a consequence, although, as argued, accrued status is not assigned fairly or consistently. Music may indeed possess/express magical and spiritual dimensions, but it is equally grounded in the more earthbound realities and mythologies of race, gender, ideology, space, place, canonization, genre and commerce.

Bibliography

Abbott, Kingsley (ed.) (2001a) *Calling Out Around the World: A Motown Reader*, London: Helter Skelter.

Abbott, Kingsley (2001b) "Interview with Carol Kaye", in Abbott, Kingsley (ed.), *Calling Out Around the World: A Motown Reader*, London: Helter Skelter, pp 93–100.

Ashford, Jack (2005) *Motown: The View from the Bottom*, East Grinstead: Bank House.

Bakhtin, Mikhail (1981) "The Dialogic Imagination: Four Essays", in Holquist, Michael (ed.), *The Bakhtin Reader: Selected Writings of Bakhtin, Medvedev, Voloshinov*, Austin: University of Texas Press, pp XX–XXX.

Barthes, Roland (1977) "The Grain of the Voice", in *Image, Music, Text*, Glasgow: Fontana.

Blaine, Hal (2003) *Hal Blaine and the Wrecking Crew*, Alma, Mich.: Rebeats.

Borthwick, Stuart & Ron Moy (2004) *Popular Music Genres: An Introduction*, Edinburgh: Edinburgh University Press.

Burgess, Richard James (2013) *The Art of Music Production: The Theory and Practice*, Fourth Edition, New York: Oxford University Press.

Dodds, Sherril (2011) *Dancing on the Canon: Embodiments of Value in Popular Dance*, Palgrave Macmillan (eBook).

Early, Gerald (2004) *One Nation under a Groove: Motown and American Culture*, Michigan: University of Michigan Press.

Edmonds, Ben (2001) "Final Frontier", *Mojo*, August, pp 56–64.

George, Nelson (2003) *Where Did Our Love Go? The Rise and Fall of the Motown Sound*, London: Omnibus.

Holm-Hudson, Kevin (2014) From a personal correspondence, December 1.

Jones, Carys Wyn (2008) *The Rock Canon: Canonical Values in the Reception of Rock Albums*, Aldershot: Ashgate.

Licks, Dr. (1989) *Standing in the Shadows of Motown: The Life and Music of Legendary Bassist James Jamerson*, Wynnewood, Penn.: Dr. Licks Publishing.

Lodder, Steve (2005) *Stevie Wonder: The Classic Albums*, London: Backbeat Press.

Marsh, Dave (1983) "James Jamerson: What Becomes of the Broken Hearted?", *Record Magazine*, 1 November, accessed 19-06-08, http://rocksbackpages.com/Library/Article/james-jamerson-what-becomes-of-the-broken-hearted.

Mayo, Simon (2008) "Interview with Martha Reeves", BBC Radio Five Live, October 6.

Moore, Allan (2012) *Song Means: Analysing and Interpreting Recorded Popular Song*, Farnham: Ashgate.

Moorefield, Virgil (2010) *The Producer as Composer: Shaping the Sounds of Popular Music*, Cambridge, Mass.: MIT Press.

Morris, Pam (1994) *The Bakhtin Reader: Selected Writings of Bakhtin, Medvedev, Voloshinov*, London: Arnold.

Negus, Keith (1992) *Producing Pop: Culture and Conflict in the Popular Music Industry*, London: Edward Arnold.

Negus, Keith & Michael Pickering (2004) *Creativity, Communication and Cultural Value*, London: Sage.

Payne, Jim (1995) "Al Jackson Jr. Interview", December, accessed 16-06-08, www.funkydrummer.com/JPpages/ajinterview.html.

Posner, Gerald (2002) *Motown: Music, Money, Sex and Power*, London: Random House.

Priestley, Howard (2012) *Love Factory: The History of Holland Dozier Holland* (self-published eBook).

Rudland, Dean (1998) Sleeve notes accompanying *Invictus Chartbusters*, Sequel Records.

Smith, Suzanne (1999) *Dancing in the Streets: Motown and the Cultural Politics of Detroit*, Boston: Harvard University Press.

Stock, Mike (2004) *The Hit Factory: The Stock, Aitken and Waterman Story*, London: New Holland.

Tagg, Philip (1989) "Open Letter: 'Black Music', 'Afro-Caribbean Music' and 'European Music'", *Popular Music*, 8(3), pp 285–298.

Trickett, Iain (2008) *To What Extent are Stock, Aitken and Waterman an "80s Answer to Motown?"*, student undergraduate dissertation, Liverpool: John Moores University.

Ward, Brian (2001) "Just my Soul Responding," in Abbott, Kingsley (ed.), *Calling Out Around the World: A Motown Reader*, London: Helter Skelter, pp 42–48.

Waring, Charles (2006) Sleeve notes accompanying *The Very Best of Chairmen of the Board*, Sanctuary.

Waterman, Pete (2001) *I Wish I Was Me: The Autobiography*, London: Virgin.

Werner, Craig (1999) *A Change is Gonna Come: Music, Race and the Soul of America*, Michigan: University of Michigan Press.

Wright, Vicky, Louvain Temps, Marlene Barrow-Tate & Jackie Hicks (2007) *Motown from the Background*, East Grinstead: Bank House.

Audio-Visual Sources

Chairmen of the Board (1970) "Give Me Just a Little More Time".

  (1973) "Finders Keepers".

  (1974) *Skin I'm In*.

Croft, Davis (director) (2008) *The 80s on Trial*. BBC4 broadcast, January 13.

Marvin Gaye (1971) *What's Going On*.

Brenda Holloway (1964) "Every Little Bit Hurts".

The Honey Cone (1971) "Want Ads", "Stick-Up".

Jackson 5 (1970) "I Want You Back", "ABC".

Freda Payne (1970) "Band of Gold".

Martha Reeves & the Vandellas (1967) "Jimmy Mack".

Rose Royce (1976) "Car Wash".

Diana Ross (1970) "I'm Still Waiting", "Doobedood'ndoobe, Doobedood'ndoobe, Doobedood'ndoo".

  (1971) "Remember Me".

Diana Ross and the Supremes (1967) "The Happening".

The Supremes (1964) "Where Did Our Love Go?"

  (1968) "Love Child".

  (1969) "I'm Livin' in Shame".

  (1972) "Floy Joy".

  (1973) "Bad Weather".

The Temptations (1966) "Ain't Too Proud to Beg", "Beauty Is Only Skin Deep".

  (1969) "Cloud Nine".

  (1970) "Ball of Confusion".

  (1971) "Just My Imagination".

  (1973) "Papa Was a Rollin' Stone".

  (1973) "The Law of the Land".

Whalley, Ben (director) (2008) *Pop Britannia*. BBC4 broadcast, January 17.

Stevie Wonder (1972) "Superstition".

2

GENDER AND DEGREES OF POPULAR MUSIC AUTHORSHIP

In an article entitled "The Men Behind the Sound of 2013" (Hoby, 2013), DJ, producer and solo artist Dev Hynes is interviewed about his work with other artists, particularly Mutya, Keisha and Siobhan (also known as the Sugababes). He comments on the widely held assumption that, in this situation, the male is the author and the females are the directed performers, "It is obviously a tricky subject. Even with the Sugababes—I'm sure people think I wrote the song but they wrote all the lyrics and vocal melodies themselves" (Hynes, cited in Hoby, 2013: 6–7). So far, so progressive; however, even this brief example acts in microcosm to illuminate some of the myriad issues connecting gender to authorship. First, Hynes is right in both acknowledging the mythologies of gender roles in popular music and, second, in giving true credit where credit is due, unlike that denied many female authors in the past. Elsewhere in the interview, Hynes reflects upon a "Twitter fall-out" after collaborating with Solange Knowles, who felt insufficiently credited in their joint project. While clearly an issue, I merely mention this matter in passing, as an example that perceived oversights in accreditation continue to dog some participants in popular music.

The bigger issue here is the reinforcement of the existing gender hegemony whereby, regardless of their contribution, female acts such as the Sugababes will almost always be produced by males. There are doubtless male vocal acts that have been produced by single female producers, as in Tricia Rose's term, an example of "resistance" (1994) to the dominant modus operandi—what Judith Butler terms "heteronormative signifying systems" (1999)—but such reversals of the norm are all too few. Richard James Burgess does note the few exceptions to the rule, but he also states that research into this syndrome finds "no appreciable increase in the number of women in music production over many decades" (2013: 194). More tellingly, attempts to get media organizations to vouchsafe information regarding male to female ratios and absolute numbers working in production areas garners a very low response rate. This suggests that the industry itself, as well as being aware of gender disparities, is actually complicit in the continuation of the phenomenon and would rather not have the resultant figures made manifest.

As a further point, bearing in mind the relative paucity of female producers, engineers, remixers, DJs, etc., it is moot that so many of the (relatively few) female producers—Kate Bush, Björk, Tori Amos, Sheryl Crow, Lauren Hill, Liz Phair, etc. (see Zak, 2001: 180)—only self-produce. Why are men behind the sound of a given year, while the women are more typically in front of the mic? Sheila Whiteley, in drawing upon the work of Simon Reynolds and Joy Press, notes that "female innovations in rock remain mostly at the level of lyrics, self-presentation, ideology and rhetoric" (2000: 8). In this chapter, through case studies and numerous examples, the breadth of patriarchal discourses running in parallel with the concept of authorship and the resulting counter-hegemonic challenges will be investigated.

While we must acknowledge the particularly patriarchal nature of the industry and the partial nature of the constructed popular music canon, this immanent and ongoing situation has already been well documented by many scholars in the field (Burns and LaFrance, 2002; Leonard, 2007; Lieb, 2013; Mayhew, 2004; McClary, 1991; Negus and Pickering, 2004; O'Brien, 2002; Whiteley, 2000). A recent point made by Tara Brabazon summarizes this syndrome well in concluding that:

> Much of the writing about popular music dismisses dance culture in favour of rock and undermines women's role in production and consumption by celebrating a few men who play guitar and focus on "political" lyrics rather than love songs.
>
> (2012: 40)

Rather, my focus in this chapter will lie in exploring the many strategies employed by female artists in challenging gender-based mythologies surrounding the authorship issue. Are there specifically female/feminine/feminist methodologies at work in this process? Can we avoid constructing an essentialized thesis seeing female authorship as "other" or distinct? Does female authorship always need to be articulated through the lens of gender?

An initial impetus comes through an exploration of some of the theories expounded by both Simon Reynolds and Joy Press in their book *The Sex Revolts: Gender, Rebellion and Rock'n'Roll* (1995). Interestingly, in their deliberate choice to assign the entire text to joint male/female authors, we experience an essentially androgynous, singular thesis. The book is broken down into three sections, which can be summarized as follows: first, the male rebel often in opposition to notions of the feminine; second, idealized images of women/femininity in male rock; and third, the imagining of a specifically female revolution (1995: xi–xii). For the purposes of this chapter, the explorations carried out in the third section are the most pertinent, although, as is often the case, the notion of authorship, or in this case female authorship, remains largely implicit and not fully articulated. Reynolds and Press explore strategies that female musicians/authors adopt as part of the writing process in a field that has proven astonishingly resistant to allowing females the license to operate as equals. Through many examples, the authors articulate the difficulties for females torn between the fact of biology and the fiction of femininity (Ibid: 234), the problems for women taking on men at their own game by adopting stereotypical male traits and also for those women forwarding a female strength that is equal but different to male strength (if indeed the two are disparate). Reynolds and Press also explore the role of image, iconography and masquerade in a field that objectifies women far more than men, yet judges them more harshly on supposed transgressions. Lastly, they investigate the difficulties posed by a dearth of role models for those women trying to forge a creative authorial role.

Even within the constructed mythology of the distinction between rock and pop (see Negus and Pickering, 2004: 54) lies a clue to the barriers placed in front of the female auteur. If, as many have argued or assumed, rock and its associated values of connoisseurship, discernment and discrimination are implicitly male, then pop, its counter, with its associated concepts of fandom, superficiality, idolatry and fickleness, remains implicitly female (see Whiteley, 2000: 13–14). Jason Toynbee has spoken of a "rock authorship [that] has constituted a fetish [that has] limited innovation and produced an elite echelon of stars" (2000: 162), and Robert Walser has mapped out the close connections between virtuosity and maleness (1993). In broad terms, the history of popular music gives us many examples of female icons, singers and dancers, but many fewer producers, engineers, band leaders or DJs. This implies that some musical roles are more readily associated with the concept of authorship (Bogdanovic, 2014). Ultimately, these myths become self-fulfilling. Negus and Pickering focus on the historical syndrome wherein females within visual art are more typically models rather than artists (2004: 120), and the same kind of iconic/artistic binary holds sway in contemporary production practices in popular music.

Empirical surveys conducted among my popular music undergraduates substantiate these gender role distinctions; even in groups, assumed subject specialists struggle to name more than a few female producers, remixers or DJs. I also carry out this kind of survey when dealing with authorship in film, with similar results. Students can compile a long list of male directors, but far fewer females, despite some recent inroads by figures such as Sophia Coppola, Kathryn Bigelow and Sam Taylor-Wood (now Taylor-Johnson). If the imbalance in the film world is marked, it is even more so within popular music. I asked a female student if she could name a single well-known female lead guitarist, and she was ashamed to admit that she could not. I did this not to belittle her, as hardly anyone can name a lead female guitarist, but to demonstrate the power of hegemony.

In terms of hard statistical analysis, in 2013, a group of about twenty final-year undergraduates were given sixty seconds to jot down as many male and female film directors as they could. They came up with twelve males and three females. The same survey relating to popular music producers resulted in ten males and two females. In 2014, a larger group of about thirty students managed to list twenty male directors and four females, and eighteen male pop producers and six female.

Nothing legislates against females taking any role in film or popular music, but the preponderance of women behind the microphone instead of behind the desk, and in front of the lens instead of behind the camera, shows that more insidious forces are at work—the issue is systemic.

Even on those rare occasions when a female musician has gained control over many aspects of her career, as with Kate Bush, any perceived creative lapses are seized upon by critics as exemplifying overambition, with the artist needing to spread the authorial load (presumably by seeking male help) (see Mayhew, 2004: 156). Janelle Monáe's perceived air of control is similarly seen as a problem by some journalists, with Dorian Lynskey terming her "possibly the most focussed, self-contained person I have ever encountered . . . talking like a politician or a businesswoman" (Lynskey, 2010) before concluding by praising a hair misfunction on stage because "it's a refreshingly unguarded moment. Her hair, at least, sometimes goes off message" (Ibid). Here, he unwittingly expresses the double-bind for the woman in pop discourse, damned for being manipulated, pandering to sexist fantasies, yet also damned for presenting a cool, calculated facade. Perhaps as a result of female artists being judged more harshly than male equivalents, image is *armour* for women in ways not so necessary for males.

I have previously explored the authorship of females such as Kate Bush, Madonna and Björk in some depth (see Moy, 2007: 72–88), but in the ensuing period since this research took place, new authors/authorships have emerged. In addition, long-standing issues have to be revisited. What has not changed is the overall degree of negotiation and compromise (although perhaps collaboration would be a more fitting term) in order for females to assume greater authorial status and identity. The strategies of these newer female auteurs indicate not only how much has changed, but also how much still needs to change before the female's role exceeds that of "muse" or "foil" (Battersby, 1989: 3) to the assumed male genius, or the female ceases to be characterized as somehow unskilled or "natural" (Mayhew, 2004: 150), as opposed to technological or virtuoso.

The remainder of this chapter will focus upon three case studies. In the first of these, I return to the world of session musicians already broached in Chapter One, but view their authorship through the frames of gender, musicology, race and accreditation. The session player problematizes the romantic view of authorship and will be returned to at greater length within a later chapter on interpretation. The second case study focuses on a relatively new solo artist, Janelle Monáe, and allows us to explore notions of image, collaboration, race and genre. The final case study explores the male/female duo, Goldfrapp, in the process asking if the division of roles is predicated upon gender and, if so, does this raise an insurmountable problem for the popular music world.

James Jamerson or Carol Kaye?

Identifying the bass player on certain Motown recordings, while fraught with controversy and conflicting anecdotal evidence, is a vital task that forms part of the investigation of the authorship process and its assignation. Unlike the very sketchy documented evidence emanating from within Motown, Carol Kaye has provided both corroborated anecdotal and some written evidence that maintains that she and her fellow session musicians played on many Motown backing tracks usually assigned to the Funk Brothers. Even Gordy himself has stated that many rhythm tracks were cut on the West Coast during Motown's heyday (see Kaye, cited in Abbott, 2001: 93–102). Direct conflict arises when different parties both claim authorship for the bass-playing on tracks such as the Four Tops' "Bernadette" (1967) and "I Can't Help Myself" (1965), Stevie Wonder's "I Was Made to Love Her" (1967), the Supremes' "Baby Love" (1964) and others in the period between about 1963 and 1969. At around the end of this period, Motown moved most of its operation to Los Angeles, and the so-called "Detroit Sound" was confined to history, or mythology. Lodder claimed that Marvin Gaye's *What's Goin' On*, released in 1971, was the first Motown album to credit session players, and Jamerson was certainly listed, among others, as a now authored participant rather than an assumed and anonymous session player (Lodder, 2005: 60–61). Jamerson played on the title track, among others—definitely.

Kaye's evidence is anecdotal but consistent and authoritative: "You can always tell your playing" (Kaye, cited in Abbott, 2001: 98); evidence is also available on her own website and in radio, filmed and written interviews). However, it must be stated that some writers, such as Licks, George and Lodder, make no mention of her whatsoever, and Posner only in passing (2002: 50), whereas one of the most respected music journalists, Dave Marsh, terms Kaye "(one of) the other Motown bassists who followed him" (1983) in his obituary of Jamerson in *Record Magazine*. In addition, others such as Dennis Coffey claim that even though there was indeed West Coast Motown recordings done in the 1960s, Jamerson would often overdub or replace the existing bass lines when the Detroit team worked on the existing backing track (Coffey, cited in Licks, 1989: 58). Conversely, Kaye has always been keen to place on record that most, but not all, Motown bass lines in this period were the work of Jamerson. Internet chat rooms favour Jamerson as the player, with many basing their opinions on sworn testaments made by Detroit musicians. The controversy over identification actually grows more problematic the more one researches the subject. This was an era of few audio-visual documents identifying anonymous session players. We do not even possess the photographic or filmed evidence to substantiate the claims of either party. Those that exist are extremely sketchy and inconclusive.

Perhaps the most comprehensive record of Kaye's work on Motown recordings comes in an interview with Kingsley Abbott in his 1993 edited collection. Kaye's recollections, backed up by others, and her own diaries, provide a great deal of detail relating to the tracks, the conditions and who else played on the sessions. She claims, with some bitterness, that many of the sessions were assumed to be demos and were thus undocumented and paid cash-in-hand before some of the tracks ended up as backing tracks on actual releases. This observation has been corroborated by George during interviews with New York-based session drummer Bernard "Pretty" Purdie, who "claimed he played on many demo sessions that Motown later released as singles with no changes" (Purdie, cited in George, 2003: 119). However, it has been documented that elements of overdubbing also took place on tracks recorded in both Detroit and Los Angeles, which further blurs the situation.

My issue here is not specifically to take sides or to prove a case, while admitting to finding both the consistency and the detail of Kaye's and others' corroborated arguments quite persuasive. Rather, the controversy raises two more fundamental issues: First, leaving aside anecdotal evidence, can we assign authorial status on the basis of the recordings themselves—the primary texts? If we cannot, then that raises another series of issues that will be returned to in due course. And, second, disputes over musicianship and accreditation go to the core of the whole authorship debate—why it matters in the past and why it continues to matter in our age of cyber-composition and virtual musicianship.

After the grey areas, disputes, omissions and (unwitting?) attempts to deceive (by some personal accounts), does the hard evidence of the recordings themselves offer us clarification? Unfortunately not. First of all, we need to explore the mechanics and technologies employed by Jamerson and Kaye to see if we can express findings related to a unique, authorial sound.

Bass frequencies, particularly on recordings from the pre-sixteen-track era, are often notoriously hard to investigate owing to their comparatively low mix level and poor audibility. It is possible to identify particular instruments—a short scale Gibson bass or a Rickenbacker model played with a plectrum does tend to sound very different to a Fender Precision, for instance. But so much depends upon other factors, it is hard to be sure. What we tend to do, as listeners or as researchers, is apply posteriori knowledge to the investigation. Thus, the sound of the bass on Andy Fraser's recordings with Free come to signify the classic Gibson sound, but only because we can see footage of him playing a particular instrument and in a particular style—a finger bassist employing a lot of partial chords and playing the gaps. Equally, documented credits stating that Stevie Wonder began making widespread use of a synthesizer to play bass lines from around 1972 strengthens the empirical evidence that allow us to clearly hear sonic distinctions on tracks such as "Superwoman" (1972). However, on other tracks, the differences between string and keyboard bass sounds are far less easy to distinguish. When the exaggerated use of portamento or the envelope filter distorts the sound, identification is easy. However, the identification of bass frequencies on *Innervisions* (1973), for instance, is often very difficult. Later, bass synth sounds could be triggered via guitars, and as technologies such as sampling began to make their presence felt in the 1980s, the resulting confusions over who (if anybody) played or programmed what pushed the authorship debate into even more confused terrain (but more on this topic in a later chapter).

In the period under scrutiny, Jamerson and Kaye both played the same instrument—a Fender Precision. Furthermore, each player rarely changed their flat wound strings and both used felt or foam muting in the bridge area to dampen their sound. However, each exemplified two opposing schools of bass playing in that Jamerson played with his fingers (or rather just his index finger), whereas Kaye played with a plectrum. It is widely assumed that an expert would, as a result, be able to tell the difference between them—possibly so. The problem remains: most of us are not so finely attuned to specific nuances in timbre. However, Kaye states that she could avoid the click that normally marks out a plectrum player by utilizing certain bass/amp settings, striking the strings close to the neck and using a flat wrist and palm damping. Conversely, she could adapt her sound and style when the session demanded it, as on her work with pop acts such as the Beach Boys or on soundtracks such as the "Theme from Mission: Impossible" (1966). In summary, as a session player, Kaye was adaptive rather than unique—a classic session player's stance, it should be noted. In addition, Jamerson's bass was directly inputted into the mixing desk (George, 2003: 125)—which normally resulted in a warmer, purer tone without distortion, but then his sound was also "limited and EQed" (Licks, 1989: 83), which can result in a less "natural" timbre. Kaye was recorded from an amp, with some compression (the same as limiting) on the tracks that she claimed she did for Motown. This evidence all acts to cloud issues of uniqueness.

Jamerson actually plays acoustic double bass on many early Motown sessions; his son still possesses the instrument, as shown in the film *Standing in the Shadows of Motown* (Justman, 2002), which has a noticeably different sound to an electric bass on many occasions (although a fretless model can confuse the issue). For instance, I would state with some conviction that acoustic bass is employed on

Stevie Wonder tracks such as "If You Really Love Me" and "Never Thought You'd Leave in Summer" (both 1971)—the slap and twang seems unmistakable. In addition, the slackly tuned drum is far removed from the tight and toppy snare of the classic Motown Sound, proving that some Motown recordings did not sound like Motown recordings by this point!

On another of Wonder's earliest hits, Lodder claims to note a bass overdub that is pick-played. As "Uptight" was recorded in 1965, this was precisely the era when, supposedly, the classic (Jamerson and Benjamin) rhythm section was in place on Motown recordings, but Lodder's notion at least partially challenges this automatic assumption. In addition, the young Stevie Wonder learned much from Benjamin, becoming a skillful drummer himself and certainly playing on most of his own later recordings. Thus, Lodder claims that Wonder was, in fact, the drummer on certain tracks as early as 1965 (2005: 39).

Licks has maintained that Jamerson sometimes overdubbed acoustic and electric bass lines onto the same track: "It was often difficult to tell that there were two basses on the same track" (Licks, 1989: 13). He may be right. Furthermore, he claims that Jamerson played stand-up bass on "Heatwave" and "Baby Love" (both 1964). With reference to the latter, a track I have heard literally hundreds of times, this claim surprises me, although again I am open to persuasion. One reason for my surprise, in addition to the actual sound of the bass track, lies in the fact that the relatively straightforward bass pattern, built on repeated singular root notes, does not appear to be Jamerson's trademark style, which is typically said to be (and experienced as) far busier, jazzier, full of startling changes in tempo and making great use of chromatic runs. On the other hand, "Baby Love", as with the previous Supremes' hit "Where Did Our Love Go" (1964), does feature a thicker, more prominent bass line than on subsequent hits such as "Come See About Me" and "Stop! In the Name of Love" (both 1965). In particular, the D bass note that underpins the D minor chord in bars five and six of the verse on "Where Did Our Love Go" really does boom and almost floods the track. This could be a result of a lack of equalization or compression, or it could be because a different instrument or instrumentalist is being employed. Also, having read Licks' claims that separate bass lines could be overdubbed in the period, I question whether I hear two on "Stop! In the Name of Love"—a low four-beat part complemented with an eight-beat part an octave above—or just one skilled practitioner at work. As the expression goes, perhaps you had to be there. To further fog the issue, George stated that "on several occasions, the electric bass of James Jamerson—though he would later deny this—was accompanied by Clarence Isabel on upright acoustic. Each would play two different lines, one a 'pulsating' and the other a straight 'running' line" (2003: 136). Is that what has been heard?

Two other points need to be noted at this point: First, Kaye, as already stated, claims she played on all of the early Supremes' hits. Second, Licks claims that

Jamerson's bass style changed radically at a point in the 1960s when he was allowed more space (and, by extension, authorial status) within recordings: "Towards the end of the year (1965), he exploded in a completely new direction . . . almost overnight" (Licks, 1989: 38). So, if early Jamerson bass tracks were totally different to his mature style, then how can we state that he had a totally unique style? In addition, evidence as to the bass player's identity is, as this section has attempted to prove, a matter of some contention. If we as listeners cannot tell the difference between an acoustic and an electric bass, or between a white female plectrum player and a black male finger player, then why does it matter who played the bass and to whom? We are, of course, dealing with extremely skilled players who would have been more than capable of playing to order and duplicating a sound or a style depending on the needs of the session. Licks is surely right to state that "by the late 60s most of Motown's bassists and arrangers tried to emulate James' style when they performed or wrote out bass lines" (1989: 60). Perhaps, ultimately, we are faced with the conclusion that the label itself and those that controlled it exerted a kind of corporate authorial identity on most of its releases.

Kaye summarizes the complex reasons leading to the playing controversies, which will probably never be completely resolved, by assigning the problems to "ignorance, prejudice and [a desire to avoid] stirring up business controversy . . . plus the fact that *they can't believe a woman did anything like that* [my emphasis] . . . plus the fact that no credits were given back in the 60s".

To these aspects must be added the issue of race. The edifice of black male authorial authenticity (and "soul") is challenged if a clean-living, Caucasian mother of three can be shown to have played the bass lines hitherto assumed to have been played by a hard-living, African American "brother". Sadly, Jamerson died young, in 1993, and he and many (indeed, most) other participants on the recordings can no longer provide a personal angle on this discussion.

As a final observation, in 2014, Kaye was interviewed by Johnny Walker on a BBC Radio 2 documentary, *The Carole Kaye Story* (Suckling, 2014). Despite covering the entire period when Kaye supposedly played on many Motown tracks, there was absolutely no mention of any contributions to songs on the label. The reasons, as with so much in this area of controversy, remain a mystery.

Janelle Monáe: Concept and Continuity

To extend the mythology of rock versus pop, we have to consider some of the really weighty distinctions in popular music, most of which have little more than a mythical, assumed reality: mainstream versus alternative, art versus commerce, the cerebral versus the corporeal. If we add to these the assumed distinctions constructed upon the bases of race, gender, genre and ethnicity, we have an overwhelming amount of evidence that perpetuates a high versus low culture divide. Marion Leonard has summarized this binary well with her phrase "the gender of genre" (2007: 24). Of course, this divide has to undergo adaptation in order to incorporate "low" concepts such as folk authenticity, roots, energy and technology in the pop construction of a fine art canon, but this process only amends history's aesthetic values; it does not fully subvert or dismantle them. The result is a situation where, in all fields of popular music analysis (journalism, media documentaries, web-based fandom or academia), authorship is only vouchsafed partially. In addition, the documenting of popular music, in terms of both journalistic and academic analysis, has been shown to be heavily biased in terms of the percentage of males to females (Ibid: 27–30). In viewing this overall process through the lens of gender, the clear conclusion is that females are largely excluded. In addition, those females inducted into the canon find that far more attention is paid to aspects such as star image and sexual iconography than when focusing upon equivalent males. Bob Dylan has so many books, conferences and treatises devoted to his oeuvre that there now exists the term "Dylanologist". I am arguing for the paucity of female equivalent neologisms—whether in the field of serious or trivial music (the distinction is used only to bolster the case, not because it has any concrete value). This is as a result of a range of aspects, most of which can be reduced to concepts and mythologies of gender. Admittedly, temporal factors ensure Dylan's legendary status, with genius often bestowed on those seen as groundbreaking. But leaving aside this issue, we can see that we are able to tick many boxes that allow for a construction of Dylan's author/canonical status. These include genre innovations, longevity and stylistic shifts, prolific sole compositions, creative collaborations, a perceived detachment from the machinations of the commercial music industry and the largely album-based status of Dylan's career.

How does a young African American female go about establishing her own authorial status, faced with a hegemonic representation of authorship predicated upon constructions of worth to which she cannot, or may not, want to subscribe? An overview of the nascent career path of Janelle Monáe may provide some answers to this question. At the time of writing, this artist has released one official EP and two albums, which obviously puts her at a disadvantage compared to most canonical artists with longevity bolstering their status. Equally, she emerges in a period where the sheer volume of music produced, and the huge back catalogue that now exists in popular music, makes it far harder to accomplish an artistic impact than was possible in the 1960s. As Reynolds has argued, so much of popular music now seems to be backward-looking and merely repeating the past, almost as if the weight of the canon acts to crush any impetus to move forward (2011). Monáe also has to struggle to overcome the stereotypes of gender, race and genre, with the knowledge that her forebearers in the broad field of female African American soul may have achieved great commercial success, and in fewer cases, critical acclaim, but these factors have not resulted in their inclusion into the authorial canon. Leonard has indicated that indie, as a genre, is more welcoming to female participants and creative agency than other areas (2007: 3). This is certainly the historical case if we compare indie to soul and its subgenres. The likes of Aretha Franklin, Whitney Houston, Diana Ross, Beyoncé Knowles and many others are known primarily for their vocal and performance prowess and their author images rather than as auteurs.

It would be an oversight not to recognize the fact that several female artists have fought hard to attain auteur status and have succeeded. In the 1970s, Kate Bush had no comparative female role models to draw inspiration from, possibly influencing her decision to surround herself with male collaborators and mentors: Richard James Burgess, Peter Gabriel, David Gilmour, Del Palmer, Jon Kelly and her two elder brothers (see Moy, 2007: 74–77). However, through a combination of will, talent, support and sheer artistic ambition, she eventually controlled all aspects of her career; furthermore, she also moved into hitherto male-dominated areas of digital technology, music production and video direction. In fact, in over- all terms, few artists, male or female, have ever had the final say over so many aspects of their career. But, as the saying goes, the exception proves the rule. What the likes of Kate Bush and, in different ways, the careers of PJ Harvey, Chrissie Hynde and Madonna provide are a much-needed lineage of female authorship to pass on to those that follow. However, all of these figures are white, and none operate solely in the fields of soul/R&B. As previously stated in Chapter One, for a variety of reasons, African American soul and its variations have often located authorship within studios, session players and production teams rather than, like the rock equivalent, within the autonomous band or individual. Does this result in a conundrum for the likes of Monáe? How does she locate herself within the inscribed mythologies of genre and race-based authorship? Thus far, her strategy seems to be to combine aspects of what might be called, for the sake of simplicity, the "rock model" and the "soul model". Here is how.

With notable exceptions, the album-based artist, and by extension the album itself, has come to be seen as the prime medium for the serious artist. Paul Stump, in accounting for the rise of progressive rock (a classic auteurist genre), argues that such developments were moving popular music away from genres such as soul and Motown, which some characterized as "the Fordist Antichrist of mass-produced pop pap" (1998: 136). Of course, rigid distinctions based on elitism are easy to counter, but the fact remains that the critical climate today still favours the rock model of authorship, and thus despite counters such as the impact of DJ authorship, the rise of single-based forms such as punk and dance (in its myriad manifestations) and the more recent impact of the internet upon purchasing and listening habits, the album as conceptual work still maintains its status. Emerging artists have to engage with this mythology. Not only has Monáe concentrated on albums rather than singles or tracks, but each of her works is deliberately set up as a concept album, and, furthermore, each concept album contributes toward an evolving multialbum saga (or *gesamtkunstwerk*). This includes an unfolding narrative, unified artwork and the construction of an alter ego or persona to drive the narrative in the guise of the android character known as Cindi Mayweather. On several occasions, tracks segue together, again, bolstering their status to be considered alongside the baroque or classical suite. This was also a device much used by progressive rock, but can be found elsewhere in African American music by female artists (for instance, Beyoncé's *I Am Sasha Fierce* [2008], Kelis's *Fleshtone* [2010] and Dawn Richard's *Goldenheart* [2013]), suggesting something of an authorial trend or ambit. It is not necessary to delve deeply into the unfolding narrative on Monáe's albums in aesthetic terms, beyond the fact that it is one of many strategies adopted by the artist that both boosts her authorial status and also, to an extent, breaks the rules of how a female African American markets herself in popular music.

The three works are all subtitled: *Metropolis* (2008) is also *Suite I (The Chase)*, *The ArchAndroid* (2010) is subtitled *Suites II and III*, and *The Electric Lady* (2013) is subtitled *Suites IV and V*. This device bolsters connotations of an unfolding oeuvre, with all the gravitas connected with such a term. The final track on the 2010 album also contains an arrangement of a Debussy piece (again, a device shared with another artist, Dawn Richard, on the concluding track of *Goldenheart*). Furthermore, the latter two works are divided, almost as an old vinyl LP was divided into sides, by beginning each suite with a track titled "Overture" (on *The ArchAndroid*) and "Electric Overture" (on *The Electric Lady*). These overtures do function in the traditional role of providing an introduction to, or recapitulation of, themes found elsewhere in the work. Through such terminology and such artistic choices, we are encouraged to view the artist as one embarking on a long career ("rock") as opposed to having less serious artistic aspirations ("pop"). It is immaterial how false this distinction might be; it is the perceptions and mythologies that result that are noteworthy.

In terms of author image, Janelle Monáe/Cindi Mayweather is the only presence, but she is not presented in an overtly sexualized manner. In fact, in terms of bare flesh, there is very little exposed, particularly in contrast to such contemporary icons as Beyoncé Knowles, Nicki Minaj or Rihanna. Theorists such as Kristin Lieb have noted the impact that platforms such as MTV (and, subsequently, You Tube, social media, etc.) have had upon female artists, as it "made beauty and sexuality a primary factor in a musician's career" (2013: xv–xvi). However, female authors must be aware of the pitfalls as well as the advantages that visual promotion can bring; we might note Sínead O'Connor's 2013 open letter to Miley Cyrus regarding her explicit use of bare flesh in promotional videos at this point. Monáe's strategy is not to pander to the more explicit demands of the video market, in terms of un/dress or the way the camera is engaged with the performer. In addition, her facial expressions are often neutral or express mild surprise. They rarely offer blatant seduction, but are more often mildly disconcerting, as found on the cover of *Metropolis*, where the figure of the woman/cyborg is disembodied, with wires protruding from the waist, elbow and shoulder. This is a direct homage to the image associated with the Fritz Lang-directed film (1927) of the same name, but without the evil characteristics connected to the film character. Even where an image connotes a projection of some kind of predator or dominatrix, as within the artwork for *The Electric Lady* that shows Monáe/Mayweather sporting a spiked "knuckleduster", her eyes still stare vaguely off to the right of the constructed viewer, somehow diffusing the potential menace offered by the accoutrement. While her album images are varied in terms of design, material and colour, it is interesting to note the artist's penchant for a more androgynous look, often based around a tuxedo, and the simple contrast of black and white in many of her publicity photos and on stage. This tendency in dress, with its connotations of business, hard work and cool efficiency, again contrasts with many of her female contemporaries. However, this look is not just about sharp style or sexual modesty. In accordance with the feminist rallying cry, the "personal is political", this uniform implicitly comments on the inequalities of race and class. Monáe has stated on numerous occasions that she is paying tribute to the struggles of her parents, who had to wear uniforms as part of their employment as janitors, truck drivers or postal workers (see Lynskey, 2010). Micropolitics become macropolitics.

Another strategy adopted to bolster the role of author is the naming of inspirations for songs and ideas within the CD booklets (for instance, "inspired by the idea of Ennio Morricone playing cards with Duke Ellington", or "inspired by Destino, Walt Disney and Salvador Dali"; Monáe, 2010, 2013). As well as giving us a clue about the artist's background and influences, these details aim to demonstrate intelligence and eclecticism, but they also show a degree of pretentiousness that again bolsters Monáe's construction of authorship. Pretension often signals ambition and connects values to art in a way that more "authentic" modes of communication do not.

As with most auteurs, male or female, black or white, Monáe relies on collaborators, including some industry big names such as Sean "Diddy" Combs and Antwan "Big Boi" Patton. However, for the most part, she writes within the broad collective known as the Wondaland Arts Society, which she helped found. Her direct writing contributions are hard to ascertain, although on most tracks, her name comes first in the credits followed by, usually, at least two others. Whereas this model of authorship is not unusual for female artists in her genre, the almost total reliance on played, as opposed to programmed, instruments does set her apart from contemporaries such as Beyoncé and Dawn Richard. It also detaches her from the modus operandi of the contemporary zeitgeist, while simultaneously her sheer range of genre influences (funk, soul, Latin, psychedelic, jazz and classical) demonstrates a postmodern sensibility. Thus, Monáe embodies the "postmodern authentic" in this openness to aspects of disunity, irony, obvious staging, the ransacking of historical models, multiple surfaces and the willing collision of art and commerce. John Hutnyk has talked about the search for authenticity being "a sham". He states that "indeed, the more sophisticated poses available . . . in the popular music scene, hold that the conscious recognition of the staged character of 'authentic' performance does not compromise, but can in effect enhance, authenticity" (2000: 90).

Reynolds and Press warn of the pitfalls of women adopting "mythological figures" or "mystical archetypes . . . it runs the risk of consolidating stereotypes (the cliché of woman as irrational, supernatural) or lapsing into essentialism (woman as biologically linked to nature)" (1995: 276). Certainly, there is little danger of the latter within the futuristic world of Cindi Mayweather. But the authors themselves provide a way beyond the impasse of the first stereotype through the trope of the masquerade. They see masquerade as a way that females can reclaim the triviality of fashion as "a reinvention of the self" (Ibid: 289). Monáe, through this postmodern playfulness with image and alter ego, can be seen to move us beyond any essentialist constraints. Whereas Reynolds and Press see this in terms of a counter-hegemonic rebellion, I see it in terms of striving for a new form of African American female authorship. It is creative rather than destructive. This version of authorship does not deny femininity's appropriation/exploitation of image, for instance. However, while Monáe conforms to the cultural norm that encourages female artists to present multiple images of themselves on CD sleeves, her denial in satisfying the male (predatory) gaze goes further in presenting counter-hegemonic images. While these still, paradoxically, function to objectify women, they do so here strictly within Monáe's own authorial terms. Neither does Monáe attempt to overturn certain aspects of traditional (male) authorship (production, technology and musicianship rest, mostly, with men). Rather, she comes up with multiple strategies to move forward the artist's authorship in ways that transcend gender- and race-based limitations. To accept that compromise is a necessary part of collective authorship is not to *be* compromised, but rather to open up avenues of creativity denied the sole author.

(Alison) Goldfrapp: She Is/They Are . . .

In contrast to Janelle Monáe's constructions of authorship, the music and author image of Goldfrapp allow us to broaden the investigation by focusing upon another female auteur who, despite some clear distinctions from Monáe, still cannot fail to work (willingly?) within several patriarchal constraints.

As the heading for this section indicates, Goldfrapp is and are, in the sense that although the act adopts the surname of Alison Goldfrapp, the name equally refers to the duo/band of Goldfrapp, including long-standing musical partner Will Gregory. Alison Goldfrapp thus functions as the semiotic signifier of the band and stands as the principal author image. Of course, naming a collective after the sur-name of one member automatically confers author status on that named member, but this may happen for a variety of reasons: commercial, iconographic or, indeed, linguistic—the connotations of Goldfrapp to an Anglophone are considerably more "exotic" and perhaps marketable than those of an act called "Gregory".

As critical outsiders essentially, we are not privy to the decisions that Gold-frapp makes relating to gender divisions and authorship roles, or to what extent such matters might ever have been raised by the members. However, discussions relating to who does what (Alison Goldfrapp is the visual conceptualist, although she and Gregory make joint decisions), and, in passing, Alison Goldfrapp's issues with age and gender have been covered in interviews. But what is evident is the degree to which, wittingly or unwittingly, the two do at least partly conform to an industry and marketing-derived division of roles predicated upon gender distinctions. There is the *assumption* that the female, as the public face/personae, is responsible for lyrics and melodies, while the male is the player and musician behind the scenes. Or, this is what we are encouraged to believe or construct. In actual fact, this assumption is partly untrue. Although the female, in this case, is indeed responsible for all of the lyrics, both members have vouched for the col-laborative nature of their music composition in numerous interviews (see Glee-son, 2008). However, the distinction in roles is further abetted by the female's high profile in videos, stage performances, photo shoots and on album covers, and by her elaborate use of makeup, costume and imagery, which is sometimes moder-ately, sometimes overtly, sexual.

Both Will Gregory's love for and use of "soundtrack timbres" (classical, Ennio Morricone) and Alison's visual art background and visualization of music and melodies account for another complementary, yet divergent, interest in visuals that are, nevertheless, made manifest in a gender-based manner. These elements are brought into a creative collision with Alison's love for Kate Bush, Prince, T. Rex and Iggy Pop. The pair's visual and conceptual worlds perhaps best meld in Alison's affection for Serge Gainsbourg and James Bond themes, which seem to infuse the duo's creations. Equally, Will's acknowledged musical influences fuse with the string-led romantic, knowingly-retro cinematic landscape so many have remarked upon. Thus, each member can be said to contribute to the essentially mixed-media world of Goldfrapp.

On the 2013 album *Tales of Us*, after additional musicians have been credited, we read the phrase, "all other instruments played by Will and Alison", with the two jointly credited as writers and producers. In addition, Alison co-directs the artwork for the album, while Will composes the string arrangements. Are these gender distinctions an issue? Shouldn't we, instead, recognize the collaborative nature of the act and celebrate the equal-but-different gender roles that acts such as Goldfrapp demonstrate? Perhaps the findings of many associated with schools of critical thought such as post-structuralism, postmodernism, and what has been termed third-wave feminism can help shed light on this dilemma. In particular, Judith Butler's work on gender and sexuality, while not really concerning itself with the specificities of popular music, can be applied and adapted to this area of gender-based authorship.

In brief and building upon the work of many diverse theorists (in particular, Jacques Derrida, Michel Foucault and Monique Wittig), Butler argues against notions of the essential or the innate when considering gender. In common with Foucault, her approach is essentially deconstructive in an attempt to reveal the performative social and historical processes that help construct myths in this field. "What we take to be an internal essence of gender is manufactured through a sustained set of acts", and gender is "a shifting and contextual phenomenon" (1999: xv, 14). If we substitute the word "roles" for the word "acts" (or "gestures", as Butler also has it), we have a way to see how the field of popular music operates when dealing with gender. At its most positive, Butler's work offers a glimpse beyond the fixity of existing practices and taxonomies—in the reclamation of the term queer and in the transformative possibilities offered by a polymorphous reimagining of gender roles. She favours a situation consisting of a "multiplicity of cultural, social and political intersections" (1999: 19) in which women may be allowed to construct the self. Butler, in common with many other theorists such as Foucault, Luce Irigaray and Wittig, want us to be able to move beyond the constructed binaries of gender. However, she has also spoken of being "not outside the language that structures me, but neither am I determined by the language that makes this 'I' possible" (Ibid: xxvi). This notion of being *partially* constrained by a signifying system has great resonance in terms of the influence of another semiotic signifying system—the music industry—which, in addition to language, uses iconography, stereotyping and mythologies to bolster a "naturalized" set of values. Thus, we must always acknowledge the realities and constraints of the existing, essentially patriarchal, domain of global entertainment and the commercial market for popular music.

We have to face the fact that popular music has to appeal to mainstream audiences, and, broadly, this appeal lies within established market values. These values state that we are faced with the choice between a studious-looking male with glasses, often bearded and with unkempt hair, and a blonde-highlighted, gamine, bisexual with long, slim legs wearing a variety of exotic/erotic costumes and adopting a number of seductive poses while singing in a breathy, high vocal register. The visual disparities alone mean that their roles are preordained—at least, if sales and success beyond a marginal level are countenanced. It can be argued that the aforementioned Janelle Monáe and Alison Goldfrapp (as well as many others—Tori Amos, Björk, Kate Bush, etc.) can certainly push boundaries, but that these boundaries, while flexible, still ultimately act to contain and limit transformative possibilities. Perhaps the metaphor of the "elastic boundary" is more useful than that of the often-termed "glass ceiling" in this case. Elastic stretches, yet also ultimately can restrain. As the full title of Butler's book *Gender Trouble* (1999) indicates, we are dealing with the *subversion* of identity within popular music roles. This is akin to what Butler sees in visual mis-performances relating to drag and cross-dressing that reveals gender itself to be a performance (see Brady and Schirato, 2011: 56). Alison Goldfrapp does not use drag or cross-dressing (although many in pop do), but instead mis-performs heteronormative signifying systems by, in pop terms, doing male things. But subversion has its limits, imposed and mythologized externally. The day that an act such as Goldfrapp has the male and the female figures more radically reversing the norms—with the male fronting the act, and the female working semi-anonymously, beyond the gendered gaze, is the day that true, fundamental transformation will take place.

Based on their longevity, eclecticism and critical and commercial success, it is hard not to conclude that Goldfrapp have found a way of collaborating that works for them. They do not operate within a theoretical terrain, but in the hard commercial world where an act is also a brand. They communicate semiologically within a market *langue* that is not of their own choosing. Despite constraints (even with the proviso that the visual emphasis on the female member is expected and hegemonic), the act has broadly transcended gender-based distinctions in other respects. Thus, they are *transformative*, in Butler's terms. In addition, the sharp turns in style and genre that are a feature of their career—taking in folk, electronica, glam and cinematic balladry—all bear witness to their restless, eclectic, yet *unified* sense of authorship and mutual purpose. *Tales of Us*, indeed.

Summary

Earlier in this chapter I posed a series of questions, among which were whether we can avoid constructing an essentialist thesis seeing female authorship as "other" or distinct and also asking if female authorship always needs to be articulated through the lens of gender. As a way of engaging with these notions, I'd like to end this chapter as it began, by exploring the implications of an article written about a female act in the *Guardian*, but this time, by male journalist John Harris (2014). In his subheading relating to the all-female band, Warpaint, Harris asks, "Could rock's future be female?" (Ibid: 28), and at various points, the assumed decline in guitar-driven rock is referenced. Subsequently, both writer and interviewees are clear when expressing the essential differences (and advantages/disadvantages) that being an all-female band confers upon both its members and the music they create. According to Warpaint's Jenny Lee Lindberg, "the way you communicate with women is very emotional" (Ibid). Lindberg places this issue in assumed opposition with male bands who "don't let their emotions get the best of them" (Ibid) and just get on with the job. Another distinction is noted by band member Emily Kokal when referring to a period when the group played with a male musician, "It's a feel thing. Sometimes when we had men in the band, the feel wasn't quite locking in. It's maybe the nature of men pushing and women receiving" (Ibid: 29). Later in the article, the notion of there still being space for women to approach guitar rock is articulated, in terms of its newness, the untapped nature of their experiences and the way that audiences see what they are doing as "thought-provoking" (Ibid). Even the band name, Warpaint, carries different connotations depending upon whether its members are male or female.

What can be concluded from this article is a simple yes to the questions posed of authorship and gender. Yes, female authorship is seen as and constructed as "other" by multiple discourses within the field—whether by participants or critical observers. Yes, femininity/femaleness is essentialized as distinct from masculinity/maleness by the same interested parties. Notions of myth apply, but these function as given, empirical realities in a terrain that is as commercially compromised as popular music. Furthermore, this is as true of so-called alternative rock as it is of mainstream pop. Wayman recounts the abuse she suffered after criticizing other female artists' sexualized images (Ibid) before recanting her use of terms such as slut. Scopophilic culture, the male gaze, the visually-obsessed world and the increasing prevalence of sexually explicit, even pornographic, imagery all contribute to a music scene that essentializes females as sexual beings. Sexuality is polymorphous, and it is naïve not to recognize that images of the all-female Warpaint dancing in videos or cuddling each other affectionately will possess an erotic charge to some consumers. The amount of flesh on view or the amount of provocative pouting (or its absence) is almost a side issue. This finding is why issues of sexuality invariably deal with the female gender and, indeed, why gender itself is often a discussion centring on females, a fact that this chapter only reinforces.

Tricia Rose, in *Black Noise: Rap Music and Black Culture in Contemporary America* (1994), while concentrating exclusively upon the black female experience in a specific genre, makes a more broadly applicable point when she states that "works by black female rappers . . . have a . . . contradictory effect; they affirm black female beauty and yet often preserve the logic of female sexual objectification" (1994: 147). To conflate expressions used by Rose and Butler, we might see this double bind in terms of a *contradictory performative effect*: one placed upon females to a far greater extent than upon males and one that sees no resolution with participants locked into mythologized forces of hegemony.

The liberal, egalitarian sensibility may yearn for more fairness and ways beyond the limitations and contradictions outlined in this chapter, for more female representation in fields of authorship dominated by males, but perhaps the old adage or, more accurately, *aspiration* of equal but different may have to suffice. The artwork for *I Am Sasha Fierce* (2009) contains nineteen photographs of Beyoncé. There are eighteen photographs of Tori Amos within *Unrepentant Geraldines* (2014). In addition, Ahonen notes the multiple photographs of Amos loosely disguised as "visual representations of song narrators" (2008: 90) on the covers album *Strange Little Girls* (2001). In addition, she notes the prevalence of multifarious author images within the oeuvre of Björk, which emphasize "Björk's autonomy and individuality" (Ibid: 48). This author image runs counter to the very collective and collaborative nature of the artist's work with mostly male producers, such as Nellee Hooper, Graham Massey, Goldie and Howie B. Thus, the promoted author images remain female to a degree that the music and productions do not.

There are a mere six photographs of Nicki Minaj within *Pink Friday: Roman Reloaded* (2012); however, this is tempered by the fact that one of the images is a fold-out, poster-sized (larger than A4) photo that features a paint-spattered Minaj dressed in micro-underwear. In terms of author image, questions of exploitation or who is exploiting who are obviously raised, but not so obviously answered. Do such expressions of gendered author image indicate submission, resistance, domination or empowerment? In the final analysis, what such an emphasis on image does demonstrate is the degree to which certain elements within explorations of authorship are and will remain deeply gendered.

In 1995, Reynolds and Press posited a hopeful projection that the future would see a more widespread representation of women in all areas of the music industry. Indeed, it is true that new female artists are emerging all the time who have a greater degree of authorial agency than has been the case in the past. In 2014, FKA twigs released her first solo album, *LP1*, having previously been employed as a dancer on other acts' videos. On her album, she writes, programs and co-produces, as well as has considerable directorial input on her videos. This does not prevent much media attention from focusing upon the explicit sexuality of her visual images and her lyrics (Beaumont-Thomas, 2014), but still indicates a young woman empowered by all aspects of her nascent career. However, such positive examples should not blind us to the fact that this may be a trend, but not necessarily a sea change, at least not to the degree aspired to by Reynolds and Press and many others. Exceptions to the rule can always be found. Direct female equivalents to authorial acts (or "empires") such as the Neptunes, Xenomania, Kanye West or Pharrell Williams are still hard to find. In terms of female authorship, great strides have been made, but a position of equality and one beyond sexual and iconic stereotyping still remains, to a degree, an aspiration.

Acknowledgment

My thanks to my colleague Danijela for her comments when reading an early draft of this chapter, March 18, 2014.

Bibliography

Abbott, Kingsley (ed.) (2001) *Calling Out Around the World: A Motown Reader*, London: Helter-Skelter.

Ahonen, Laura (2008) *Constructing Authorship in Popular Music: Artists, Media and Stardom*, Milton Keynes: VDM Verlag.

Battersby, Christine (1989) *Gender and Genius: Towards a Female Aesthetics*, London: Women's Press.

Beaumont-Thomas, Ben (2014) "Private Dancer", *the Guardian Guide*, 9 August, pp 8–11.

Brabazon, Tara (2012) *Popular Music: Topics, Trends and Trajectories*, London: Sage.

Brady, Anita & Tony Schirato (2011) *Understanding Judith Butler*, London: Sage.

Burgess, Richard James (2013) *The Art of Music Production: The Theory and Practice*, Fourth Edition, New York: Oxford University Press.

Burns, Lori & Mélisse LaFrance (2002) *Disruptive Divas: Feminism, Identity & Popular Music*, London: Routledge.

Butler, Judith (1999) *Gender Trouble: Feminism and the Subversion of Identity*, London: Routledge.

Foucault, Michel (1979) *The History of Sexuality, Volume 1: An Introduction*, London: Allen Lane.

George, Nelson (2003) *Where Did Our Love Go? The Rise and Fall of the Motown Sound*, London: Omnibus.

Gleeson, Sinead (2008) "Archive Interview: Goldfrapp", *State Magazine*, 6 March, accessed 27-03-14, http://www.state.ie/features/interview-goldfrapp.

Harris, John (2014) "Fab Four", *the Guardian*, 21 June, pp 28–29.

Hoby, Hermione (2013) "The Men Behind the Sound of 2013", *the Guardian*, 27 December, pp 6–7.

Hutnyk, John (2000) *Critique of Exotica: Music, Politics and the Culture Industry*, London: Pluto.

Leonard, Marion (2007) *Gender in the Music Industry: Rock, Discourse and Girl Power*, Aldershot: Ashgate.

Licks, Dr. (1989) *Standing in the Shadows of Motown: The Life and Music of Legendary Bassist James Jamerson*, Wynnewood, Penn.: Dr. Licks Publishing.

Lieb, Kristin (2013) *Gender, Branding, and the Modern Music Industry*, London: Routledge.

Lodder, Steve (2005) *Stevie Wonder: The Classic Albums*, London: Backbeat Press.

Lynskey, Dorian (2010) "Janelle Monáe: Sister from Another Planet", *the Guardian*, 26 August, accessed 13-03-14, http://theguardian.com/music/2010/aug/26/janelle-monae-sister-another-planet/.

Marsh, Dave (1983) "James Jamerson: What Becomes of the Broken Hearted?", *Record Magazine*, 1 November, accessed 19-06-08, http://rocksbackpages.com/Library/Article/james-jamerson-what-becomes-of-the-broken-hearted.

Mayhew, Emma (2004) "Positioning the Producer: Gender Divisions in Creative Labour and Value", in Whiteley, Sheila, Andy Bennett & Stan Hawkins (eds.), *Music, Space and Place: Popular Music and Cultural Identity*, Aldershot: Ashgate, pp 149–162.

McClary, Susan (1991) *Feminine Endings: Music, Gender & Sexuality*, Minneapolis: University of Minnesota Press.

Moy, Ron (2007) *Kate Bush and Hounds of Love*, Aldershot: Ashgate.

Negus, Keith & Michael Pickering (2004) *Creativity, Communication and Cultural Value*, London: Sage.

O'Brien, Lucy (2002) *She-Bop II: The Definitive History of Women in Rock, Pop and Soul*, London: Continuum.

O'Connor, Sinéad (2013). "Sinéad O'Connor's Open Letter to Miley Cyrus", *the Guardian*, 3 October, accessed 15-03-15, http://www.theguardian.com/music/2013/oct/03/sinead-o-connor-open-letter-miley-cyrus.

Reynolds, Simon (2011) *Retromania: Pop Culture's Addiction to Its Own Past*, London: Faber & Faber.

Reynolds, Simon & Joy Press (1995) *The Sex Revolts: Gender, Rebellion and Rock'n'Roll*, London: Serpent's Tail.

Rose, Tricia (1994) *Black Noise: Rap Music and Black Culture in Contemporary America*, Middletown, Conn.: Wesleyan University Press.

Stump, Paul (1998) *The Music's All That Matters: A History of Progressive Rock*, London: Quartet.

Toynbee, Jason (2000) *Making Popular Music: Musicians, Creativity and Institutions*, London: Arnold.

Walser, Robert (1993) *Running with the Devil: Power, Gender and Madness in Heavy Metal Music*. Middletown, Conn.: Wesleyan University Press.

Whiteley, Sheila (2000) *Women and Popular Music: Sexuality, Identity and Subjectivity*, London: Routledge.

Zak, Albin (2001) *The Poetics of Rock: Cutting Tracks, Making Records*, Oakland: University of California Press.

Audio-Visual Sources

Tori Amos (2001) *Strange Little Girls*.
  (2014) *Unrepentant Geraldines*.
Beyoncé (2009) *I Am Sasha Fierce*.
FKA twigs (2014) *LP1*.
Four Tops (1965) "I Can't Help Myself".
  (1967) "Bernadette".
Marvin Gaye (1971) *What's Goin' On*.
Goldfrapp (2013) *Tales of Us*.
Justman, Paul (2002) (director) *Standing in the Shadows of Motown*, film documentary.
Kelis (2010) *Fleshtone*.
Nicki Minaj (2012) *Pink Friday: Roman Reloaded*.
Janelle Monáe (2008) *Metropolis: The Chase Suite, Special Edition*.
  (2010) *The ArchAndroid: Suites II and III*.
  (2013) *The Electric Lady: Suites IV and V*.

Martha Reeves & the Vandellas (1964) "Heatwave".

Dawn Richard (2013) *Goldenheart*.

Lalo Schifrin (1966) "Theme from Mission: Impossible".

Suckling, Chris (producer) (2014) *The Carole Kaye Story*, BBC Radio 2 documentary, broadcast 2-06-14.

The Supremes (1964) "Baby Love", "Where Did Our Love Go".

(1965) "Come See About Me", "Stop! In the Name of Love".

Stevie Wonder (1965) "Uptight".

(1967) "I Was Made to Love Her".

(1971) "If You Really Love Me", "Never Thought You'd Leave in Summer".

(1972) "Superwoman".

(1973) *Innervisions*.

3

THE SINGULAR AND THE COLLECTIVE

The Writer as Auteur

Before the likes of Buddy Holly and the Beatles combined hitherto separate roles within popular music, there was a clear historical demarcation between writers and musicians. This should come as no surprise when we compare popular music to the orchestral tradition or to folk, jazz or even to theatre or cinema. With notable exceptions, we do not expect a cellist to write their own concerto, but rather we experience Jacqueline du Pré's interpretation of Elgar (although, of course, this can be read as an act of authorship in itself). Equally, we do not expect a stage actor to write their own script. For every figure like Woody Allen (writer, actor and director), there are dozens of respected actors whose every word or, at the most extreme, every gesture is the result of the director's vision—or so we assume or have been told. For the most part, traditional folk performers tapped into an oral repertoire, as self-composition was indeed frowned upon in some quarters (see Brocken, 2003). There are whole areas of jazz that rest upon concepts of spontaneity and improvisation (again, another version of authorship; I will return to this issue in Chapter Five) rather than on players writing original works. However, there are no hard and fast rules. As noted in the Introduction, Toynbee's research into the authorship of Charles Mingus does demonstrate important exceptions, but exceptions prove the rule (2000: 201). Why should popular music be any different?

In this chapter, several facets of authorship will be explored: principally, the historical path leading to the widespread phenomenon of the "multitasker" and tensions between the solitary composer and collective authorship, and between the constructed divided status of band members versus session players. The essentially collaborative nature of popular music has already been posited. Within this scenario, how can creative demarcations exist between the sole author and group authorship, and between the composing group musicians and outsiders, often referred to as session musicians? How can we draw the line between the mere hired hand and the creative outsider?

One dimension of the auteur process culminates in the situation where a musician may also be the composer, arranger, producer, mixer and even have significant input into areas such as design, choreography, audio-visual direction, marketing, business and promotion. What factors allow for this situation to emerge, and is pop a special case in this respect?

As explored in Chapter One, concepts of authorship vary across genres and ethnicities. For the most part, soul and R&B authorship was quite rigid and hierarchical in the early-1960s, with most successful acts being vocalists and little more. The concept of the band as a playing and singing unit was developed more fully by acts such as the Beatles and those who followed them, who worked in a different generic and geographical terrain. Many such acts have run successfully as virtual dictatorships, with only some members being granted the status of auteur. Examples might include Mick Jagger and Keith Richards in the Rolling Stones, Paul Weller in the Jam, and Brian Wilson in the Beach Boys. Other acts have operated on a far more collective and democratic basis, particularly if we examine compositional credits; we might consider the work of the likes of U2, Nirvana, REM and Black Sabbath in this regard. This is not to say that individual compositional aspects in a four-piece band are divided up on the basis of 25% shares, but, more importantly, that this signals that the band wants the process of accreditation to be seen as collective. In addition, we must leave aside questions of star image and iconography, which are explored elsewhere.

Some acts start off as ostensible democracies, but then an exploration of ongoing authorial credits illuminates an internal power struggle. While the impact of success and the disparity in the perception of musicians' roles often results in a bias leading to the atomization of the composing leader over and above that of the democratic unit, the opposite can occur, as the explorations in this chapter will show.

Within the very term popular music rests the seeds for a radical challenge to established notions of authorship. The weight of tradition and hierarchy and the lack of antecedent role models must bear down upon the member of an orchestra, militating against this individual doing anything more than learning to play their instrument to a high standard, reproducing the work of composers and interpreting conductors to an assumed level of expertise. The popular music musician suffers less of these constraints, although they existed in the past and have not disappeared, as demonstrated when we witness the modus operandi of the boy/girl band or the recent success of talent shows such as *The X Factor, Pop Idol* and *The Voice* in the UK (and global equivalents).

When Buddy Holly (and others such as Chuck Berry) emerged in the mid-1950s as players, singers and composers, their creative breadth was unusual, but not without precedent. Although Holly is closely associated with his backing group, the Crickets, as the very title suggests, Buddy Holly and the Crickets indicates an automatic distinction between leader and band members. However, this distinction was as much about authorship as star image and status and was an implicit portent of changing times. In writing many of his songs and contributing to arrangements and production, he was not the great transgressor that his orchestral equivalent would be seen to be. He was only working in a field largely discounted in the 1950s as throwaway, light entertainment, and the creative demarcations were assumed rather than more rigidly inscribed. In addition, he was working in a creative and geographical backwater (based for a time around a studio in Clovis, New Mexico) and, ultimately, recording for small, independent or subsidiary record labels. According to Spencer Leigh (2009), Holly initially signed for the major label Decca, and recorded in Nashville under producer Owen Bradley. However, artist and producer had creative disagreements—the artist wanted more say over production and arrangements. Holly's contract was later not renewed, and he subsequently signed with the Decca subsidiary Brunswick and also, unusually, signed as a solo artist with Coral, another small label. These business arrangements allowed Holly to assume greater creative control and to become an early example of the popular music auteur in the brief period before his untimely death in 1959 at the age of twenty-two.

The influence of the likes of Holly and Chuck Berry on the Beatles has been well documented, both in numerous biographies (written and television) and interviews. What is more significant for this chapter is their legacy as creative authors. First, it is important to note that many of their British contemporaries never fully, or even partly, made the transition from being players and interpreters to being writers (examples include the Searchers, Gerry and the Pacemakers, the Swinging Blue Jeans, etc.). The Beatles never had an inferiority complex in relation to the perceived model of popular music composition constructed by the US (and the British) press in the 1950s. Lennon and McCartney were composers almost from the outset of their working relationship and appeared never to see their ethnicity or nationality as a barrier. In contrast, even after the Beatles' emergence as quality songwriters (see Mann, 1963), near-contemporaries such as the Rolling Stones and the Animals still relied, at least initially, upon cover versions. The possibly apocryphal, or at least embellished, tale of Stones' manager Andrew Loog Oldham locking Jagger and Richard in a room as a way of compelling them to develop as writers may be a myth, but it is a myth whose construction tells us a lot about the shifting values of the time (Loog Oldham, 2001). Not only was it seen as vital that the Rolling Stones compete with the Beatles as creative artists, but also it was recognized that they needed the financial independence garnered by composers and, ultimately, to become owners of their own publishing. Other British bands forming in the wake of the beat boom, such as the Move and the Small Faces, were largely self-composing creative units (with Roy Wood and Steve Marriott/Ronnie Lane, respectively, as the main writers), and indicate how rapidly authorial shifts occurred between about 1963 and 1967. As is so often the case, authorial role models encouraged a new perspective among the burgeoning and soon-to-be-termed rock scene.

It is important to emphasize the partial and evolutionary nature of these developments in authorship. At the same time as these shifts were occurring, there still existed the light entertainment world of rigid demarcations. Many solo artists such as Cilla Black, Dusty Springfield and Tom Jones were, in effect, completely reliant on interpreting others' work. This also applies, in overall career terms, to some of the most significant global performers of the age such as Elvis Presley, Frank Sinatra and, more recently, Barbra Streisand and Celine Dion. During the Beatles era, there were also numerous jobbing musicians clocking in for three-hour sessions and playing music almost by rote, with little or no creative input or artistic recognition. Even Eric Clapton, whose status as a player and composer was almost without parallel by this era, performed without a credit on the Beatles' eponymous 1968 album. Whether he appeared as a special guest is immaterial, he still had the actual status of a session player, although doubtless he was either paid more than standard Musicians' Union rates or possibly did it "for art" (in which case some would argue that he actually did *not* have session man status).

Some session players belatedly gained genuine critical, if not financial, status (as we saw with the Funk Brothers, for instance). Others such as Jimmy Page and John Paul Jones tired of the creative constraints and formed or joined creative units such as the Yardbirds and, more significantly, Led Zeppelin. The very fact that Jimmy Page later obtained global status and other session players such as Big Jim Sullivan remained largely unknown sheds light upon the cult of authorship that rock journalism and the paradigm of authenticity helped to cultivate. It is highly significant that researchers are often reliant on obituaries or Wikipedia biographies in order to gauge the true worth of the session player.

Hal Blaine, drummer often associated with the California-based group of session players some refer to as the Wrecking Crew, has claimed to have played on over 35,000 tracks. He has performed on more than forty No. 1 US hit singles and over 350 top ten records by artists as diverse as the Beach Boys, the Byrds, Frank Sinatra, Elvis Presley, John Denver and the Tijuana Brass (Blaine, 2003). However, quantity is a negative signifier in "rockist" circles, suggesting a production-line mentality at odds with the romantic model. It is difficult to suffer for your art when playing three long sessions in a day—in aesthetic, if not in physical, terms. Carol Kaye claimed that it was difficult for a session player to turn down work in the 1960s, as this would get you a bad reputation in that competitive world, based on availability, adaptability and economic imperatives (Kaye, cited in Suckling, 2014). Blaine played on "Goodbye to Love" (1972) by the Carpenters, although, as with most of his work, only a few drum experts could identify anything personal in his style. However, more easily recognizable in dealing with session player authorship is the work of the lead guitarist on the same track, Tony Peluso. In this chapter, however, the focus falls on constructed roles and status rather than on the actual performance aspects of the session player. Thus, this track and Peluso's work will be returned to in a future chapter.

According to Dave Laing (2012), Big Jim Sullivan helped pioneer the use of guitar effects such as the wah-wah and fuzzbox. These were heard on Dave Berry's hit single "The Crying Game" and P.J. Proby's "Hold Me" (both 1964). During his session career, Sullivan played on over fifty major UK hits, usually in the middle-of-the-road vein. Page was similarly prolific and contributed to muzak as well as recordings by the Who, the Kinks, Them and Marianne Faithfull (Page, 1993). Page and Sullivan shared session duties on occasions. Although unknown to the wider public, their historical significance cannot be overlooked:

> The sound of British pop music in the 1960s was largely the creation of unsung recording-session musicians who accompanied the solo singers of the era and were frequently enlisted to improve the efforts of well-known pop groups. The principal guitarists of this elite team were Jimmy Page . . . and Big Jim Sullivan.
>
> (Laing, 2012)

Paradigms of Authenticity

This begs the question why Page is a household name in popular music circles and has even had poor quality demos released commercially (demonstrating notions of the auteur's formative years), whereas Sullivan remains relatively unknown outside of "muso" circles. The answer is simple: Page later became a multitasker within a self-contained authored group and thus an exemplar of the authenticity paradigm. This paradigm's construction by journalists, fans and, to an extent, academics dates from the period in the late 1960s when pop becomes rock. Simon Reynolds sees many rock critics as superimposing an outdated model of art values upon popular music. He personifies them as:

> cultured, educated individuals who nevertheless love what parent culture stigmatizes as juvenile, trivial and empty. Burning with an inferiority

complex towards the 'high' culture in whose discourse they are themselves fluent, their overweening desire is to validate pop culture.

(1990: 11)

This validation helps construct binary oppositions between art and commerce and helps to build a canon of worth. Thus, it functions in a parallel fashion to the construction of the auteur in film theory outlined in the Introduction. Deena Weinstein refers to the art versus commerce binary as "a (useful) romantic illusion" before deconstructing its authority (1999: 57–69). She states that in the rock era, "the myth of the irreconcilable opposition between art-authenticity and commerce was established: henceforth musical discourse had a literary discourse to police it, indeed, to normalize it . . . the binary has become the guiding myth-structure of rock" (Ibid: 59, 60).

However, the writer then falls into the same binary trap by claiming that "one need only look at the top-selling records year after year to realize that authenticity is not a concern of the general music-consuming public" (Ibid: 66). This opposition between serious rock fans and casual pop fans, as well as being merely an ungrounded claim, can be challenged by another ungrounded claim. I find it a false assumption that fans of, say, Justin Bieber, One Direction or Lady Gaga do not treat their objects of fandom and desire equally as serious, authentic artists. Indeed, as these mostly relatively young and immature fans progress (or *regress*) into adulthood, they leave behind simple "faith" and instead start to construct identities upon those very same binaries that Weinstein exposes. They leave behind a belief in authenticity and replace it with a binary code of distinction based upon specific tropes of authenticity. A twelve-year-old Justin Bieber fan will not criticize Bruce Springsteen's inauthenticity. That same fan, a few years later, disowning their adolescent tastes and having discovered an identity constructed around the ideal of a rock canon, may well criticize Bieber's inauthenticity. They now possess a binary paradigm that supersedes the youthful "I like/I don't like" with the adult "this has authentic value/this does not".

For Robert Pattison, the basis of this new credo lies in an updated version of vulgar romantic Pantheism: "The artistic virtues of rock and Romanticism are originality, primal order, energy, honesty and integrity" (1985:188). However, this aesthetics, modeled on the values of prior art movements and paradigms, has not resulted in all pop being granted the status of serious art within the canon. As explored within Chapter One, this can result in the construction of a partial and self-perpetuating oeuvre that has typically, and almost inevitably, reflected the tastes of certain social groupings, males, academics, the bourgeoisie, Anglophones, at the direct expense of other social groupings such as women, ethnic minorities and the masses. For Robert Walser:

Rock critics' own preoccupation with art rock reflects their acceptance of the premises of the classical model. Performers who haven't composed their own material—'girl groups', Motown, soul singers—have rarely won critical respect comparable to that granted artists who better fit the model of the auteur.

(1993: 7)

Clearly, the authenticity paradigm served its purpose in helping to validate both popular music as a form and also the tastes and values of its devotees. However, in an age characterized by increasing diversity, technological innovation, genre hybridity and many of the challenges posed by a postmodern aesthetics, the lingering echoes of this position have become more critically exposed (see Moore, 2012: 261–271). This exposure has not prevented its continuing, and largely unquestioned, romantic adoption within popular music journalism and fan-based criticism. Authorship and authenticity—often entwined—remain mythologized and a given. Walter Benjamin (1999) was challenging notions of the authentic aura surrounding the work of art in the 1930s, and his influence can be felt in the more recent theories expounded by the likes of Roland Barthes (1972) and John Berger (1972). The latter attempted to democratize the audience for semiotic deconstruction by producing televisual essays relating to the religiosity or mystification of traditional readings of artworks in the 1970s. However, the field of popular music has remained, to a large degree, in the thrall of romantic mythologies. Within academia, the authenticity paradigm has been challenged and deconstructed, but its close link to the concept of authorship, as argued in the Introduction and Chapter One, has largely remained implicit.

Hugh Barker and Yuval Taylor's recent take on authenticity deconstructed this edifice in myriad ways—and from the very outset. Its full title, *Faking It: The Quest for Authenticity*, immediately sets up the constructed nature of searching for something that may not exist, outside of mythologies. Early on, they state that "Nirvana had always *appeared* (my emphasis) absolutely genuine in everything they did" (Barker and Taylor, 2007: 2). There is a world of difference between the use of the term "appeared" and the choice of a less nuanced term such as "were". The authors claimed that this "notion of authenticity" dates back to at least the period of the eighteenth century (Ibid: 58). Deconstruction is as much about the choice, or interrogation of signifiers, as it is about the underlying concepts. Barker and Taylor's wide-ranging account, taking in genres and individual examples from blues, country, rock and roll, disco, punk, grunge and hip hop, constructs a convincing case for the long-standing (and continuing) existence of the authenticity paradigm and provides many examples of its manifest limitations. Working within the metagenre of dance music, Jeremy Gilbert and Ewan Pearson argue that through explicit challenges to structural and timbral conventions, dance music offers a jouissance that moves it beyond the binaries of rock and pop (1999). Upon their and others' work rests this book's attempt to wrestle with the dimensions of authorship that are so integral a part of this paradigm. It is only through a rigorous investigation of authorship and its linguistic construction within different roles in popular music that a true deconstruction of this paradigm can occur.

Richard Rorty states that:

> Interesting philosophy is never an examination of the pros and cons of a thesis . . . but implicitly and explicitly, a contest between an entrenched vocabulary which has become a nuisance and a half-formed new vocabulary which vaguely promises great things.
>
> (1986: 4)

Examples of the entrenched vocabulary would include the unchallenged use of terms such as "real", "honest", "genuine", "authentic" and "'cred'(ible)" (see Ahonen, 2008: 83–86, 101–103). And yes, these terms have become a nuisance. In this study, the new vocabulary centres around the concept of authorship, one that so often seems barely able to speak its name. Ahonen speaks in this new vocabulary when she states that:

> I take the position that there exists no firm and unchangeable notion of authenticity that is applicable to all styles and genres of music. I adopt the critical perspective of cultural studies and post structuralism, which understands authenticity as a socially and historically formed construction that is constantly being reshaped within different musical practices.
>
> (2008: 101)

So much comes back to authorship. The reason why the world of popular music knows of Jimmy Page and not Big Jim Sullivan is not fundamentally about the quality or breadth of their work—that is merely to do with distinctions based upon subjectivity. It is rather that perceived or constructed mythologies of authorship *allow* for subjectivities to result. Holm-Hudson notes that the documentation of Page's career is retroactive—because of his subsequent authorial status. Equally, had Sullivan become part of an authored group such as Led Zeppelin, we would probably know a lot more about his early session career (2014).

It is not a question of whether the guitar work is better on Led Zeppelin's "Stairway to Heaven" (1971) or Thunderclap Newman's "Something in the Air" (1969); some will prefer the former and some the latter. More problematic is that Page's role can be corroborated by scholarly, biographical and anecdotal sources; Sullivan's cannot. Whereas one website will state that Sullivan played on Newman's track or on David Bowie's "Space Oddity" (1969), another source will disagree or, at least, cast doubt on the veracity of what are often just anecdotal memories. Sullivan's own records were sketchy, and few others would have made a written record of his work. He was a session man, whereas Page was an auteur with a documented oeuvre.

What is more significant is that the Led Zeppelin track is canonical, authored by Page and his creative unit and produced by him as well. These factors all bear down on individual and collective constructions of worth and value and become naturalized. The implicit concept of authorship and its associated partly formed vocabulary help shape taste without us even noticing.

Session players remain largely authorless, but the very lack of credit begs a critical deconstruction of this crucial signifier at this point.

Credit

Credit is a term that has a complex epistemology. Its English etymological roots lie in the sixteenth century as a term signifying belief or credibility. Interestingly, credibility is still a key aesthetic signifier in contemporary popular music discourse. Certain acts or genres are said to "have cred", and certain others do not.

Credit can be money obtained that others have earned and will lend to you, the borrower, at a price. Similarly, the session player gives credit to others via the skills that are otherwise unavailable and at a price. Thus, the perceived disparity in status between the lender and the borrower is duplicated in both financial and musical circles.

Credit can be applied, grudgingly, as in "you have to give credit" to a sporting performance by a team who scores against your favoured team. In this sense, credit has to be earned; however, it is not rewarded with financial recompense but rather with praise. Similarly, the uncredited session player gains recompense, whereas the credited author gains praise (yet also recompense, but almost as an unacknowledged byproduct rather than the prime motive).

The colloquial expression "you wouldn't credit it" suggests that something surprising or even unbelievable has occurred. Perhaps the uncredited work of the session player suggests that such occurrences pass almost unnoticed as the result of the perceived lack of status within the session player world. Within the authenticity paradigm, it may be considered surprising that the nonauthor can create moments of distinction and beauty within popular music. Another reason why one might not credit a session player is that it might cost someone somewhere a share of the authorial coffer.

To be considered a credit to a family or a school is to have worth conferred. It is to sustain or build a reputation. A student gains credits through passing courses or modules on their degree. These credits, when sufficient in number and grade, confer status and recognition—an undergraduate becomes a graduate. A session player who, like Page, forms a band and assumes (an assumed) greater creative role might equally be said to have graduated to the role of author.

To have a bank account in credit is positive and to have a bank account in the red is negative, in both financial and psychological terms.

In contemporary parlance, if you have zero credit on your mobile phone, this means in communicative, social terms that you cease to exist. The session player with zero credits similarly only exists in the sonic sense, not the social sense.

Somebody or someone's work can be a credit to themselves or others or their art form as in a reward but, again, not in the sense of financial recompense.

What all such connoted meanings of the term share is the notion that credit results in the author receiving credit that is based on creativity rather than mainly or solely on income (artistic value versus commercial value). Thus, the art versus commerce binary distinction at the core of the authenticity paradigm is reinforced linguistically. Therefore, as in Foucault's terms, an exploration of authorship in addition becomes a historical and social exercise in philology.

What then makes manifest the praxis of credit and accreditation in popular music? Before embarking upon an in-depth study of Genesis and their relationship to collective authorship and accreditation, a brief view into how the process of accreditation allows us to explore deeper structures of power and status must be referenced. The example is the album *Trilogy* (1972) by Emerson, Lake and Palmer (ELP).

At the very outset, the name of the act, along with near-contemporaries such as Crosby, Stills and Nash, connotes a kind of collective singularity—the band name is constituted by the names of its individual members. This connects to the authorial unit known as the "supergroup", which is formed by members bringing inherent creative status to a new act. In the case of ELP, all three members had achieved varying degrees of success with previous groups and, certainly in the case of Emerson and Palmer, had the reputation of being rock virtuosi. Emerson had played with the Nice between 1967 and 1970 on four albums and had a small hit single in the UK in 1968 with "America". Lake had composed, sung, played bass and helped produce King Crimson's debut album *In the Court of the Crimson King* in 1969. Palmer had played briefly with both the Crazy World of Arthur Brown and Atomic Rooster, including the latter's debut album in 1970. All three joined to form ELP in the summer of 1970 and had immediate success. Their third album, *Trilogy*, was a top-five hit in many countries including the UK and US.

The elaborate gatefold sleeve album, designed by graphic auteurs Hipgnosis, features an airbrushed illustration of the three members' fused torsos with their faces staring out over a sunset. The inner image features time-lapse photography, allowing multiple band figures to be distributed pictorially within a forest location. The original album cover has the authorial credits in a small box in the far left of this photo-montage. However, the reduction in size necessitated by the

CD design now renders these credits near-illegible, and so the 2011 remastered version adds the credits to the gatefold image, underneath the sunset. This gives the inadvertent impression that the three members are now visually noting this accreditation in some way. The elements of accreditation relevant to this discussion are as follows: "Produced by Greg Lake, arranged by Emerson Lake & Palmer, lyrics by Greg Lake . . . all tracks written by Emerson/Lake/Palmer except 'Hoedown' written by Emerson/Lake/Palmer/Aaron Copland." This accreditation differs from the 1972 rubric in that the section beginning "all tracks" is missing from the original internal legend. As is often the case, the reason for this can only be conjectural, but it certainly has the effect of apportioning a more collective sense of authorship to the three members. In fact, the original rubric divides up the credits to individual tracks, with Emerson and Lake contributing the lion's share. Palmer is only listed as co-composing two tracks, "Hoedown" and "Living Sin". Is this a case of rewriting history or indicating that youthful egos are now somewhat suppressed? We must note that the original listing did feature the unusual (for rock music) collective arrangement credit, which may have been for reasons of democracy or to note a different form of financial consideration that had been apportioned. And on another level, the band were always quick to acknowledge, in terms of accreditation, the contributions of the likes of Bernstein, Copland, Mussorgsky and Sibelius, even if this did not extend as far as occasions when Emerson sneakily dropped in a phrase lifted from others' work in many ELP compositions without noting the originating author.

In terms of this overall discussion, perhaps genre considerations can be said to play some part. As we will see when the focus shifts to Genesis, as exemplars of progressive rock, the bands may have shared a sense of liberalism or collectivism far removed from the values of, say, Tamla Motown, or even commercial pop in general. While Palmer was certainly the junior member, by virtue of his role and perhaps his age (he was born in 1950, as compared to Lake in 1947 and Emerson in 1944, which is a big difference in group terms), there certainly seems an attempt, both on the original album and its rerelease, to value the authorial contributions of all.

Clearly, in sonic terms, Palmer's percussion work cannot be said to have the timbral, melodic or lyrical impact of the other two members. Normally, the musical leadership/authorship of such a trio, almost unique in their near-total replacement of lead guitar with keyboards, would lie with Emerson, particularly as his range of sounds and sheer virtuosity makes his work stand out. In addition, vocal contributions are countered by the great reliance on extended instrumental passages. However, if we combine Lake's roles as sole lyricist, sole vocalist, bass, electric and acoustic guitarist and producer, we can judge his overall authorship to match that of Emerson. It is true that the accreditation reflects this hierarchical disparity (between E, L and P!), but there has still been an effort to, as the old

adage has it, "give credit where it's due". Palmer may have been the junior partner, but certainly compared to most drummers, he was given a remarkable degree
of credit. In this, he was unusual, which brings us to another unusual act with
another, even more prominent percussionist. . . .

The Politics of Authorship: A Case Study of Genesis

> Genesis was a collaborative venture—a co-operative—all the royalties were
> being split equally, and there was quite a lot of idealism.
>
> (Gabriel, cited in Fielder, 1984: 90)

Two principal factors helped diminish the role of the session player in popular
music. First, the growing desire of the rock band to be autonomous and wholly
responsible for their art, and second, the impact of new instrumentation and technologies such as the synthesizer, the drum machine, the multitrack tape recorder
and the sequencer; all of which allowed musicians to either reproduce existing
sounds themselves or to work outside the constraints of real-time virtuosity hitherto, at least partly, the preserve of the hired hand. However, at this point, it should
be acknowledged that certain session players such as Paul Beaver and Bernie Krause
made important uncredited contributions to acts such as Simon and Garfunkel,
the Doors and the Monkees as a result of their skills with the aforementioned
new instruments and technologies. Holm-Hudson notes that they "'graduated'
to authorial status, releasing three albums for Warner Brothers in the early 1970s"
(2014). Similarly, Robert Margouleff and Malcolm Cecil moved in the opposite
direction. Their expertise on early synthesizers was employed within their group
Tonto's Expanding Headband (on albums such as *Zero Time* [1971]) before they
became central to Stevie Wonder's early-1970s' work (for instance, *Talking Book*
[1972]). Perhaps unsurprisingly, although they were far more than just session
players on Wonder's albums (being also credited with programming, engineering
and associate production), the duo still achieved far more authorial status when
they moved from authoring their own projects to helping author those of another.
Wonder's huge impact in this period ensured their share of reflected glory, which,
to be fair, they were in no small measure responsible for creating—as mentors as
much as musical contributors (Lodder, 2005: 72–75).

The term band supersedes group as the collective noun for so-called "serious" music at around the same time that rock supersedes pop. This section takes
us through and beyond this era. By drawing upon a linear case study, it will focus
upon the aforementioned first principal factor, and also how the inter-band relationship had an impact upon credits and compositional roles.

A brief historical overview of Genesis is a difficult task, bearing in mind the
longevity of the act and the many personnel changes. Nevertheless, it is necessary

for the purposes of this chapter. Genesis formed in 1967 with, among the numerous in the group, three musicians who were to form their core until 1971: Tony Banks, Peter Gabriel and Mike Rutherford. These three were joined by Phil Collins and Steve Hackett before the release of their third album, *Nursery Cryme*, in 1971. Gabriel left the band in 1975 and Hackett in 1977. After this point, the core of the band reverted to Banks, Collins and Rutherford until the eventual (assumed) end of the band, barring a period where Collins left, to be replaced by the vocalist Ray Wilson and session drummers on the *Calling All Stations* album in 1997. Apart from a hiatus from around 1998 to 2006, the band functioned as a performing and composing entity for some four decades, becoming one of the most successful acts in the history of the rock era.

Beyond these bare biographical details lies the more complicated history of composition and credits. Their first album, *From Genesis to Revelation* (1969), credited all compositions to Banks, Gabriel, Rutherford and their then guitarist, Anthony Phillips, but gave no credit to their then drummer, John Silver, who left shortly after the album was recorded. Even at this early stage, the near-complete collective credit seems to have been as much ideological and about representing a united front as actually noting individual contributions. Rutherford commented:

> Initially Ant and I wrote together, just as Tony and Pete were doing. The songs on the first album . . . were mainly written by either of the two pairs although there were a couple that we all collaborated on.
>
> (Rutherford, cited in Fielder, 1984: 18)

For a period, the band, with new drummer John Mayhew, shared a country cottage in Surrey and essentially lived a secluded band life, which prompted a burst of collective writing that resulted in the bulk of the material found on their next album, *Trespass* (1970). This process, already established by bands such as Traffic in the late 1960s and euphemistically referred to in the press as "getting their heads together in the country", indicated both the organic nature of rock band existence and composition, but also the sheer intensity and will expected of the so-called serious musician in this period. It also, of course, aped the romantic model of the creative retreat, and its relative claustrophobia encouraged members to argue: "It seemed to be part of the creative process . . . we used to care so much about each bit, you know . . . you could lose sleep over it, I mean, it was that important" (Banks, in Fielder, 1984: 22). Rutherford also claimed that this somewhat monastic existence actually stymied social interaction and made them "rather insular as individuals" (Ibid). Phillips left in 1970, citing stage fright as well as the almost obligatory musical differences, but the aforementioned communication problems also had an impact.

Phil Collins joined in 1970 and was shocked by the tense atmosphere, punctuated by fierce arguments and members storming out of rehearsals. "The dynamic I was entering into was far more fragile than I had anticipated; it was very highly strung ... my job became the diffuser of tension" (Banks, Collins, Gabriel, Hackett and Rutherford, 2007: 96, henceforth credited as "Genesis"). Years later, Banks confessed to being difficult and "subject to tantrums" (Genesis, Ibid), and Collins recollected that "Steve and I were watching this tennis match of abuse" (cited in *Come Rain or Shine* [Mathile, 2007]). However, in this atmosphere, most of the songs for the next studio album, *Nursery Cryme* (1971), were recorded, while the band toured and felt transformed by Collins' drumming and light-hearted attitude. This album, with most guitar duties handled by Steve Hackett, was collectively credited in the same way as previous albums, although Collins, not really considered a writer at the time, did contribute his first lead vocal on the song "For Absent Friends" and sang co-lead on "Harold the Barrel". An interesting aside is that this writer, a long-standing fan of the band, did not recognize this fact for many years. This might suggest several things: first, that Collins' voice was similar to Gabriel's, particularly in their quieter moments; second, that Collins was a far more integral vocalist to the group sound, even at this early stage, and thus his voice registers as less of a timbral shift to the listener; and last, that on some level, if a contribution is uncredited, it is harder to perceive—accreditation triggers acknowledgement in two senses.

Social class differences, which will be more fully explored ahead, did also result in something of a divide between the old and new members, but still the collective credit signaled communality, at least on one level.

Gabriel had always had an interest in the theatrical side of presentation, and from 1972, his costumes and half-shaven head began to garner the band more publicity. This in itself created tensions between the "actor" and the "players" (Collins, cited in Fielder, 1984: 82, 94) and encouraged the establishment of the front man as assumed leader, "which was never the case" (Ibid), although iconic elements will often prevail in the visually oriented world of popular music. Gabriel's occasionally bizarre costumes were sometimes sprung upon the band live, with Banks admitting that they would never have been agreed upon through democratic process (Genesis, 2007: 124). The next album, *Foxtrot* (1972), again presented as a collective series of compositions, marked their first real commercial success. The sleeve note credit also stated that "all titles [were] composed arranged and performed by Genesis". In fact, Gabriel was by now composing a greater percentage of the lyrics, and the solo guitar piece "Horizons" was evidently a composition by Hackett. Democracy, in the form of what Gabriel referred to as "the popular vote" (cited in Fielder, 1984: 62), still decided what would stay or go, in compositional terms.

Selling England by the Pound (1973) followed the now-standard compositional pattern, with the sleeve note dropping the word "performed" found on the previous album and replacing it with "produced."The band actually co-produced the album with John Burns. "More Fool Me", only the second Collins lead vocal from the Gabriel era, was actually credited as "vocals Phil", thus raising his performance status to a small degree. He also performed the song live on the subsequent tour, accompanied only by Rutherford on guitar and backing vocals. Some debate among the fan community along the lines of "he really can sing!" actually prefaced his later switch in roles and its wide acceptance. Again, the notion of ostensible proof of creativity and authorship can be raised at this juncture.

The Lamb Lies Down on Broadway, a double album from 1974 that many consider their finest achievement, was credited as a group composition. However, this glossed over the reality that Gabriel wanted to compose all of the lyrics but was unable to because of external factors. He did compose most of the lyrics, but his contribution to the music was relatively marginal. Brian Eno, the conceptualist then beginning to forge a huge reputation beyond his initial role as a member of Roxy Music on their first two albums, was credited with "Enossification" in recognition of some production input on certain tracks. In addition to Gabriel, Hackett was also beginning to be marginalized in compositional terms, although not in accreditation. Despite previously describing the band as a "lifeline" during the breakup of his marriage, by this point, he described himself as "an innocent bystander on *The Lamb*":"It happened despite me, not with me" (Hackett, cited in Fielder, 1984: 84, 92).As is so often the case in art, creative and emotional turmoil contributed to a work whose legacy has endured. Gabriel left the band after the subsequent world tour to forge a successful solo career.

Many assumed that the band would break up at this point, but Collins proved the best replacement as vocalist, at first on an assumed temporary basis, but soon his new joint role became permanent.

The first Genesis album as a four piece was *A Trick of the Tail* (1976).The album actually outsold its predecessor, but signaled a shift in compositional accreditation. The old collective model was replaced with named authors. For Banks, "I'd got slightly fed up with the fact that people thought Peter had written everything, so we decided on this album to credit each song to whoever wrote it" (Genesis, 2007: 167). Although the sleeve credit still read, "all material arranged and performed by Genesis", only two tracks were composed by the remaining four members, and one of these, "Los Endos", was for the most part an instrumental recapitulation of themes from other songs. Collins had a co-credit with Banks on one other song, but, mainly, songwriting duties were split between Banks and Rutherford (two songs) and Banks and Hackett (one). The two remaining songs were Banks' solo compositions.What can be read from this shift in accreditation? It can only be conjecture. Perhaps the tensions or resentments relating to authorship had built up, particularly with regard to the previous album, and this was a way to redress them. Perhaps it was felt that certain members were not pulling their weight and did not deserve equal shares of credit (and income). Or perhaps a leader was emerging, in creative terms. Most probably, as Banks stated, the individual members felt that they needed to emerge from the shadow of the front man, with all the perceptions of creative leadership which that had provoked. Simply, in terms of accumulative accreditation, Banks led and was followed by Rutherford, with Hackett and Collins relatively minor contributors. Was it a way of forcing Hackett out or at least marginalizing him? He admitted that for his last two years with the band, he simply "trod water" (Hackett, cited in Fielder, 1984: 95). Collins' vital dual role certainly granted him integral status and further cemented his relationship with other band members.

The next album, *Wind and Wuthering* (1976), saw the relationship between the four splintering, with Hackett leaving after the 1977 tour. Bill Bruford, who drummed with Genesis live for a period, illuminated the class issue alluded to earlier, which had an impact upon personal relations, as well as shed light upon issues of specifically English middle class ethnicity:

> I'm from the same public school background which I think throttles your emotional expression. Phil doesn't have that problem—he's a song and dance man. Mike and Tony have a much harder time trying to express what they are trying to say.
>
> (cited in Fielder, 1984: 99)

It should also be added that the class/school background of the members contributed to the subject matter of the songs. Banks commented that "it was difficult for us to write about reality. In the early days . . . we tended to use myths and legends . . . to avoid having to say anything real" (Genesis, 2007: 33).

This notion of authorship being predicated upon factors such as class, background, nationality and genre is well explored by Sarah Hill, Kari Kallioniemi and Kevin Holm-Hudson in the edited collection of essays entitled *Peter Gabriel: From Genesis to Growing Up* (Drewett, Hill and Kärki, 2010). Hill talks of Gabriel, who "like many of his peers . . . utilized the distancing nature of progressive rock to explore issues or personal and cultural identity, what it meant to be English and what being English *sounded* (her emphasis) like" (Hill, 2010: 15). Kallioniemi notes Gabriel's antipathy toward the English Public School system before situating him, Genesis and other fellow-travelers within the English tradition of eccentricity (2010: 31–42). He explores the impact that such eccentricity has upon the subject matter and style of Genesis compositions and even notes the significance of the design of the band's label, Charisma, which features an image of Lewis Carroll's Mad Hatter from *Alice's Adventures in Wonderland*. Such English surrealism is made manifest in many Genesis songs, such as "The Musical Box" (1971). Holm-Hudson shows how many of Gabriel's strategies for coping with Charterhouse Public School manifested themselves through music, with the young Gabriel loving the soul singing of Otis Redding, among others (2010: 43–55). However, for the most part, an explicit manifestation of elements of soul within Gabriel's work had to wait until he became a solo author and was freed from the authorial expectations placed upon the band.

The detached *froideur* within the band around the time of *Wind and Wuthering* made negotiations over songs difficult, with Hackett feeling that his works were rejected in favour of inferior efforts by others. This resulted in Hackett gaining three co-credits, which showed a greater contribution than on the previous album, but for him, this was clearly not enough. Collins claimed that at one point, Hackett asked for the running time to be divided up equally, in terms of the four writers, but that was never going to work (cited in Fielder, 1984: 101). Part of the problem stemmed from Hackett becoming more strident. In the early days, he had been content to "just be a guitarist" (Genesis, 2007: 106), but the authorial dynamic was not flexible enough to accommodate his wishes. Banks again dominated, with three solo and three co-compositions. He admitted later that at this point, he "was controlling it too much" (Genesis, 2007: 192). Rutherford had one solo and three co-compositions, and Collins, two co-compositions. Interestingly, the practice of always slightly amending the sleeve note credits continued on this album with "all tracks arranged by Genesis".

The aptly named *And Then There Were Three* emerged in 1978, with the title carrying connotations of defiance, resignation and perhaps even a degree of obstinacy. Suffice to say that Banks still contributed the majority of songs as a solo and co-writer, although "Scenes from a Night's Dream" was claimed to be the first Genesis lyric written wholly by Collins. Interestingly, manager Tony Smith has stated that "for Tony, Genesis was his solo career" (cited in Mathile, 2007).

The now-established pattern of credits was broken with the release of *Duke* in 1980. As well as five of the twelve tracks being band compositions, Collins garnered his first solo composition credit. The change was not dramatic but signaled a shift that was only to make more comprehensive moves in the years following. The principal factor determining the emergence of Collins and the reemergence of group compositions seems to have been a result of the hiatus following the previous album. As well as Rutherford and Banks releasing (relatively unsuccessful) solo albums, Collins took a leave of absence to move to Canada and try to save his marriage. In this period, he began writing prolifically, with several songs being based directly on his emotional state and thus being read as autobiographical. Some were later to emerge on his first solo album, *Face Value*, in 1981, but a few entered the Genesis canon, despite their emotional directness being something at odds with the group's past efforts, which had traditionally tended to avoid the tropes of love, loss and feelings in favour of historical or fantasy narratives, moods of detachment or third-person observation. However, for Rutherford, this album was essentially a return to old collective ways of writing (Genesis, 2007: 218).

Collins claimed that *Abacab* (1981) happened at "the first time that we really talked to each other . . . and that's why, as far as I'm concerned, the group almost starts there" (cited in Fielder, 1984: 105). What an astonishing claim for a man who had worked with the other two musicians for around ten years at this point. The album was a band production and featured six group compositions and one solo song each from the trio.

The group then made the remarkable decision to call their next album, simply, *Genesis* (1983). In the history of pop album etymology, there are principally two reasons for an eponymous title: First, it is the debut album and presents a new "brand" to the public (for example, the Ramones, New York Dolls, the Smiths, the Pretenders, etc.). Second, it is the strident, stripped-down notion of simplicity or "this is who we are" that you find with the Beatles, Elton John, the Byrds or Blur. The vast majority of eponymous albums are the debut work; it is actually very unusual for subsequent albums to be self-titled by a band or individual (the contrary auteur Peter Gabriel entitled his first three albums *Peter Gabriel*). As well as this blatant statement of identity, the compositional credits reverted to the collectivist model of the period up to 1976. The term collectivism is deliberately chosen. The unfolding story of Genesis accreditation is implicitly *political* and *ideological*. As well as the increasing amount of social comment in later-period songs, Banks, in his own modest, self-effacing middle class English way, later commented, "We make more than enough money now . . . I definitely feel over-privileged; I can't avoid that, because I have socialist tendencies" (Fielder, 1984: 122). Authorship is one important way in which these tendencies manifest themselves.

All songs on *Genesis*, as well as *Invisible Touch* (1986) and *We Can't Dance* (1991), were group-composed. Furthermore, this most English of bands began to write in a more collective manner, with song ideas being gestated through long jamming sessions. Hitherto, ideas would be presented to the other members and then rehearsed. This had an impact on the songs, which in many cases became more direct and obviously commercial in their broad accessibility. The impact resulted in *Invisible Touch* selling an estimated 15 million copies worldwide. By this point, Banks referred to their writing as "a totality, three people writing almost as one" (Genesis, 2007: 282). This was a band that could sell out several nights in stadiums, with more than 250,000 people watching four shows at Wembley in 1987. Certainly, at this point, they were among the biggest bands in the world. This is not to say that collective processes made their music better or worse than other methods, but the increasing levels of affection and empathy that all of the members have referenced were reflected in the way their compositions were now achieved and also *presented* to the outside world.

One more studio album under the name of Genesis emerged, *Calling All Stations*, in 1997. Collins effectively went on extended leave, and the decision to recruit a new vocalist, Ray Wilson, and use session drummers to take Collins' place backfired on every level. Although Wilson contributed to three group compositions, which suggested that he was a member rather than merely a hired hand, the album was poorly received and sales were relatively low. It seemed that the core of just two of the classic lineup was too few even for hardened fans. After a long hiatus, Banks, Rutherford and Collins reemerged in 2007 to play a series of dates culminating in a performance in Rome's *Circo Massimo* in front of around 500,000 fans—their biggest ever concert and probably their last. Collins announced his retirement from music in 2011, citing health problems relating to bodily damage incurred over decades of drumming.

As the core band members decreased, other players were recruited to augment their live sound. In addition to Bruford, who stayed for a brief period, two other musicians would ultimately have a long-standing relationship with Genesis: drummer Chester Thompson and guitarist/bassist Daryl Stuermer. Despite all participants never apportioning terms such as session player to Thompson and Stuermer, they never became members, only guests. It was made clear that they would not be contributing to albums or writing songs. They thus inhabited that liminal zone between the polarities of hired hand and band member. Having said that, on the sleeve credits for the 2007 concert DVD *When in Rome*, their names are listed under Genesis in alphabetical order as part of a five piece. The accompanying documentary, *Come Rain or Shine* (Mathile, 2007), which maps the planning and logistics behind the tour, does almost wholly focus on the three core members—Stuermer and Thompson remained players rather than authors. Stuermer did, in one of the rare sequences when he speaks, perhaps unwittingly illuminate another key distinction between the three and the two when he stated, with some surprise, that he and Thompson actually practiced on a regular basis (cited in Mathile, 2007), whereas the other three did not. But we might read this as an indication that these players were jobbing musicians who needed to remain employable rather than members of a band only recently reconvened after a long hiatus.

Shifts in credits tell us a great deal about a lot of things, but what of the songs themselves? How did the emergence of Collins as a writer and the turn toward looser, collective methods of composition have an impact upon Genesis' material? Leaving aside distinctions based on aesthetics, what can be stated is that late-period Genesis (barring *Calling All Stations*) sold many more records than during the Gabriel period or in the immediate post–Gabriel lineup. There could be many reasons for this, but one indisputable fact is that the band became more authorially commercial. The songs, as a body (there are important exceptions), became more direct, rhythmically simple, danceable, funkier and radio friendly.

This was true of lyric matter as well as the music. Early Genesis lyrics often directly adapted ideas from classic works. These ranged from Greek mythology ("The Fountain of Salmacis" [1971]) to T.S. Eliot ("The Cinema Show" [1973]) and Jack London ("White Mountain" [1970]). What might be termed social comment did not feature extensively in the early oeuvre, but it did exist, albeit often couched within somewhat whimsical or fantasy narratives—"Get 'Em Out by Friday" (1972) dealt with dislocation caused by new town planning, and "The Knife" (1970) railed against dictatorship.

It is tempting to point to Collins as the prime mover in these changes, but that is too simplistic. Collins has gone on record as bemoaning the lack of emotional directness in some Genesis songs, claiming his own tendency toward the straightforward: "Being a kind of direct emotional writer and singer, you know, I say I love you, I miss you and I want you" (cited in Mathile, 2007). Banks, on the other hand, stated in 1986 on the subject of the song "The Brazilian" that "it's kind of much closer to the kind of stuff I do on my solo albums. So if you like 'The Brazilian' then buy them, um, its, its . . . which no one does!" (cited in Mathile, 2007). This was said with amused resignation rather than acrimony.

After their late reformation, Banks was still eager to emphasize his role:

> to take the group a little bit away from doing the kind of straight pop songs all the time. I love doing pop songs . . . but I always want to try and make certain we do a bit of the other . . . songs like "Domino".
>
> (cited in Mathile, 2007)

While there is some truth in his creative preference, there are many songs associated with Banks ("Afterglow" [1976]) and Rutherford ("Your Own Special Way" [1976], "Follow You, Follow Me" [1978]) that are directly romantic and redolent of profound feelings of love. He also co-wrote all their biggest single hits in the group's later period. The aforementioned instances of social comment became more prevalent and couched in less allusive terms during Collins' tenure as lead vocalist and writer, although both Banks and Rutherford were an integral part of this lyrical shift. Among the subjects tackled were the moral issues of TV evangelism ("Jesus He Knows Me" [1991]), pornography and the war in Lebanon ("Domino" [1986]). As for the "lack of swing" that Thompson initially found difficult to accommodate, several years down the line, the three core members would be "talking about making it more funky, and I'd come all set to give it the old Genesis treatment" (Thompson, cited in Fielder, 1984: 106). The common thread seemed to lie in the willingness of the members to be adaptive and discard assumed creative roles or audience assumptions. Certainly, members past and present have vouchsafed the notion that fewer writers can result in less compromises and more manageable and liberating ways of working (Genesis, 2007: 85, 192).

Their methods changed, their writing and playing evolved, and in both interpersonal and commercial terms, it was for the better.

In a sense, this overview of one band and its relationship to authorship gives us that rarity in terms of popular music biography—a tale of ultimately happy closure that ends on a high point. When looking back on their entire career, Collins commented that the band had grown much closer: "You realise what you meant to somebody else, what we've meant to each other" (cited in Mathile, 2007). Most art forms (and biographical accounts) seek a narrative arc, preferably with a few misfortunes, resentments, tragedies and disappointments surfacing along the way. A huge factor in the growing contentment expressed by band members lay in the writing methods that in some sense took them back to, or even took them beyond, their original all-for-all philosophy. They ultimately found a model that worked for them. It is one that in overall terms is all too rare in the field of popular music.

Summary

Popular music grates against established canonical constructions of authorship, whether based on individualistic literary and art models or more modern applications in fields such as cinema. But it cannot wholly dispense with them. In the process, it asks if there can be an authorial ideal for both creativity and subsequent critical appreciation, or is the whole concept contingent upon circumstance and individual and collective dynamics. These issues have been the culmination of a long struggle with notions of authenticity. As an art form, popular music has long felt the need to justify itself as worthy of serious, critical attention. Partly, this justification has been built upon what can be termed a "validation process" that consists of adopting romantic values and paradigms of worth, value and authorial creativity. However, the shifting climate of critical aesthetics and popular music practices has rendered many of the old, rigid critical distinctions between the individual and the collective highly problematic. As this chapter has attempted to show, the politics of creativity and accreditation shed a great deal of light upon shifting perceptions of authorship. Issues of credit/accreditation have been shown to play a huge part in popular music's internal constructions of authorship and the subsequent wider perception of these constructions. This linguistic and legalistic representation of authorship is much overlooked in popular music studies and deserves further scholarly research and emphasis.

In 2014, the five members of Genesis that took the group through its early period of success all participated in an extensive documentary entitled *Genesis: Together and Apart* (Edginton, 2014). This BBC broadcast was an edited version of a longer programme entitled *Genesis: Sum of the Parts*. Both titles are, of course, significant for discussions of authorship. Perhaps more significant was seeing the five former members in a line offering their views and memories. The body language was certainly tense, restrained and, at times, gave some indication of the extent of the earlier issues that prompted the departure of Gabriel and Hackett. Nevertheless, seeing these five names under "Genesis" in the end credits indicated a collective ease in including those who had actually left decades ago. Of course, the documentary ties in with (yet) another compilation of old Genesis and solo material (*R-Kive* [2014]), and Hackett has gone on record to express disappointment with editorial decisions that resulted in his own solo work being largely overlooked (cited in Kreps, 2014). However, the overall authorial intentions were still noble—that in popular music, individuals are part of something bigger, and accreditation should acknowledge this fact.

Ahonen rightly notes "the media's insistence on isolating a front figure that will give the music its face" (2008: 142). But despite the huge success of Collins' solo career, this never detracted from the relative facelessness of the Genesis band image or established the front man as any more than just an inevitable focal point. Certainly, for Genesis, the authorial ideal took them on a long and circular path away from and back to collectivism, from a youthful brittle and angst-ridden idealism to a middle-aged take on the noble concept of "all titles done by all".

Authorship in this chapter has been shown to shed light on so many aspects: class, ethnicity, genre, Englishness, interpersonal relationships, commercialism, guest musicians and longevity. Authorship issues, or disputes, have driven many bands apart—the myth of musical differences so frequently evoked is often based in reality. However, for Genesis, it is hard not to conclude that authorship issues actually kept the band together and strengthened their emotional and creative bonds. Collective authorship became inseparable from their sense of brotherhood and fundamental to their very reason for existing.

Bibliography

Ahonen, Laura (2008) *Constructing Authorship in Popular Music: Artists, Media and Stardom*, Milton Keynes: VDM Verlag.

Barker, Hugh & Yuval Taylor (2007) *Faking It: The Quest for Authenticity*, London: Faber & Faber.

Banks, Tony, Phil Collins, Peter Gabriel, Steve Hackett & Mike Rutherford (Genesis) (2007) *Genesis: Chapter and Verse*, London: Weidenfeld & Nicolson.

Barthes, Roland (1972) *Mythologies*, London: Jonathan Cape.

Benjamin, Walter (1999) "The Work of Art in the Mechanical Age of Reproduction", in Arendt, Hannah (ed.), *Illuminations*, London: Pimlico, pp 211–244.

Blaine, Hal (2003) *Hal Blaine and the Wrecking Crew*, Alma, Mich.: Rebeats.

Brocken, Michael (2003) *The British Folk Revival, 1944–2002*, Aldershot: Ashgate.

Drewett, Michael, Sarah Hill & Kimi Kärki (eds.) (2010) *Peter Gabriel: From Genesis to Growing Up*, Farnham: Ashgate.

Fielder, Hugh (1984) *The Book of Genesis*, London: Sidgwick & Jackson.

Fielder, Hugh (2000) Sleeve notes accompanying Genesis Archive CD box set.

Gilbert, Jeremy & Ewan Pearson (1999) *Discographies: Dance, Music, Culture and the Politics of Sound*, London: Routledge.

Hill, Sarah (2010) "From the New Jerusalem to the Secret World: Peter Gabriel and the Shifting Self", in Drewett, Michael, Sarah Hill & Kimi Kärki (eds.), *Peter Gabriel: From Genesis to Growing Up*, Farnham: Ashgate, pp 15–30.

Holm-Hudson, Kevin (2010) "How Peter Gabriel Got His Mozo Working", in Drewett, Michael, Sarah Hill & Kimi Kärki (eds.), *Peter Gabriel: From Genesis to Growing Up*, Farnham: Ashgate, pp 43–56.

Holm-Hudson, Kevin (2014) From a personal correspondence, December 1.

Kallioniemi, Kari (2010) "Peter Gabriel and the Question of Being Eccentric", in Drewett, Michael, Sarah Hill & Kimi Kärki (eds.), *Peter Gabriel: From Genesis to Growing Up*, Farnham: Ashgate, pp 31–42.

Kreps, Daniel (2014) "Genesis Guitarist Steve Hackett Blasts 'Biased' Documentary", *Rolling Stone*, 5 October, accessed 6-10-14, http://www.rollingstone.com/music/news/genesis-guitarist-steve-hackett-blasts-biased-documentary-20141005.

Laing, Dave (2012) "Big Jim Sullivan Obituary", *the Guardian*, 3 October, accessed 15-03-15, http://www.theguardian.com/music/2012/oct/03/big-jim-sullivan.

Leigh, Spencer (2009) "The Day the Music Died", *the Independent*, 23 January, p 4.

Lodder, Steve (2005) *Stevie Wonder: A Musical Guide to the Classic Albums*, London: Backbeat.

Loog Oldham, Andrew (2001) *Stoned*, London: Vintage.

Mann, William (1963) "What Songs the Beatles Sang", *the Times*, 27 December.

Moore, Allan (2012) *Song Means: Analysing and Interpreting Recorded Popular Song*, Farnham: Ashgate.

Pattison, Robert (1985) *The Triumph of Vulgarity: Rock Music in the Mirror of Romanticism*, Oxford: Oxford University Press.

Reynolds, Simon (1990) *Blissed Out: The Raptures of Rock*, London: Serpent's Tail.

Rorty, Richard (1986) "The Contingency of Language", *London Review of Books*, 17 April, pp 3–6.

Toynbee, Jason (2000) *Making Popular Music: Musicians, Creativity and Institutions*, London: Arnold.

Walser, Robert (1993) *Running with the Devil: Power, Gender and Madness in Heavy Metal Music*, Middletown: Wesleyan University Press.

Weinstein, Deena (1999) "Art Versus Commerce: Deconstructing a (Useful) Romantic Illusion", in Kelly, Karen & Evelyn McDonnell (eds.), *Stars Don't Stand Still in the Sky: Music and Myth*, London: Routledge, pp 57–69.

Audio-Visual Sources

Atomic Rooster (1970) *Atomic Rooster*.

Dave Berry (1964) "The Crying Game".

Berger, John (director uncredited) (1972) *Ways of Seeing*, BBC television documentary series.

David Bowie (1969) "Space Oddity".

The Carpenters (1972) "Goodbye to Love".

Phil Collins (1981) *Face Value*.

Edginton, John (director) (2014) *Genesis: Together and Apart*. BBC Documentary, broadcast 4-10-14.

Emerson Lake and Palmer (1972) *Trilogy*, "Hoedown", "Living Sin".

Genesis (1969) *From Genesis to Revelation*.

(1970) *Trespass*, "The Knife", "White Mountain".

(1971) *Nursery Cryme*, "Harold the Barrel", "For Absent Friends", "The Fountain of Salmacis", "The Musical Box".

(1972) *Foxtrot*, "Get 'Em Out by Friday".

(1973) *Selling England by the Pound*, "The Cinema Show".

(1974) *The Lamb Lies Down on Broadway*.

(1976) *A Trick of the Tail*, "Los Endos".

(1976) *Wind and Wuthering*, "Afterglow", "Your Own Special Way".

(1978) *. . . And Then There Were Three*, "Follow You, Follow Me".

(1980) *Duke*.

(1981) *Abacab*.

(1983) *Genesis*.

(1986) *Invisible Touch*, "Domino", "The Brazilian".

(1991) *We Can't Dance*, "Jesus He Knows Me".

(1997) *Calling All Stations*.

(2014) *R-Kive*.

King Crimson (1969) *In the Court of the Crimson King*.

Led Zeppelin (1971) "Stairway to Heaven".

Mathile, Anthony (director) (2007) *Come Rain or Shine*, DVD documentary, Virgin.

The Nice (1968) "America".

P.J. Proby (1964) "Hold Me".

Suckling, Chris (producer) (2014) *The Carole Kaye Story*, BBC Radio 2 documentary, broadcast 2-06-14.

Thunderclap Newman (1969) "Something in the Air".

Tonto's Expanding Headband (1971) *Zero Time*.

Stevie Wonder (1972) *Talking Book*.

4

THE INTERPRETER AS AUTEUR

The last chapter established a critical distinction between band musicians and session players, with the associated use of terms such as art versus commerce being acknowledged. Part of the received myth of authorial distinction rests upon the assumption that writing, as a creative activity, has more status than interpreting; the former is about origination, and the latter about a form of duplication, albeit with an important personal twist. The interpreter is there to bring something of the self to bear in terms of creativity, talent, technique or trademark sound, but this is not considered by some to encompass the same status as having generated the original creative act (see Ahonen, 2008). The tensions inherent in this scenario are well explored in the documentary *Twenty Feet from Stardom* (Neville, 2013), which, within the context of this chapter, could be paraphrased as "twenty feet from authorship". However, it would be a mistake not to acknowledge that historical processes are always at work, rendering any absolutist connotations of terms at the very best, partial (and thus *partisan*). By way of example, Negus and Pickering's exploration of creativity maps out the historical shift that has seen the positive connotations of imitation and mimesis replaced by those connected to innovation and creativity (2004: 9).

Partly, qualitative distinctions within authorship stem from differing linguistic discourses. It is hard to imagine an author in a band justifying their contribution to a song they disliked by stating that they just counted up the dollars while ticking off the minutes, although this has been done by top session player Carol Kaye (cited in Bewley, 2013). Equally, Kaye's frequent references to "putting food on the table" and "having three kids", while doubtless genuine, are not issues typically raised by those who are considered (and who consider themselves) authors.

Statements such as "go make the money . . . whatever they want, I'll do it" and "you just thought one dollar, two dollar, three dollar and you went home to your kids" (Ibid) have the effect of turning a creative process into a mere job—and an hourly paid one at that. Yet, Kaye demonstrated many of the attributes of the true artist, a love for music and playing, an admiration for many of her peers, and expertise on bass and guitar that is remarkable for someone of her advanced years who has suffered health problems. In addition, she demonstrated, through playing riffs and bass sequences, some of the many occasions when she claimed to have transformed bass lines by taking an original progression and making it more interesting, funky or rhythmically complex. This is *interpreting* rather than *writing* in the accepted (and legal) sense of the word (Kaye got no composing credits). However, as listeners unaware of the original lines, we hear them as written elements. Whether Kaye in fact wrote the bass lines on tracks performed by the Four Tops, Stevie Wonder, Mel Tormé and the Righteous Brothers is for others to judge or guess. Kaye claimed that the bass line that she *invented* (her term) on Sonny and Cher's "The Beat Goes On" (1967) meant "a nothing song became a hit" (cited in Bewley, 2013)—easy to say, harder to substantiate. As indicated in Chapter One, this remains a largely undocumented area of considerable dispute. Nevertheless, the issue that Kaye raises regarding interpretation opens up a whole field of study.

"A Whiter Shade of Pale": Courting Controversy

In 1967, Procol Harum released their debut single "A Whiter Shade of Pale" (originally credited to Reid and Brooker). In addition to its global success at the time of its release, the song has been the most played track in public places in the last seventy-five years in the UK, according to Phonographic Performance Limited (BBC news channel online source, 2009). Originally, the song was credited to its lyricist and music writer. An initial issue related to authorship requires that the song be judged as unique, in that no other sounds exactly the same. However, while there cannot be shades of uniqueness, there were clearly, what has been called, "creative influences" at work in the composition process. In addition to lyrics referencing Geoffrey Chaucer's "Miller's Tale" and possibly paraphrasing John Milton's "the light fantastick", scholars have identified several Bach compositions that the organ motif may be referencing as well. Moreover, underlying the lyrics and organ lines, the bass line can be said to adopt the model of the "major chord with descending baseline or DESH (diatonic elaboration of static harmony). This results in the progression C-B-A-G under a C major chord. Variations or close adoptions of such a pattern can be found throughout popular music, in songs from the likes of David Bowie, Slade, the Beatles, Nina Simone and Madonna, to name but a few. Perhaps the closest in terms of connoted feel and instrumentation can be found within the Percy Sledge song "When a Man Loves a Woman" (1966).

Nevertheless, similarity does not become a judicial issue unless deliberate plagiarism can be proven, the consequence being that most of the field of popular music authorship can be said to rest quite legally, and to varying degrees, upon prior authorial influences. What is more of concern here is the protracted series of court cases and judgments that took place between 2006 and 2009. In 2006, Matthew Fisher, organ player for Procol Harum, brought legal action, claiming a share of composing royalties for his contribution to the song. As an aside, a session drummer, Bill Eyden, played on the song for the standard fee at the time of £15.15 shillings (£15.75p). The song has, of course, made millions for the band members, but with the bigger share going to the songwriters and owners of the publishing rights.

Brooker claimed that Fisher only began to mention his grievance around the time that he left the band in 2003:

> I am shocked and dismayed that after Matthew had worked with us quite happily . . . without him once alleging that his role . . . was anything other than that of a musician, it is only now that he claims he recalls writing part of the song. People can draw their own conclusions from this.
>
> (cited in anon, 2006)

At the subsequent court case, Fisher was awarded 40% of the musical copyright of the song. This was overturned on appeal based on the period of time it took Fisher to make his claim (cited in anon, 2008). However, despite the copyright remaining with Reid and Brooker, Fisher was awarded joint authorship, but was not awarded either copyright royalties (past, present or future) or any ongoing control over the song's exploitation. In 2009, Fisher appealed against this decision, and the case was heard in Britain's Supreme Court—the House of Lords—for the first time in a copyright case. The Lords ruled that the time delay was not a factor, and Fisher was awarded 40% of future royalties. Ultimately, these rulings resulted in a compromise, with Fisher gaining both a credit and some future income and Reid and Brooker losing some of their future royalties.

As well as proving that the legal system is as much about *interpretation* as hard facts, this case does also throw some light over instrumental *interpretation*. In another play on words, we might conclude that Fisher's musical part was instrumental in both senses of the word, as it contributed hugely in terms of timbre, prevalence, mix and connoted mood. However, in strict authorial terms, this is not a factor. It is not the degree of authorship that matters; nor does it matter if the lyricist took two hours and the music composer two weeks to author their contributions. If Fisher's playing has been considered compositional, then what about the other band members' contributions? What about the session player? This case proved that history could be rewritten, but only within certain bounds.

Fisher may well have had the money from his many years working with the band to gamble on a court case in order to obtain more recompense (although a "no win, no fee" has been claimed). Maybe it was just about the accreditation. . . . Many others in his position are not so fortunate. The classic Marxist notion of the economic base determining the superstructure rings true in this case. Authorship can be negotiated in terms of finance and income as well as status and recognition, and this factor is instrumental in both its continuing importance and the controversies it can provoke.

Authorship and the Cover Version: A Different Angle

Explorations of the myriad creative and authorial issues raised by cover versions (from biographical, journalistic and academic positions) are widespread within popular music writing (see Ahonen, 2008; Homan, 2006; Plasketes, 2010; Sweeting, 2005). It is not my intention in this section to retread existing theories, but rather to broach a relatively overlooked aspect of the cover version wherein an artist revisits (re-covers? recovers?) their past material. To this end, I will be focusing on songs found within Tori Amos' album *Gold Dust* (2012). In addition, a briefer exploration of aspects of authorship by other mature artists (Kate Bush, Rod Stewart) will also inform my analysis of the question of age and authorship.

It has to be stated that Tori Amos' album of reworkings is rare but not without precedent. Certain orchestral conductors have adopted the same process (Herbert von Karajan, for example), which, as with the later example of Frank Sinatra, seems to be predicated as much on the desire to exploit the improving fidelity of recording processes as stemming from a more strictly creative, artistic impetus.

Ahonen (2008: 86–94) explores the work of Amos, her album *Strange Little Girls* (2001) and, in particular, her cover of Eminem's track "'97 Bonnie and Clyde" (1999). On *Strange Little Girls*, Amos takes a selection of songs written by men, most of which explicitly broach issues of gender and sexuality. She, in effect, regenders them by virtue of the narrative and vocals both being represented by a female artist/protagonist. As Frith has noted, pop is about "double enactment . . . a star personality and a song personality" (1998: 212), but in the case of Amos augmenting Eminem's divided authorship, we actually can talk of multiple enactments being brought to bear here, with the authorship of the interpreter and of her gender adding to the levels of inserted and implied meaning. This is in addition to any constructions of autobiography or self being read into the narrative. In the case of this song, these levels can only be symbolic (Eminem is not a murderer!). As well as broaching this complicated process, Ahonen also explores implications for authorship when an artist whose status rests at least partly on notions of authorship decides to become an interpreter: "By covering songs instead of performing self-written material, Amos poses a challenge to her acclaimed status as an auteur" (2008: 88). Ahonen concludes that "because of their author images as innovative and original artists, auteurs can take advantage of the familiarity of cover versions, without losing their credibility and fame as skilled musicians" (Ibid: 100).

Before taking research into other areas by focusing upon Amos' album *Gold Dust* (2012), it is useful to provide some biographical information about the artist.

Since releasing her first solo album in 1992, Amos has pursued a long and varied career, releasing many albums, touring globally (sometimes solo and sometimes with other players), and achieving critical and varying amounts of commercial success. In the UK, her second album, *Under the Pink* (1994), reached the top of the album chart, and a remix of her song "Professional Widow" was similarly successful in the singles chart in 1996. It is fair to judge her more recent releases as less successful in chart terms (Amos' 2014 album *Unrepentant Geraldines* entered the UK album chart at 13; the next week, it had dropped to 99, suggesting that almost all her fans are long-standing and purchased the album upon its release). However, the artist has a dedicated fan base, owns her own publishing, has her own recording studio in Cornwall and, more recently, became a recording artist on the renowned, largely classical label Deutsche Grammophon (a subsidiary of Universal, which releases her nonclassical works). This label has seemingly had its own authorial impact upon Amos' work. In the accompanying documentary to *Night of Hunters* (2011), Amos states that "Deutsche Grammophon approached me about doing a twenty first century song cycle" (cited in Barnes, 2011). The artist references her relative lack of knowledge of the whole classical tradition before noting the collaborative nature of the authorship process on this album. This consisted of working closely with Alexander Buhr, executive producer for the label. In the documentary, Buhr talks about the long-standing practice of the variation whereby composers would use an existing theme as inspiration—what he termed "honouring the source" (Ibid). Amos is eager to present this creative process as not about "thieving" and seems to be drawing upon the authority of her executive producer, the label and the classical tradition in order to justify this working rationale.

The method was this: Buhr would send Amos pieces to consider, and Amos would then compose a song based on the original music. This music was subsequently arranged, usually for an octet, by her existing orchestral collaborator, John Philip Shenale. Other authorial components were the physical setting of Amos' house in Ireland, the energy of which Amos references, as well as the freedom wrought by not being on location, and the many themes and oppositions brought to bear in the cycle (hunter/hunted, male/female, fire/water, day/night, etc.). As is so often the case, authorship on *Night of Hunters* is diffused through many different agents of creativity.

In the sleeve notes to *Gold Dust*, Amos references a long-standing desire to play many of her early songs with new orchestral arrangements, and after rehearsing and performing material with the Metropole Orkest, she notes that:

> I began to see new pictures in my mind . . . it was as if the orchestra were revealing to me subtle meanings of my own songs I had not yet discovered. This is when collaboration turns into an intimate back and forth conversation.
>
> (2012)

Subsequently, the album consisted of fourteen songs spanning her entire career (with a slight bias toward earlier work), and in collaboration with Amos, an orchestral arranger and the orchestral players, a new suite of songs was fashioned that eschewed the amplified instrumentation of some earlier arrangements in favour of piano, organ and orchestra. Three of the songs had originally been arranged for orchestra but were reworked.

In a sense, *Gold Dust* is a continuation of the process begun on two previous albums. In 2003, Amos released *Tales of a Librarian*. This album was the artist's final release on EastWest before moving to Universal. The album was, broadly speaking, a compilation, but with some additional tracks and some rearrangements of existing tracks. It thus did not neatly fall into the long-standing syndrome known colloquially as the "contractual obligation album", wherein artists who leave a label or have been let go do not wish to allow their old label the rights to release new tracks before moving on. The contractual obligation album typically consists of a live concert recording or a greatest hits/best of compilation. Amos' authorship manifests itself in both her own choice of tracks and her desire to revisit and subtly amend old performances.

A further move into authorial areas of adaptation came with *Night of Hunters* (2011), where, as discussed earlier, Amos composed a song cycle based upon musical themes by a wide variety of orchestral composers, including Chopin, Debussy, Satie and Schubert. She also employed her daughter and niece to sing lead vocals on certain tracks in order to represent different characters within the narrative. *Night of Hunters* was her first album not to feature electronic instruments and the first to feature her compositions as adaptive and interpretive components rather than as complete entities.

As an aside, Amos and her daughter also collaborate on the track "Promise" from 2014's *Unrepentant Geraldines*. It is fascinating to hear the maturation process within the authoring of Natashya Hawley's vocal performance, as the results of a different environment and musical education continue to make their presence felt on the youthful voice. Amos' voice, in comparison to her daughter's, has a precise, almost formal diction, whereas Natashya's is more melismatic and redolent of soul-singing in terms of phrasing and timbre. The juxtaposition of these two disparate examples of vocal authoring is fascinating, particularly as the more aged voice appears not to have aged over many years and the younger voice has been truly transformed in a short space of time.

The degree of transformation on *Gold Dust*'s tracks, compared to the original recordings, is variable. On "Yes, Anastasia", for instance, the original 1994 recording lasts 9.33 (the orchestra joins at 4.49), whereas in the later version, the orchestra joins *in media res* (with the line beginning "thought I'd been through this") and only lasts for 4.17. The shorter version replaces the long sense of brooding in the buildup with an abrupt entry that is more jolting, but nonetheless effective, as a dramatic device. In addition, the newer version sees Amos' melody double-tracked to a much greater extent than on the original. This aspect is found throughout *Gold Dust*. The reason for this is not evident, but certainly is not due to any diminution in the artist's vocal capability or power. Although the very highest note in the new version does put some strain upon the voice that is not evident in the original, in other respects, Amos' voice is remarkably unaltered by the passage of time, as previously indicated. Indeed, on many occasions, the delivery of words or notes seems less mannered and more assured.

Barthes' theories of "grain", characterized as "the body in the voice as it sings" (1977:188), posits a qualitative divide between an everyday, understandable voice (drawing upon Julia Kristeva's term "pheno-song") and a voluptuous, ecstatic voice that exceeds the bounds of general communication ("geno-song") (Ibid: 182). While Barthes is surely correct in judging our relationship to voices to be "erotic" (Ibid: 188), his distinction between voices of pheno-song and geno-song is open to challenge when considering Amos' voice authoring. Her early vocal efforts, replete with growls, moans and whispers, do not necessarily evoke a state of jouissance in the listener because their very self-consciousness can force a sense of detachment, as we are made too aware of the bodily processes employed. Her later vocal efforts, it can be argued, do more to exceed the everyday response of *plaisir*, as they are less self-conscious and ultimately encourage a sense of interpretive abandon. Amos does *less* with her voice as her career progresses, but achieves *more*.

Another significant development in the newer version of "Yes, Anastasia" is the much fuller orchestral palette offered by a greatly increased number of players and instruments. On the original version, there are six violins, three violas, three cellos and one bass listed in the album credits. On the newer version, rather than a string section, we have closer to a full orchestral lineup, consisting of eighteen violins, five violas, six cellos plus contrabass, flute, oboe, French horn, trumpet, trombone, clarinet, harp, percussion and saxophone. The sleeve notes do not tell us how many of these instruments contribute to the newer version of "Yes, Anastasia", but in terms of timbres and sheer presence, we can assume that the numbers of players and instruments far exceed those found on the original arrangement.

The newer version of "Precious Things" retains the almost manic hammered piano triplets of the original, but dispenses totally with the rock instrumentation and highly mixed, reverberant, syncopated drum rhythms that make this track one of the most intense (in terms of timbres and distortion) found in the artist's whole back catalogue. In the process, the connoted mood is displaced from amplified components onto acoustic and vocal elements. On other tracks, particularly those already possessing an orchestral component, the changes are more subtle. Vocally, the melodic and harmonic arc is never overthrown, but, instead, the incremental shifts in metre and precise inflection do still result in an almost sublime transformation. On "Flying Dutchman", the original downward melisma on the word "sight" is replaced by one that travels up and then down on the newer version. At another point, the original's single-tracked refrain on the chorus that repeats the title is replaced with a multitracked delivery on the newer version.

As a final aside on artists interpreting their own songs, Holm-Hudson has rightly noted the significance of other dimensions of this authorship syndrome, particularly within "Garth Brooks' construction of Chris Gaines, David Bowie's parade of characters ranging from Ziggy Stardust to the Thin White Duke in the 1970s, or even fictional group constructions such as Spinal Tap or The Rutles" (2014). There is clearly more scope for ongoing research into this field of reinterpretation and authorial reinventions of songs, acts and personae.

Vocalists such as Joni Mitchell or Robert Plant find that the passage of time necessitates a considerable amount of downward transposition in melodies in order to accommodate their more mature vocal ranges. Interestingly, Mitchell released *Both Sides Now* in 2000, which consisted largely of her interpretations of standards, plus two of her own songs. The title track was originally on her 1969 album *Clouds*. Unlike Amos, Mitchell first came to public prominence as a songwriter, with Judy Collins covering "Both Sides, Now" in 1967. This reflects upon the soon-to-be outdated authorial process of the pre-rock era. It was indeed the likes of Mitchell, James Taylor and Leonard Cohen who did much to pave the way for a new model of authorship—the autonomous, multitasking singer-songwriter. It is that creative legacy that so many, including Tori Amos, have built upon.

Authorship and the Age Issue

The results of artists revisiting old material can only be gauged subjectively, but do, regardless of personal preferences, have an impact upon the precise nature of the vocal authorship. In a television documentary entitled *Forever Young: How Rock'n'Roll Grew Up* (Rodley, 2010), Robert Wyatt comments on Mitchell's vocal reworking of her early song "Both Sides, Now", which is transposed down by "about an octave . . . it's so moving because you suddenly think, God, it's taken her three decades and now she understands the song she wrote when she was in her youth." It is true that some might judge that maturity does render the song and lyric with a gravitas in a more fitting manner than on the original, but this is because a cover necessitates a reflection back upon the primary text. If this factor were our only reference point, few would surely have criticized the young voice (and she was already twenty six when the original was released) as incapable of handling the sentiments suggested by the lyric. (We can all reminisce and express world weariness at whatever age.) Conversely, Amos' voice, albeit over a less extensive period than Mitchell's, shows little signs of needing to adapt to the aging process. The vocal shifts are more truly the result of creative, authorial decisions rather than forced upon the artist.

Authorship choices for the aging popular-music performer have become a more salient issue as the pop/rock meta-genre and its participants have aged themselves. Indeed, scholarly research has recently begun to engage with the issue of aging in popular music (see Bennett and Taylor, 2012; Homan, 2006; Whiteley, 2005). There are a variety of strategies adopted by the aging auteur to deal with the passage of time. An interesting angle on aging and authorship was raised by Rod Stewart when he released his 2013 album entitled, perhaps knowingly, *Time*. For most under the age of thirty, Stewart will perhaps be known as a covers artist. Prior to *Time*, he had released such works as *Merry Christmas, Baby* (2012), an album of covers, and five volumes of albums subtitled *The Great American Songbook* (2002, 2003, 2004, 2005 and 2010). However, prior to 2001's *Human*, every Rod Stewart solo album had included at least one self-composition or at least co-composition. As a result of possessing one of the most instantly recognizable voices (and hairstyles) in popular music, Stewart's authorship rests as much upon image and vocal grain as upon his ability to write. In addition, in commercial terms, his albums always garner very respectable sales figures and invariably high chart-placing in many territories, regardless of who has written the songs.

What needs to be acknowledged at this point is that, often in collaboration with others, his early solo work (and group work with the Faces) contains many songs that would now be considered classics ("You Wear it Well" [1971], "Maggie May" [1970], "Stay With Me" [1971], etc.). Stewart was never prolific and usually needed a musical collaborator ("Mandolin Wind" [1971] being a rare solo composition). However, his writing contributions, partially as a result of a combination of critical acclaim and commercial success, do confer authorial status. As his career progressed into the new century, he ceased to compose. Years later, he commented with admirable candour on the subject of the creative muse: "Song-writing's never been a natural art for me . . . I just thought it had got up and left me . . . maybe I'd got nothing to write about anymore" (cited in Hann,

2013). With the encouragement of long-term collaborators, Stewart co-wrote twelve tracks on *Time*, but with a seemingly autobiographical frankness largely absent from his earlier lyrics (which Hann characterized as "picaresque tales . . . music-hall bawdiness" [Ibid], as opposed to personal confessions). Perhaps the contemporaneous influence of his print autobiography (Stewart, 2013), which was generally praised, had some impact upon his lyrics, which reflected upon his youth, his divorce, his children and the death of his father, among other topics. This return to authorship seems to have struck a chord with his fan base. As previously noted, his albums always sold well, but *Time* surpassed many recent efforts and reached the top 10 of the album charts in twelve countries, giving Stewart his first British No. 1 album since 1976.

If this statistical success does allow us to make any conclusions that move beyond mere conjecture, then it must reflect upon both the way that the promotional process seized upon the artist's return to authorship and how his audience responded positively, if implicitly, to the rebirth of the auteur. Both of these dimensions have acted to confer increased status upon this elder statesman of rock. The notion of authorship's connection to quality also needs to be raised. Although authorship does not necessarily confer worth or status, Stewart choosing not to write for a number of years, fearing that a lack of inspiration would result in substandard work, does speak volumes for his creative honesty. Of course, another perfectly valid interpretation would view Stewart as a rich, aging rock star whose popularity is assured and who is too lazy to compose, so he takes the easy way out and covers others' work. It is for the individual interpreter to construct a critical stance, but regardless of the conclusions drawn, the catalyst for the exploration of the issues rests, yet again, upon the episteme of authorship.

Kate Bush and "Moments of Pleasure"

In Chapter Six, I will turn my focus to those extra-musical elements within the music scene (such as audiences, scenes, the market, the use of new technologies, etc.) that can be considered to play an authorial role. The origins in any scene lie within an individual's relationship to music. At this point, I want to preface later arguments by focusing upon my individual "authored" response to two versions of Kate Bush's "Moments of Pleasure" and, in the process, taking the issue of authorship and age into new areas.

The original version of "Moments of Pleasure" is found on the 1993 album *The Red Shoes*. The song can be read as highly autobiographical in its reflection upon events and on people who the artist knew, several of whom have died. Among those mentioned are Alan Murphy, her former guitarist; Bill Duffield, a lighting engineer who fell to his death before a concert during the artist's only tour in 1979; her mother and aunt; and Michael Powell, director of the film *The*

Red Shoes (1948), who Bush met shortly before his death. As a final note of poignancy, the original orchestrations were written by Michael Kamen, who died prematurely at the age of 55. In an earlier analysis of the song, I commented, "This track carries a huge emotional charge....To these lyrical themes is added a mood of gravitas and loss that only ageing and the inexorable march of mortality can have upon us all" (cited in Moy, 2007:116).

Since my analysis of and comments on this track, Kate Bush has returned to the song as part of the project entitled—appropriately for the purposes of this book—*The Director's Cut: Collector's Edition* (2011). On the *Collector's Edition*, this consists of a compilation of rerecorded tracks from two earlier albums and a remastering of the original albums *The Sensual World* (1989) and *The Red Shoes* (1993). The notion of the director's cut (from an artist always heavily influenced by film and the film auteur) extends into all areas of authorship. As well as referring to the contributors as the "cast" and self-crediting "visual concepts and direction", iconography deepens the connections between film and music authorship. The front cover of the CD box consists of an image of a sepia roll of film, with each frame reproducing a shot from earlier album artwork. Inside the CD booklet, a large tinted black-and-white photo shows the director/producer/editor with a roll of film in hand, clutching a pair of scissors, somewhat strategically seeming to be in the process of choosing which image of the past to relegate to the cutting-room floor.

This was an interesting musical/authorial project, as it gave Bush the chance both to correct (from a personal viewpoint) the mixes on earlier tracks and to reinterpret some old songs. On "Moments of Pleasure" (1993), the artist radically reworks the original track in several ways: the newer version is much sparser, slower and longer; the key is dropped considerably; and the soaring chorus melody and orchestral swell that gives much of the original its emotive push are dispensed with. Instead, the chorus melody is wordlessly chanted in a choral fashion by a group of deep male voices. Toward the end of the new version, some lines are dropped. Bearing in mind that in the original section, each line acts as a brief epitaph to those who have passed, this effectively means that two people who the artist originally pays tribute to, and most touchingly, have now been written out in narrative terms, which emphasizes the creative singularity (and brutal single-mindedness) of the sole auteur.

Of course, creative choices should remain paramount to the auteur, but we have to consider the interpretation of the phonologist as well as the originator. The newer version has a restrained dignity that the somewhat melodramatic arrangement of the original cannot match, but the original allows for a catharsis and intensity that are now absent. In addition, the missing tributes are incomprehensible in terms of their denial of autobiography. The author's own history has been edited, but this then has a repercussive effect of editing the phonologist's own past. Thus, the "mere" reinterpreting of an existing text can have a far great aesthetic impact than listening to a new, authored track. I will return to the figure of the remixer in an expanded form in Chapter Five. In this brief example, the remix/remixer (as the production equivalent of the interpreter) explicitly foregrounds the authoring process in a manner that the simple, original, authored text cannot.

Authorship and "Trademark Sounds" Example One: Al Jackson Jr.

Interpretation is a broad and nebulous term. As well as those aspects of the topic already covered in this chapter, one further area ripe for analysis in a book concerned with author roles is that of the instrumentalist and the construction or perception of trademark sounds. As I previously argued, part of the reason for Matthew Fisher's authorship claims connected to "A Whiter Shade of Pale" relates both to the extent of his contribution to the track, but also to the assumption that his playing is personal, albeit drawing upon prior influences and playing a Hammond organ with its own authorial timbres. Having dealt with the controversies that accrue from personal sounds, I now want to delve deeper into the specific area of instrumental authorship, both by returning to the experience of the band member and also the session player.

In Chapters One and Two, the issue of instrumental authorship was broached in relation to players associated with Tamla Motown. After the confusion and controversy stirred at least in part by the poor documentation of the Motown organization, in conjunction with an unwillingness to talk according to some sources (see George, 2003), it comes as something of a relief to move on to another musician whose individual contribution is far simpler to assign, yet whose claims for uniqueness shed further light on the authorship issue.

One of the great rivals to the Motown soul model was the Stax/Volt organization, formed in 1957 by two white business collaborators, Estelle Axton and Jim Stewart, and based in Memphis, Tennessee. In comparison to Motown, Stax/Volt was in the South, possessed a far more racially mixed group of musicians, and operated using an authorial model much closer to what was becoming the rock norm in the 1960s—namely, that semi-autonomous groups contributed direct and varied creative input to their work. The principal group to embody these aspects was Booker T. & the MGs, comprising Booker T. Jones on keyboards, Donald "Duck" Dunn on bass, Steve Cropper on guitar and Al Jackson Jr. on drums. As well as being a performing and composing group in their own right, this band also became essentially the house backing musicians for others such as Sam & Dave, Otis Redding and Carla Thomas. This group's contribution to popular music is well documented, but for the purposes of this chapter, I want to concentrate on the role of drummer Al Jackson Jr.

Jackson's work and style provides us with an instant contrast to the efforts of Motown's session drummers and, in particular, Benny Benjamin. First, Jackson was equally adept at playing three- or four-beat rhythms, unlike Benjamin, who Licks claimed was uncomfortable with shuffles (in formal terms, 6/8 or 12/8 time signatures, often incorporating dotted crochet stresses). On tracks utilizing these rhythms (e.g., "How Sweet It Is" [1964] or "Beauty Is Only Skin Deep" [1966]), "Pistol" Allen would be the drummer of choice (Licks, 1989: 31).

According to Jim Payne, other contributory factors to Jackson's Stax sound included the "very dead sounding" drum heads he used and the fact that the studio itself was situated in an old "movie theatre" (Payne, 1969, from an interview with the drummer). As well as helping to shape the Stax sound, Jackson later made important contributions to the work of Al Green, recorded elsewhere in Memphis at Willie Mitchell's Hi studios. Stax rhythm tracks were far removed from the Motown model. As well as being generally sparser, with a small brass section replacing the customary Motown strings, beats per minute tended to be more deliberate and the drums kept very simple, with few of the trademark tom-to-snare eighth or sixteenth rolls so reminiscent of Motown. Jackson's rolls did utilize such intervals, but on Otis Redding tracks such as "Respect" (1965), "Love Man" (1967) and "(I Can't Get No) Satisfaction" (1965), these rolls stayed resolutely on the snare or, occasionally, the kick drum and sometimes lasted for a whole bar, unlike the shorter, more explosive Motown rolls of the period. Jackson would make use of the snare crochet beat, but far more sparingly than on Motown tracks. He was more typically a classic proponent of the snare on the backbeat style. On ballads such as "These Arms of Mine" (1962, later rerecorded) and "My Lover's Prayer" (1966), he barely plays at all beyond the most skeletal beats. The aforementioned "dead" sounds of Jackson's simple snare roll on Eddie Floyd's "Knock on Wood" (1966) indicate a drummer who was basic and functional rather than elaborate or jazzy. Economy was always Jackson's motto.

Most Stax tracks were built upon the solid, simple basis of a twelve-bar blues walking-bass style, and Jackson's work does nothing to detract from this feel. According to Cropper, aspects that singled out Jackson's style included the fact that he "never shuffled a ride cymbal", preferring to play "straight fours" with "a sort of half shuffle thing on the foot" (cited in Payne, 1969). For Cropper, this results in a song as simple as "Green Onions" (1962) actually having a unique feel. Equally, his doubling of the speed of the beat during the slow part of Otis Redding's "Try a Little Tenderness" (1966) engenders the (ostensible) ballad with a huge amount of latent tension that is ultimately resolved during the climax of the song, which presents another highly distinctive element. According to Cropper, Jackson just came up with it in the studio and everybody else went along. This gives us concrete evidence of the authorial dimension attached to both an instrument and an associated player that popular music mythology often overlooks in authorial terms. Jackson was also credited as co-composer on many songs throughout this period—again, an unusual practice for a drummer.

Jackson's work on many of Al Green's best known hits is worth exploring in some detail. Significantly, by this time a session player after the partial demise of Booker T. & the MGs, Jackson was not the only drummer to work with Green on his albums. Howard Grimes would play on many tracks, but Jackson was usually chosen for the singles. The reasons for this are hard to ascertain, but may have something to do with his style being more singular. Having said that, label owner Willie Mitchell is on record (in 1973) as stating, "There's two people you can put in a studio and I wouldn't know which of them is playing—that's Al Jackson (of the M.G.'s) and Howard Grimes" (cited in Abbey, 1973). Mitchell assigned the label's authorship to the identical machines, studio and musicians. It may be in Mitchell's interests to mythologize the chronotope of Hi rather than differentiating between individual players, but concrete evidence is sketchy, as with Motown.

One feature that became a virtual trademark for both the drummer and Green was the practice of overdubbing, or doubling up the snare and tom-tom on the normally snare-only backbeat. According to Payne, this later became widely copied (1969). Such was Jackson's comfort with the tom-tom that it is claimed that he played whole gigs hitting the rim and head of the drum if the snare head broke (Ibid). Again, a very pragmatic, some might say lackadaisical, approach to musicianship that paradoxically resulted in a more creative, authorial style! On many Green hits such as "I'm Still in Love with You" (1972), "Look What You Done for Me" (1971) and "Call Me" (1972), the hypnotic, metronomic tom-and-kick rhythm is the principal counterpoint to the vocalist's melismatic, pleading style. The production style of Mitchell and Hi studios meant that there was very little variation between tracks, leading us to that true oxymoron, "standardized yet unique", or as Negus and Pickering summarized the dichotomy, "creativity [is] both ordinary and exceptional" (2004: vii).

Doubtless, Jackson was not the first to double the snare and the tom on the backbeat. However, it became his characteristic trademark both through the frequency with which it was employed—so it ceased to have novelty value—and also by virtue of the commercial success of the recordings to which it contributed; it gained wide recognition. But we must always be clear that "the relative distinctions between innovation and novelty are shifting and fluid" (Negus and Pickering, 2004: ix). Furthermore, "creativity is obviously associated with newness, but knowing what is significantly new may require guesswork as much as mature judgement" (Ibid: 9). Nonetheless, with the benefit of close research, trustworthy sources and, above all, the willing acknowledgement of the workings of mythology, our encounters with many of these Al Green hits does effectively take us back to a time, place, space and unique sonic experience.

"Trademark Sounds" Example Two: Tony Peluso

In addition to timbre in itself, another way in which a personal approach to instrumentation can become apparent is as a result of different genres or styles coming into close contact (or even confrontation) within a recording. In the early 1970s, after a few hits in a very traditional ballad style, the Carpenters released "Goodbye to Love" (1972). Along with the customary middle-of-the-road arrangement and the deep, languid vocal grain of Karen Carpenter, the song featured two prominent guitar solos (from 1.24 to 1.49 and from 2.55 to 3.39) courtesy of session player Tony Peluso. According to co-composer Richard Carpenter, Peluso was given the creative license to move away from a soft sound: "No, no, no, not like that, play the melody for five bars and then burn it up! Soar off into the stratosphere" (cited in Coleman, 1994: 127). Despite the fact that Peluso was initially invited to play with the Carpenters because of his attacking style, he gives credit for the decision to (mis)place a powerful solo in a soft ballad to Carpenter. Thus, the authorship is partially displaced from the self-effacing session player or, at least, shared with the band leader.

In addition to the prominence in the mix and the duration of the solos, another interesting authorial dimension lies in the "squawking" harmonics that are very noticeable, particularly when short, repetitive notes are being played. Of course, harmonics, whether engendered by amplifier, foot pedal or microphone settings, or the tonal qualities of the guitar (Gibson SGs seem to be prone to producing harmonics, as found in the work of Tony Iommi, for instance), is not uncommon in rock. However, they were certainly uncommon in 1970s' soft-rock ballads. The process known as "pinched harmonics", whereby the thumb or index finger can be used to dampen a string and bring harmonics to the fore, may also have been a part of Peluso's repertoire. Again, what needs to be emphasized is that regardless of whether Peluso employed this device, his playing produced the same effect, which is more commonly found in blues rock and, more recently, heavy metal.

Despite Coleman claiming that Peluso was sent hate mail by Carpenters' fans (presumably for some kind of "betrayal" of their sound or style), the success of this track and sound ensured a long career for Peluso as a member of the Carpenters' touring and recording band. Some have gone so far as to anecdotally claim that this track helps to at least prepare the ground for the subgenre of the power ballad. This became increasingly popular over the next few years in the hands of acts such as Journey, REO Speedwagon, Starship and Bonnie Tyler.

Of course, many guitarists can claim to possess their own trademark sound, some partly as a result of building their own guitar (Queen's Brian May). With the help of his father, May constructed his guitar from a variety of found parts over two years. As well as this authored guitar possessing two names given to it by May, a replica model is now available, and the instrument has its own bodyguard on tours (Huntman, 2014). Other players construct a trademark sound through a combination of unique effects and playing style (Robert Fripp's "Frippertronics", with his band King Crimson, and also as a guest player with the likes of Brian Eno, Blondie, David Bowie [on "Heroes" (1977)], Peter Hammill, etc.), or there are those players who bring a specific existing guitar model to wide attention via new innovations in genre and technique (the Byrds' Roger McGuinn, with his twelve-string Rickenbacker). However, Peluso's authorship reflects upon his interpretive status rather than as a composing player or band leader. As will be explored in Chapter Five when we explore the role of the "humble remixer", the paradox lies in the fact that the relatively anonymous, unacknowledged session musician can make more of a difference to a creative text, maybe as a result of differing expectations or prior knowledge, than the star auteur.

Many artists have drawn upon players endowed with the status of instrumental auteurs in order to enhance their own work. The results can be varied. Fripp's contributions are often sympathetic to the track he appears on, but still instantly recognizable (for instance, Blondie's "Fade Away and Radiate" [1978] or Brian Eno's "St. Elmo's Fire" [1975]). In other circumstances, such contributions can smack of standardization or redundancy. Kate Bush had always drawn upon the contributions of others. On her first album, *The Kick Inside* (1978), she was backed by session players who had achieved limited success as band members of Cockney Rebel and Pilot (see Moy, 2007: 12). Later in her career, she drew upon folk musicians such as Donal Lunny and John Sheahan, but, again, these musicians had little in the way of star status, and, as a result, less critical baggage was attached to any notion of authorship. Bush then began to utilize more "iconic" star players as her career progressed (Jeff Beck, David Gilmour, Nigel Kennedy and Prince, for example). Eric Clapton contributed to her track "And So Is Love" (1993). However, "to all but the most sonically astute of listeners, [Clapton's] blues fills could have been the work of any journeyman session musician, so the purpose of his contribution remains unclear" (Moy, 2007: 116). Perhaps such special guests were friends, perhaps Bush was a long-term admirer (and vice versa), or perhaps I am just unwilling or unable to identify the kind of trademark sound that I have, admittedly, been attempting to explore elsewhere in this section. This could well reflect a personal prejudice against "big name" syndrome and a certain antipathy to Clapton's own genre and playing style. As ever, questions of authorship *speak us*.

Recollections from the (In)side: Interviews with Two Musicians

In order to gain a different perspective on some of the issues and debates raised in this chapter, I carried out ethnographic research into the careers of two musicians in the form of informal interviews. First, I spoke to Tony Turrell (interview,

April 7, 2014), whose career in the music industry spans over twenty years. During this period, he has played keyboards, sung backing vocals, arranged songs, programmed and remixed material, and recorded and performed in many different countries, occasionally as part of a Prince tribute act. His most high profile role has been as accompanist to Fish, ex-Marillion, for a period of several years. In addition, he has also worked with Thomas Dolby. As well as touring extensively with Fish and having the role of live "musical director", Turrell co-wrote several songs, including two on the 2003 album *Field of Crows* and six on the 1999 album *Raingods with Zippos*.

I was interested in finding out if Tony experienced any status issues in terms of how he was treated by others when acting as accompanist or, in the traditional parlance, as "side man" (no negativity intended) to the star/auteur figure of Fish. He stated that although he was "on a wage" and some participants treated him as a session player, the caveat was that he co-wrote material, which elevated his role. In terms of composing, this resulted in what Tony called "an equal split" when it came to apportioning accreditation and, subsequently, royalties. As a consequence, for the most part, his relationship with Fish was amicable and collaborative, with him being treated as a creative partner. When Tony became Fish's musical director on an extensive tour, he was paid more than the other musicians. But it was an informal arrangement, based on him working more than the others, and did not result in any internal hierarchical divisions. The only real disagreements came as a result of the band leader being in what Tony described as a "bubble-like" mindset where "everything that happened was Fish World" and wherein others' commitments were not fully appreciated. Thus, his backing musicians were expected to "drop everything" in order to fulfill tours or recording sessions. Clearly, this stance was what might be termed auteurist insofar as Fish's creativity or vision was considered more important than events in others' lives.

Where Tony originally did experience real animosity was from long-standing fans of Marillion/Fish. One of his first encounters with a fan resulted in him being told that he "would never replace" the keyboardist whose role he had assumed. Equally, online posts relating to various adopted roles were extremely vitriolic and upsetting. Committed, or even fanatical, fans can feel betrayed by personnel/author changes in acts that they feel they "own".

In terms of authorship, Tony clearly inhabited many of the roles associated with this concept. However, the interview also illuminated his personality as a self-effacing accompanist. He commented on his keyboardist role as providing an underpinning bed of sound on which other, more lead elements build, and this was reinforced by his consistent deferring to others rather than emphasizing his own personal creativity. He also stated, "I've never wanted to be a front man . . . keyboards serve as a secondary foil to the guitar" (2014). In a sense, his character determined an accompanist's role to be most suitable for him, in a form of authorial homology. Likewise, Tony admitted to getting bored easily, so, again, the "idea of being a session guy always sat well with [him]" (2014), and the resulting variety of music was suitable. He only really became part of a band (The Reasoning) late in his career and found it a difficult transition in some ways. Other musicians looked down on commercially unknown bands, whereas in being a side-man (despite the gender connotations, side-woman is not really a term in industry discourse) with Fish, conversely, he was treated generally better. Was this status via association with an auteur? Roles such as backing musician or side-man may signal a position lower in the hierarchy than leader or star-image, but in many cases, they accurately define a different form of authorship well suited to those who inhabit these vital, titled roles.

In some senses, his role as accompanist or session player allowed for more authorial fulfillment than being a member of an autonomous, creative band unit, which challenges rock mythologies of authorship. This demonstrates that any assumptions relating to authorial roles are contingent upon individual circumstances. No hard and fast rules apply.

Alex Germains (interviewed July 15, 2014) shares many career similarities with Tony Turrell insofar as he has jumped between roles over the course of a long career in music. Alex took up the bass at seventeen and joined a band called Jake Bullet, which became the nucleus of the Mountaineers. Over a period of several years, Alex became more proficient, took up guitar and also began to write, arrange and produce material. The Mountaineers signed to Deltasonic, a Liverpool label that had great success with the Coral and other acts. After releasing an EP, they moved to Mute—a long-established indie label that achieved high international chart places with the likes of Depeche Mode and Moby. For a while, the band was on hiatus while one band member toured globally playing keyboards with Echo and the Bunnymen. After releasing an EP, the Mountaineers released the album *Messy Century* in 2003 to acclaim but little success. The band was dropped by the label around the end of 2004. Alex continues to write and perform, often improvising music to visual images.

What is most significant for the purposes of this chapter is the relatively brief period that Alex spent after also joining Echo and the Bunnymen. The band had lost long-standing bassist Les Pattinson and needed a replacement to record backing tracks for the album that was to become *Flowers* (2001). Alex provided the bass lines and sang backing vocals. The two principal members were happy for Alex to compose his own bass lines, although all compositions are credited to McCulloch and Sergeant. Alex was given a one-time payment for his work, but he also receives playing royalties for the album, which was not a big success. Additionally, he played some live dates with the band, which ultimately hastened his exit. He recollects being sacked for "inadvisable comments" when he "replied to a comment on a fan forum that was disparaging about [him]" (Germains, 2014).

Moreover, he remembers that a fan of the band had reviewed a gig and praised the two principal members before then dismissing the other players in terms such as: "There were just a couple of no-marks on keyboards and bass". Alex replied, "I'll have you know that I was the no-mark on bass and that I wrote all my own bass lines on the album, so be more respectful!" (Ibid). For the other members, he had obviously transgressed his role limitations with this retort. This led to one of the management team phoning Alex and "letting him go" with a statement to the effect that "you can't be saying things like that. The fans are very loyal and demanding and expect things to be a certain way" (Ibid). These comments chime very much with Tony Turrell's experience with fans of Fish and Marillion almost claiming an authorial right over how their band should sound and responses to who is or should be considered an authoring member. In recollection, Alex says that "when people ask you what you do you say you're in the band but it's not really true in terms of the narrative that surrounds the band" (Ibid). And, of course, that narrative is composed by many interested parties, including fans.

Summary

It is interesting to reflect upon the historical shifts in status associated with covering or interpreting others' work. Within popular music, qualitative divisions between writers and interpreters hold sway to a greater or lesser extent depending upon many external factors. In addition, the revisitation by artists of their own earlier creations only serves to further cloud the binaries of creator and interpreter. Some of the many findings in this chapter stand opposed to the assumed distinctions between session player and creative band member. They are further reinforced within the film documentary *Twenty Feet from Stardom* (Neville, 2013). This film mainly concentrates on female backing singers from the 1960s onward. Not only do some participants support Turrell's preference not to be in a stable composing unit (a band or similar), but they go further in actively appreciating the creativity of the backup singer. How? They point to creativity as a consequence of no constrictive set list to perform, no fan expectations, less rigid genre boundaries and the fact that everyday can bring an unexpected new challenge. Thus, there are issues relating to variety, eclecticism and improvisation that many overlook. These concepts take us into the realms of true creative authorship and encourage us to look beyond the "one dollar, two dollar" assumptions relating to these authorial roles.

Bibliography

Abbey, John (1973) "Willie Mitchell", *Blues & Soul*, accessed 23-04-14, http://www.rocks backpages.com/Library/Article/willie-mitchell.
Ahonen, Laura (2008) *Constructing Authorship in Popular Music: Artists, Media and Stardom*, Milton Keynes: VDM Verlag.

Amos, Tori (2012) Sleeve notes to *Gold Dust*.

Anon. (2006) "Procol ex-Organist Plays in Court", BBC News Online, 13 November, accessed 7-10-08, http://news.bbc.co.uk/1/hi/entertainment/6142290.stm.

Anon. (2008) "UK Court Overturns Whiter Shade of Pale Copyright Ruling", 4 November, accessed 20-11-08, http://sourcewire.com/releases/reldisplay.php?relid=38008&hilite=.

Anon. (2009) "Whiter Shade Most Played Song", BBC News Online, 13 April, accessed 21-11-13, http://news.bbc.co.uk/1/hi/entertainment/7996979.stm.

Barthes, Roland (1977) "The Grain of the Voice", in *Image, Music, Text*, Glasgow: Fontana, pp 179–189.

Bennett, Andrew & Jodie Taylor (2012) "Popular Music and the Aesthetics of Ageing", in *Popular Music*, volume 31/2, May, Cambridge: Cambridge University Press, pp 231–243.

Coleman, Ray (1994) *the Carpenters: The Untold Story*, New York: Harper Collins.

Frith, Simon (1998) *Performing Rites: On the Value of Popular Music*, Cambridge: Harvard University Press.

George, Nelson (2003) *Where Did Our Love Go? The Rise and fall of the Motown Sound*, London: Omnibus.

Germains, Alex (2014) Interview, Liverpool, July 15.

Hann, Michael (2013) "Rod Stewart: I Thought Song Writing Had Left Me", *the Guardian*, 19 April, accessed 13-02-14, http://www.theguardian.com/music/2013/apr/19/rod-stewart.

Holm-Hudson, Kevin (2014) From a personal correspondence, December 1.

Homan, Shane (2006) *Access All Eras: Tribute Bands and Global Pop Culture*, Maidenhead: Open University Press.

Huntman, Ruth (2014) "Me, my Dad and 'the Old Lady'", *the Guardian*, 18 October, p 3.

Kennedy, Maev (2009) "Organist Wins Battle for Recognition for a Whiter Shade of Pale Riff", *the Guardian*, 30 July, accessed 15-03-15, http://www.theguardian.com/music/2009/jul/30/lords-ruling-whiter-shade-pale.

Licks, Dr. (1989) *Standing in the Shadows of Motown: The Life and Music of Legendary Bassist James Jamerson*, Wynnewood, Penn.: Dr. Licks Publishing.

Moy, Ron (2007) *Kate Bush and Hounds of Love*, Aldershot: Ashgate.

Negus, Keith & Michael Pickering (2004) *Creativity, Communication and Cultural Value*, London: Sage.

Payne, Jim (1969) "Al Jackson Jr. +", accessed 16-06-08, http://staxrecords.free.fr/aljacksonpage.htm.

Plasketes, George (ed.) (2010) *Play It Again: Cover Songs in Popular Music*, Farnham: Ashgate.

Stewart, Rod (2013) *Rod: The Autobiography*, London: Arrow.

Sweeting, Adam (2005) *Cover Versions: Singing Other People's Songs*, London: Pimlico.

Turrell, Tony (2014) Personal interview, Liverpool, April 7.

Whiteley, Sheila (2005) *Too Much, Too Young: Popular Music, Age and Gender*, London: Routledge.

Audio-Visual Sources

Tori Amos (1994) *Under the Pink*, "Yes, Anastasia".

(1996) "Professional Widow".

(2001) *Strange Little Girls*.

(2003) *Tales of a Librarian*.

(2011) *Night of Hunters*.

(2012) *Gold Dust*, "Yes, Anastasia".

(2014) *Unrepentant Geraldines*, "Promise".

Barnes, Barry (director) (2011) *Tori Amos: Night of Hunters*, DVD documentary.

Bewley, Jonathan (producer) (2013) *Carole Kaye: Session Legend Interview*, accessed 21-10-13, http://www.youtube.com/watch?v=q4JWqK6r6n4.

Blondie (1978) "Fade Away and Radiate".

Booker T. & the MGs (1962) "Green Onions".

The Carpenters (1972) "Goodbye Love".

David Bowie (1977) "Heroes".

Kate Bush (1978) *The Kick Inside*.

(1989) The Sensual World.

(1993) "And So Is Love", "Moments of Pleasure", *The Red Shoes*.

(2011) *The Director's Cut: Collector's Edition*.

Echo and the Bunnymen (2001) *Flowers*.

Eminem (1999) "'97 Bonnie & Clyde".

Brian Eno (1975) "St. Elmo's Fire".

Fish (1999) *Raingods with Zippos*.

(2003) *Field of Crows*.

Eddie Floyd (1966) "Knock on Wood".

Marvin Gaye (1964) "How Sweet It Is".

Al Green (1971) "Look What You Done for Me".

(1972) "Call Me", "I'm Still in Love with You".

The Mountaineers (2003) *Messy Century*.

Neville, Morgan (director) (2013) *Twenty Feet from Stardom*.

Powell, Michael (director) (1948) *The Red Shoes*.

Procol Harum (1967) "A Whiter Shade of Pale".

Otis Redding (1962) "These Arms of Mine".

(1965) "(I Can't Get No) Satisfaction", "Respect".

(1966) "Try a Little Tenderness", "My Lover's Prayer".

(1967) "Love Man".

Rodley, Chris (2010) *Forever Young: How Rock'n'Roll Grew Up*. BBC television documentary.

Percy Sledge (1966) "When a Man Loves a Woman".

Sonny and Cher (1967) "The Beat Goes On".

Rod Stewart (1970) "Maggie May".

(1971) "Mandolin Wind", "Stay With Me", "You Wear It Well".

(2001) *Human*.

(2002, 2003, 2004, 2005, 2010) *The Great American Songbook* (vols. 1–5).

(2012) *Merry Christmas, Baby*.

(2013) *Time*.

The Temptations (1966) "Beauty Is Only Skin Deep".

5

THE PRODUCER/REMIXER
AS AUTEUR

In recent years, various writers have begun moving beyond the false binaries relating to constructions of artistic and technological authorship. In the fourth edition of his book *The Art of Music Production: The Theory and Practice* (2013), Richard James Burgess maps out the many roles of the modern music producer in ways useful to those wishing to forge a career in the industry. However, his book is very much more than a simple "how to" manual. He establishes six "functional typologies" (Ibid: 12) that not only help us distinguish the different styles of production (and producer), but also suggest that there is no clear demarcation between what have been seen historically as opposing roles (such as producer/arranger, producer/engineer or producer/player). All aspects of production, whether technological, musical or interpersonal, are all situated along a continuum of creativity.

In a similar vein, a series of essays entitled *The Art of Record Production: An Introductory Reader for a New Academic Field* was published in 2012 and edited by Simon Frith and Simon Zagorzki-Thomas. This title is particularly interesting for the inclusion of the words "introductory" and "new". It has become increasingly difficult to break new critical ground in popular music studies as a result of the rapid proliferation of courses and book titles over the past twenty years. Nevertheless, the argument that this book does indeed broach a new aspect of the discipline—whether assumed or de facto—forms the basis for some of the principal critical dilemmas raised by this chapter. Throughout the text, various writers argue that romantic myths separating the individual and the collective author (and the technologist from the musician) are built upon false bifurcations. This is a stance that many of us working within the scholarly field would support. As stated in Chapter One, Bakhtin's notion of the dialogic (cited in Morris, 1994) is needed to ensure a critical path moves between and beyond such binary positions.

Particularly pertinent for the purposes of this chapter is another important point raised by Phillip McIntyre. In assuming that individuals can only contribute collectively in an environment such as the studio, he asks, "how then do we explain what happens creatively in the studio if we can't rely on the tenets of romanticism" (McIntyre, cited in Frith and Zagorski-Thomas, 2012:150). In other words, how can creative activity (and by extension authorship) be apportioned, if there is not a system, a location or a set of techniques that are all utilized? McIntyre argued that an overreliance on individual creativity, resulting in "psychological reductionism", has been countered by its opposite, "sociological reductionism", wherein the individual ceases to have any role. The way beyond this binary impasse has been seen to lie within a form of (Bakhtinian) synthesis that "has recognised that a confluence of factors, which includes social, cultural and psychological ones, needs to be in place for creativity to occur" (Ibid: 151). Other writers such as Negus and Pickering have also been at pains to move debate beyond outdated dichotomies. They argue that creativity "certainly does not imply a sender/receiver or encoding/decoding model of communication" (2004: ix).

Another text, Virgil Moorefield's *The Producer as Composer: Shaping the Sounds of Popular Music* (2010), while providing a valuable scholarly reappraisal of the producer-as-artist, falls into the trap of presenting a linear account of "great men" (a common failing in historiography), which maintains that only a significant, or signature, contribution would allow for the establishment of an auteur figure. Others such as McIntyre (cited in Frith and Zagorski-Thomas, 2012: 149–162) or Albin Zak (2001) take a more holistic approach to production and all of its participants in arguing that there cannot be creative distinctions between "composer" and "non-composer" based on the specific *degree* of contribution. Zak's research into (the nebulous nature of) studio roles does much to challenge the auteurist approach to the record producer, in showing that the "humble" engineer can also play a huge role. In almost metaphysical terms, he describes their work as requiring "a deft, sometimes invisible hand. For their manipulation of sonic reality must become for the listener a reality in itself—not an apparent replacement or a representation" (2001: 169). He goes on to quote Kevin Killen, an engineer, who argues that any absolute distinctions between producers and engineers have no basis beyond simple etymology, "it's all nomenclature" (Killen, cited in Zak: 170). Burgess argues that the Digital Audio Workstation (or DAW) has further blurred the lines "between technical and musical contributions" (2014).

Within this new critical scenario, outdated distinctions between individual and collective creativity and technological craft/artistic creativity are superseded by a more fluid model that sees all studio contributions as essentially "equal but different". As Toynbee states, "technological innovation is very much a cultural phenomenon" (2000: 99), and the two worlds fuse within the empirical listening experience. However, Burgess adds the caveat that "from a pragmatic perspective of attempting to teach the topic and encourage aspirants it is necessary to differentiate between skillsets . . . equal but different—worth differentiating in order to understand the fundamental skills required" (2014).

This is all well and good, but still bypasses a fundamental issue regarding authorship and production—"most listeners don't know what the producer does" (cited in Frith and Zagorski-Thomas, 2012: 153). This is true not only of the casual fan, but also of many scholars in the field (I count myself among this number, at least to a degree). Timothy Warner, in one of the first in-depth attempts to analyze the works of a specific producer (Trevor Horn), indicates the difficulty facing us when he states: "Being a closed environment, assigning specific artistic responsibility to each element of the finished product is virtually impossible" (2003: 35). Burgess talks of the "speed and transparency of suggestions and counter-suggestions" (2014) making it difficult to assign or even remember from whence contributions emanated. So bearing this in mind, how do we proceed? First, we use the notions of dialogue, synthesis and confluence to fashion a holistic frame through which to view the authorship of the producer or, rather, the authorship of *production* (what Ahonen calls "diffused authorship", 2008: 166). Second, we avoid falling into the trap of relying upon technological jargon, which, as with musicological jargon, does little more than to reinforce distinctions and preclude interdisciplinarity. And, third, we recognize that anecdotes, myth-spinning and unscholarly sources can all play their part in (unwittingly?) dismantling assumptions and ignorance about "behind the scenes" methods of authorship.

In brief, a producer can make decisions related to:

How and where recordings will take place (studio or chronotope as auteur).
Who, if anyone, will help create (collaboration as auteur).
What equipment will be used (technology as auteur).
How the budget will be spent (economics/marketing as auteur).
Choice of material, arrangements, structure, playing (traditional authorship as auteur).
Administration, paperwork, documentation (business infrastructure as auteur).
Balance between humans and technological systems (relationships as auteur).

Bearing in mind this breadth of roles, which alone account for the importance of the position, we might ask if the producer's role as an enabler *should* (or today *does*) remain subservient to the artists, the performances and the songs. How much should we be made aware of the production process in recordings? Isn't production merely the process that allows for art to emerge? The producer Quincy Jones described himself as a "culminator" (cited in Moorefield, 2010: 84), which seems a vague but appropriate summation. Sam Phillips talked about the need "to open up an area of freedom within the artist himself" (cited in Zak, 2001: 174), and, clearly, that almost hippie-like notion of "getting the right vibe" is of vital, if unquantifiable, importance.

In the following section, while trying to avoid the pitfalls set by a "history of great men" approach, three producers, each representing a different modus operandi, will have their relationship to authorship scrutinized. Phil Spector will symbolize the traditional "organic mode", wherein recordings based on performances partly in real time and space were realized. Trevor Horn will symbolize the "transitional mode", which incorporated elements of live, overdubbed and early sequencing and sampling processes into the end mix. Liam Howlett will symbolize the "virtual mode", which has moved the balance between playable and programmable methods largely (and totally within certain genres) in favour of the latter.

There have long existed producers that become names and have a public persona, from Shadow Morton and Mitch Miller in the 1950s, to Phil Spector and George Martin in the 1960s, to Trevor Horn in the 1980s, to David Guetta and Pharrell Williams in the contemporary period (and, yes, the position of producer is heavily gendered). Certainly, as time has gone on and as a result of the producer's shifting role (many are now DJs, players and performers), the public profile of the producer has never been higher. For Emma Mayhew:

> production credits have become significant to the discourse of contemporary musical criticisms. Discussions of the overall sound of a track or album often include identifying the producer(s) as an authorial presence within the recorded text.
>
> (cited in Whiteley, Bennett and Hawkins, 2004: 149)

The *Guardian* ran advertisements in 2013 offering Metropolis master classes with figures such as Timbaland. With a sepia-toned photograph presenting the auteur stroking his chin and resembling a 1940s' jazz musician or film star, the advertisement offered a standard attendance fee of £249 or a "first class" ticket costing £349. In addition to watching the producer dissecting some of his tracks and demonstrating his production processes, the higher price offered extras including a "one-to-one signing" (anon, 2013). Of course, Timbaland has a public profile superseding that of a mere producer. Others with a more backroom role (such as Jimi Hendrix's engineer Eddie Kramer) garner a lower fee.

However, even such examples of the burgeoning celebrity cult of the producer still do little to contribute to a widespread knowledge or appreciation of their roles as auteurs. A few relatively brief examples of the historical reasons for this ignorance need to be investigated at this point.

Phil Spector

One of the few producers from the pre-rock era to have gained (and maintained, partly the result of his notoriety and recent criminal acts) a high public profile is Phil Spector. Virgil Moorefield argues that Spector and George Martin gained high public profiles as a result of their "embracing subjectivity" (2010: xv). However, this is a problematic assumption. It is a reasonable guess that many nonspecialist music fans would have heard of Spector's name and the creative process with which he is closely associated—the "Wall of Sound". Certainly, some of his methods of working and producing have been hugely influential, and much of his work from the period 1962 to1970 is posteriori, instantly recognizable. Burgess is happy to utilize the term auteur when referring to certain producers in stating that "[Afanasieff, like] all auteur producers employs a level of control that creates a signature identity" (2013: 12). While this may be true for the expert producer-as-listener, the less specialized fan may struggle to identify such sonic trademarks. Again, authorship in such cases may be assigned rather than explicitly identified. But to return to Spector, the more one explores, the more a mono-lithic (excuse the pun) view of his precise influence upon recordings begins to be challenged.

The first point to make is that his output was only prolific for a few years. From 1966 onward, he worked far more sporadically, and the Spector sound mutated, moving from mono to stereo and making some concessions to generic shifts happening from the mid-1960s. Some of his work with both George Harrison and John Lennon is not particularly "Spector-esque". Of course, his role with such artists was not the multitasking role of writer, arranger, player and producer, as it was for the likes of the Crystals and the Ronettes. However, on most of his early productions, he worked with the Wrecking Crew and was also assisted by engineer Larry Levine and orchestral arranger Jack Nitzsche. Moorefield (2010: 10) states that Levine and Nitzsche were "consistent presences . . . from 62–66" and that writing credits were usually shared between Spector and others such as Ellie Greenwich and Jeff Barry. Accounts of Spector's recording sessions vary widely, with Mick Brown (2008) claiming that the atmosphere was often tense and intimidating. However, Blaine (2003: 53–56) painted a far more positive picture, portraying Spector as full of energy and humour, being very hands-on, and actively moving from one role to another. Carol Kaye spoke of a party atmosphere when she worked on Spector's sessions with Ike and Tina Turner, and claimed that such sessions were the first she had participated in where players got feedback through headphones (Kaye, cited in Suckling, 2014). Spector even placed his own microphones (not normally a producer's job). However, Blaine did state that engineer Levine "had some tricks, and every time he came up with a new one Phil would beam and want to use it on the record" (2003: 55). Although very anecdotal, such comments do demonstrate a sharing of the creative load and Spector's willingness to incorporate others' artistic input.

Most of the so-called "classic" recordings took place in the Gold Star Studios in Los Angeles. However, according to Blaine (Ibid: 68), the recordings subsequently moved into United/Western and Brian Wilson's own studio (for later Beach Boys sessions). Much of their early work was recorded at Gold Star, with Levine engineering and the Wrecking Crew making varied contributions (Moorefield, 2010: 16). This raises the issue of the specific space having a creative dimension. Thus, authorship is more diffuse and more closely connected to a chronotope than on first glance. The reasons for Spector's relative critical and commercial decline are multiple, but one factor must be the fragmentation of the time and space confluence, which substantiates the conclusion that while he was an important—probably the most important—component in the production process, he was not the overarching auteur assigned by rock mythology. Barbara Bradby's research into Spector and girl-group music reaffirms the notion that "as the products of a complex division of labor, these recordings cannot be ascribed to any one 'author'" (Bradby, 1988, cited in Frith and Goodwin, 1990: 342). In addition, as previously stated in an earlier chapter, the single male auteur myth that overlooks the contribution of female creativity plays its part in the process whereby Spector, along with terms such as the Wall of Sound, become a kind of critical shorthand, with Spector himself functioning as a metonym and a public face for a series of processes few truly comprehend and that he was only one (admittedly vital) component of. Burgess is persuasive when arguing that "the term auteur does not imply a single author but the imparting of a dominant characteristic to the work" (2014). Within this scenario, the notion of Spector as auteur-producer can be subtly shifted from its more monolithic connotations.

Some scholars have willingly subscribed to and helped substantiate romantic myths of the sole auteur in the context of production. Moorefield is surely correct in claiming that the producer "takes responsibility" (Ibid: xvii), and, equally, that over time, "the cultural ear . . . becomes more aware of the production aspect of a track" (Ibid: xvi), with economics having an important role: "cheapness encourages the all-in-one figure" (Ibid: xvii). However, he has overemphasized the breadth of the individual's role. A statement such as "there have been instances of the producer totally determining the sound of the act, as for example in the case of the English band Joy Division" (Ibid: xvi) is highly debatable, as well as offers no substantiation. Partly, the issue is one of terminology. In a later chapter, referring to Trent Reznor's "signature sound—his is hard, abrasive, grating, yet also connected to the American song writing tradition, however obliquely" (Ibid: 70), adjectives do little to actually define Reznor's work as distinct from contributory factors such as genre, technology and collaborations—in short, all of the elements that help deconstruct myths of the singular auteur.

As time progressed, many of the myths of authenticity acted to militate against the producer-as-auteur gaining widespread currency across all genres. Even today, focus on producers tends to be concentrated in fields such as EDM, pop and rap—or non-rock forms in broad terms. For Frith, "rock ideology . . . disparaged mechanized music [and] tended to restrict critical analysis to matters of composition and performance" (Frith and Zagorski-Thomas, 2012: 207). The studio itself was seen to be "a setting for artifice while rock's appeal rests on its 'roughness'" (Ibid: 211). The notion of live performance as the ultimate terrain within which authenticity is literally "proven" thus cast producers in a compromised role, the suspicion being that they represented the commerce element acting in opposition to the creative element of the musicians (Ibid). The notion that qualitative distinctions between terms such as commerce and creativity must be challenged is very well expressed in Negus and Pickering's work on the industry. They go further in maintaining that in many instances, it is commerce that actually *provokes* creativity (2004: 46–47).

As ever, debates relating to producers and authorship do as much to reflect upon individual interpretive strategies as upon any overarching critical thesis. Moorefield took issue with Zak's notion of the "recordist" in stating, "I do not believe that everyone present in the studio is what Zak has called a 'recordist' and hence automatically involved in the process of production" (2010: 71). Admittedly, this disagreement may be as much to do with the semantics of terms such as player and producer and whether we want to rigidly compartmentalize creative roles. But what Moorefield and Zak's divergence of opinion exemplifies is the difference between a romantic construction of authorship and a post-structuralist deconstruction of authorship—the latter seeing the concept as a fluid episteme including notions of the "death of the author" (see Barthes, 1977: 142–148) and the birth of the reader as at least the partial determiner/originator of meaning and worth. And, for what it is worth, I am with Zak on this issue.

Trevor Horn

More recently, the producer Trevor Horn's work has moved the issue of the producer-as-auteur into new areas, partly as the result of more sophisticated technologies encouraging a reappraisal of the producer's role. Moorefield encapsulates this historical shift as moving from "the illusion of reality" to "the reality of illusion" (2010). However, the longstanding debate over the individual versus the collective and how we exactly pin down the contributions of those behind the desk only continue and indeed proliferate. One practical way to manifest the confusions of the listener is through a brief study of Horn's work, culminating in the production credits of the band Propaganda.

Trevor Horn graduated to production after being a musician and composer, best known for the Buggles' "Video Killed the Radio Star", a global hit in 1979. This track was unusual in terms of Horn's subsequent career in that, according to Mark Cunningham, the song was played on instruments rather than sequenced or programmed (1996: 270). Burgess played drums on this track, with the instruction to play with "a machine-like precision" (2014). Horn's period of greatest commercial success spanned the 1980s and included work with ABC, Malcolm McLaren, Yes, Frankie Goes to Hollywood and Seal. As part of the Art of Noise, he was an early innovator in exploring the creative possibilities of the Fairlight CMI—one of the first digital samplers. On the band's first album, Horn was credited as "musical director" and co-composed six of the nine tracks (Warner, 2003: 101).

His production work on Malcolm McLaren's *Duck Rock* (1983) made great use of "field recordings"—a long-standing process. However, he was among the first to then sample (authored citations of prior texts) and manipulate these recordings and incorporate them into a sound collage. This became one of his trademarks, although on this album, he was also heavily reliant on Anne Dudley. In addition, J.J. Jeczalik, another future member of the Art of Noise, was responsible for the sample production (Warner, 2003: 52). The technological limitations with early samplers can be said to have affected the authoring process in this period. Because of the limited memory space, short samples tended to be used repetitively, and this became a trope both of the era and of those such as Horn closely associated with it. McLaren had comparatively little creative input into the project, but he possessed the important author image and was the overall conceptualist who helped market the album.

Despite the collaborative processes that Horn utilized, it was his name that came to be associated with a particular sound/method of working, whereby often small instrumental sequences would be augmented with samples and programmable elements before being cut and pasted into a radical mix having very little to do with organic notions of real time and playing capability. In addition, Warner viewed his work with Yes as typifying a dynamic relationship between moments of timbral complexity and "drops" to sparse passages (Ibid: 67–68). These were also to be a feature with later projects such as Frankie Goes to Hollywood and Propaganda. As with other producers, such as Spector, it can be argued that Horn's role was indeed significant but partly determined by technologies (early samplers such as the Fairlight CMI and their "grainy" timbre), collaborations, and the chronotope of the recording studio (Sarm West and East) and the record label (ZTT). Particularly important was the creative input of Anne Dudley, who wrote, arranged and co-composed many of his commercial successes, as well as Jeczalik and Steve Lipson. Lipson began working with Horn in 1983 on Frankie Goes to Hollywood's "Relax", and the two continued collaborating for several years.

The group Propaganda had a moderate amount of success with the single "Dr. Mabuse" (1984) and the album *A Secret Wish* (1985). Although Horn only produced a few tracks on the album, the remainder (produced by Lipson) sound to the unenlightened to be the work of the same person, but this is the crucial point. We, as listeners, are easily fooled by publicity relating to the star quality of the producer, with Horn as one of the major names in this period. Warner notes "important similarities" due to "technology, technique and taste" (2003: 113) between the work of Horn and Lipson. What is particularly interesting is Warner's repeated desire to emphasize the collaborative authorial credits within a text ostensibly devoted largely to Horn. In the extensive interview with Horn that concludes Warner's book, the subject himself was equally at pains to share accreditation. On the subject of collaborators, Horn states, "they have an enormous input into what I do" (cited in Warner, 2003: 152).

We are willingly seduced by mythologies of the single, named creator, whereas evidently, Propaganda's work was partially determined by technology, genre and even the zeitgeist. Burgess references Horn's methodology and his "vision" (2014), so this is not to say that another producer, working within the same set of physical and technical circumstances, would have produced work indistinguishable from Horn or Lipson, but that Horn's position as an auteur is, to a degree, dependent upon specific temporal, technological and collaborative factors.

Conversely, Rick Rubin's sheer eclecticism as producer—he has worked with acts as diverse as Run DMC, Limp Bizkit, Dixie Chicks, Johnny Cash, Nusrat Fateh Ali Khan, Mel C, Tom Petty, Justin Timberlake and AC/DC—precludes any notion of a trademark sound. Rubin produced four out of the eleven tracks on Adele's *21* (2011), but most would struggle to identify them based on any notion of a personal style. Rubin may well be hired for his technical expertise, experience, ability to deal with people or for what his name brings to the project, but in terms of output, his productions prove that *creativity* is not the same as *authorship*, as it has been historically understood.

One of the biggest problems in dealing with production and authorship is that we usually have no prior text or alternative production with which to compare the finished work. How would Trevor Horn have produced Johnny Cash's *American Recordings* (1994)? We can guess, but it remains pointless conjecture; he did not and Rick Rubin did—end of story.

Yet, before this chapter itself descends into the realm of pointless conjecture, there are ways that a producer's role can be defined and identified, provided we are allowed to stretch terms somewhat and use individuals that elide the roles of player, writer and producer. At the end of the chapter, the creative role of the mixer/remixer will be investigated, but at this point, the role(s) of the assumed auteur of the Prodigy's Liam Howlett can help illuminate our critical dilemmas.

Liam Howlett/The Prodigy

Frith quoted Paul McCartney, who in 1974 sought to minimize George Martin's perceived influence in saying, "We don't mind him helping us, it's great, it's a great help, but it's not his album, folks, you know" (Frith and Zagorski-Thomas, 2012: 215).

This seemingly over-defensive reaction, characterizing Martin as something of an outsider or, at least, not one of the band, exemplifies the importance of authorship to involved parties, even those whose status as great auteurs was secure and long before 1974. However, if we consider the position of Liam Howlett, as principal songwriter, producer and arranger of the Prodigy, a different light can be shed on an individual who in this case was an integral component in a band, yet who was at the same time partially displaced as the public face of the act by shifts in genre, marketing and musicians' roles during the group's career.

Howlett's musical roots lay in hip hop and DJing. The Prodigy formed in 1990 and was an unusual conglomerate in that they moved between the authorial and performing modes of dance and rock. For Ben Thompson, their success is due to the "irresistible fusion of dance technology and rock dynamics" (1998: 1). Indeed, one of the reasons for their enduring popularity resides in their ability to cross over genres and draw influences from funk/rock acts such as Red Hot Chili Peppers as well as from hip hop and rave music. Certainly, in their early days, despite always performing live (an obvious rock trait) as opposed to merely producing music to be played or mixed in clubs (an obvious dance trait), Liam Howlett was effectively the only player, writer and producer. The other three members of their early recording career, Keith Flint, Leeroy Thornhill and Maxim Reality, concentrated on dancing and a limited amount of MCing in a live context. Howlett is unusual within dance/DJ circles in having some formal musical skills; he took piano lessons for eight years (Ibid).

The first album, *The Prodigy Experience*, was released in 1992. Despite always basing some of their sound upon samples, hardly any are credited. At the time, the band was associated with the partly illegal rave scene, and this may have contributed to their outsider status and the decision not to fully acknowledge sources. Howlett was credited as the writer, producer, engineer and recorder on all of the tracks. Flint and Thornhill were credited as dancers, and Maxim as MC. The second album, *Music for the Jilted Generation* (1994), credited other (outside) writers and producers as well as listing samples. Howlett's contribution was still considerable, but not quite to the same extent as on the first album. The third album, *The Fat of the Land* (1997), which broke the band internationally credited a wide range of writers including Flint and Maxim and those who composed the sampled elements.

How do these significant shifts in accreditation illuminate the issue of production and authorship? First, the band went "legitimate" in terms of the full acknowledgement of sampled sources. The reasons for this are not clear, but may well reflect an end to the free-for-all situation that existed in the earlier days of digital sampling. Second, the nature of the Prodigy's recorded output shifted from a largely synth-and-sample DJ mix to a more recognizably song-based terrain featuring rap-style vocals and elements resembling verses and choruses. From the second album onward, players were credited for contributions to individual tracks. Not only did this shift give the band much bigger singles (e.g., "Firestarter" [1996], written by Howlett, Flint, Horn, Dudley, Jeczalik, Morley, Langan and Deal, and "Breathe" [1997], written by Howlett, Flint and Maxim), but also the rising public profile afforded to the hitherto peripheral Keith Flint by his new role, which effected an authorial change in terms of public image.

Ahonen's research into author image shows how difficult a group such as Coldplay has found it to not be mediated and perceived as simply consisting of a leader/auteur and backing musicians because of the high public and stage profile of Chris Martin (2008: 126–130). Andrew Goodwin talks of stars (which Flint effectively became) as providing "a point of identification" (cited in Ahonen, 2008: 32). Stage performances in the period of their greatest success see Howlett as the principal, sometimes the only, player, but trapped behind a bank of keyboards, samplers and laptops. As a result of stage presence and contributory factors such as costume and specular mediation, the visual authorship and public perception of the band inevitably shift to Flint (and Maxim to a lesser extent). In this sense, the adoption of Toynbee's notion of "social authorship" (2000) made possible by dance's challenge to rock's performance and image authorship can be considered.

On the fourth album, *Always Outnumbered, Never Outgunned* (2004), there were several composing credits to Neil McLellan (also co-production and programming), but little mention of Maxim or Flint. Did this signal a move by Howlett to reestablish the band as a production project rather than an image-led pop group? The credits to Howlett playing "keys, guitars, drums and analogue shit" certainly marked a radical shift toward conventional accreditation. Conversely, the more recent *Invaders Must Die* (2009) featured wide and varied accreditation, with not a single track credited solely to Howlett.

Part of the critical dilemma in exploring this case study is the paucity of documentation afforded the new generation of digital/sample/DJ-based producers. The principal research sources consist of a small number of biographies giving little real insight and a few journalistic interviews that admittedly do dig deeper into working methods. However, it can be considered significant that, seemingly, Howlett's work has not yet been considered worthy of complex, critical analysis. His role(s) in the Prodigy—also including his input on videos and artwork—clearly distinguish him as an auteur in terms of his breadth and musical prominence. Equally, while there is clear progression in the albums over the course of a now long-standing career, there is also some recognizable stylistic continuity—another authorial trope.

One of the stand-out qualities of the Prodigy's oeuvre is the level of distortion imposed upon both existing samples and newly composed elements. With this, the tracks are immediately experientially distanced from most within the metagenre of dance. In addition, Howlett's reliance on breakbeat drum patterns on most of the tracks, as opposed to the more customary four-to-the-floor patterns of dance genres such as house and techno, give the tracks a feel closer to hip hop and drum and bass. Although essentially composing via the mediums of sequencing software (Reason) and a laptop "studio", Howlett's affection for vintage analogue keyboards produced by companies such as Korg and Oberheim and his use of "loads of old valve stuff" do provide a historical spread of timbres, giving the keyboard riffs and motifs some of their "trashy" character (Howlett, cited in Sillitoe, 2004). On the *Always Outnumbered, Never Outgunned* album, retro elements were mastered using the more contemporary Pro Tools software. Something in this mélange of old and new technologies, a singular approach to sampling, added to Howlett's playing skills and the harsh collision of genres such as hip hop, rock and EDM, which helped fashion this unique sonic world. Howlett's work, while considered and sophisticated, is not subtle, and the lack of acoustic instruments and timbres aids our identification of his modus operandi.

Unlike some of the anonymous techniques of the traditional producer, Howlett's use of samples, some of them highly recognizable, do render his trademarks as more easily accredited. For instance, the opening sounds on the album *Music for the Jilted Generation* (1994) originate from a speech given in the film *Blade Runner* (Scott, 1982). The band's breakthrough hit "Charly" (1991) made similar use of speech from an old public information film warning children of the dangers of going out alone without telling their parents. The controversy of the title (a slang drug term) and the use of a decontextualized child's voice proved a portent for later, even more contentious creative choices within tracks. One such example is "Firestarter" (1996), which allied Flint's "Essex Boy" rapping/persona to a backing track making use of the Breeders' "SOS" (1993) and the "hey, hey, hey" element, also sampled by the Art of Noise on their single "Close to the Edit" (1984). Howlett talks about the desire to make the hook based upon a sound as opposed to a vocal, which is a process ideally suited to sample-based recordings. However, Howlett's trademark style was to combine samples with original elements of musical composition. This method of authorship allows for others to attempt to reproduce tracks to a high degree of accuracy. This "reverse engineering" (or literally *deconstructive*) process on Prodigy tracks such as "Voodoo People", itself an "authored performance" by engineer Jim Pavloff (2010), allows a unique insight into the work of a figure such as Howlett.

"Voodoo People"

Pavloff's method is to isolate small elements of a track and then attempt to reproduce them or locate them in the case of samples. These elements are then engineered, mixed and linked to closely resemble the original track. The process, which is extremely time consuming and painstaking, produces elements that are then edited in order to compact the whole viewing procedure into a few minutes.

"Voodoo People" is principally built upon small sampled sequences from longer musical tracks. The principal sampled sources are the Last Poets' "Right On" (1970), Johnny Pate's "Shaft in Africa" (1971) and Led Zeppelin's "Whole Lotta Love" (1969).

In addition, Pavloff claims that a guitar riff from Nirvana's "Very Ape" (1993) is then replayed by someone other than the original player. This is thus not a digital sample, but more of an influence or example of plagiarism, depending upon your viewpoint (most samples are uncredited on this track listing). In terms of original composition (in the accepted sense), Howlett's contribution mainly consists of a lead synth line, which actually functions as one of the principal lead hooks—so, although short, it is memorable, extended, manipulated and repeated between 2.24 and 3.15 and from 5.31 to 6.22, which is the end of the track. It is also worth noting that Howlett's multiple roles allow him to think of note choice and note manipulation as part of the same process, as he is responsible for both. There is no mediator between the player and the producer in the Prodigy. Pavloff reproduces close to the exact timbres of this line using these techniques and processes: changing the pulse width, overdrive, using cut-off filter, mix saturator, equalization and various forms of echo such as chorus, room reverb, ping-pong delay, short delay and hall reverb (2010).

As a nonmusician and nontechnologist, what matters more to me than the naming processes here is the extent to which manipulation and distortion of the original elements take place. If we add to this finding the frequent use of timbres that have a "dirty" feel, such as distorted heavy or metal-guitars, we are clearly closer to the terrain of rock in terms of production and timbral choice. However, in terms of structure and flow, this track, in combination with many others within the Prodigy oeuvre, exhibits a closer connection to dance/EDM than it does to rock. If most rock and pop *songs* are built upon a dynamic of tension/resolution consisting of verse/chorus/middle, then most dance *tracks* are built upon a dynamic of tension/resolution consisting of buildups and drops. In terms of a personal aesthetics, song structures are experienced as trying to efface their constructed nature by use of mythologies of flow, with gradual shifts in intensity and affective response. The buildups to the transcendent moment of the chorus, key change or solo are often incremental (the listener is *teased*, by two or three verses before the chorus, etc.). Within the dance track, the structure is made more manifest, with components being added often at the start point of the bar, usually around multiples of four, in addition to the almost inevitable 4:4 time signature. Considering the impact both visually and sonically of the other band members in the Prodigy, as previously broached, we again have elements that we can relate to dance and others that can relate to rock in terms of authorship.

While other acts such as the Chemical Brothers also operated in a liminal terrain between dance and rock and as both DJs and musicians, the Prodigy (and Liam Howlett's contributions) still stand alone. I must confess to the reason for choosing Howlett, insofar as his role as much more than a producer does make it easier to judge his contribution. In addition, the lack of acoustic instruments in his work does function to make the samples and mixes more easily identifiable. Many of the component parts contribute to the perhaps mythical audience construction of sounds as edgy, aggressive and even brutal, yet they also have the personalized imprint of the true auteur. They can fill a dance floor, energize an arena or triumph at a huge festival—a band for all seasons (and venues). Ultimately and paradoxically, the techniques of the contemporary virtual producer, reliant on laptops, samples, software and Pro Tools, can stand out as authored in ways that more organic or collaborative methods cannot. Toynbee sees Howlett as not conforming to the "utilitarian division of labour" (2000: 131) found in dance; he does perform, produce, write and DJ. These are elements of "rock's expressionism, inscribed in stage performance and the 'great work' format of the album" (Ibid). In this, there is a reason to see a way between the bifurcation of "Author-God" and "consumption based through combination in 'social authorship'" (Ibid: xv). Constructions of rock- and dance-based authorship collide fruitfully within Howlett's oeuvre.

Remix, Remaster (With Thanks to Bryan Ferry and Richard Hamilton)

Once tape-based, multitrack recording became widely available in the early 1960s, the intrinsic connections between linear time and space began to fracture. The live mix, with all its capacity for undoable mistakes, began to be superseded by processes that allowed producers and engineers to mix, or more accurately remix, after the backing tracks had been recorded. The famous weekly meetings at Motown where Berry Gordy and producers would discuss the merits of recordings and decide whether songs should be released, rerecorded or remixed have been well documented (George, 2003). It was also common practice for records to be mixed differently for stereo and mono in the 1960s, or for album tracks to be edited or remixed as single releases, with an eye upon a different market. For example, Steeleye Span's "Gaudete" (1973) in its original form features a slowly faded-in vocal that pans slowly between the stereo channels before slowly fading out. When released as a single to tie in with the Christmas holiday, the stereo panning was dispensed with, as were the extensive periods of fade-in and fade-out because they would not have fit into the commercial radio format of the time. (Radio programmers hate "dead air".) What difference this made to sales or reception is difficult to judge, but the remixed version did give a folk act, singing an ancient hymn a capella and in Latin, an unlikely hit (reaching No. 14 on the charts) in the UK.

Controversies around the use of technology and the aesthetics of reception have long existed when considering remixes. Some Beatles aficionados maintain that the mono mixes, particularly on their early albums, are superior to the stereo versions. Such disputes do help support the rereleasing of the complete catalogue of the Beatles' mono albums in a box set, or Paul McCartney overseeing a revisionist remixing of *Let it Be* (1970) with what was titled *Let it Be . . . Naked* (2003). Among many other changes, this new version removed the orchestrations of Phil Spector that so annoyed McCartney when he discovered what one auteur had done to another auteur's work without permission (Hurwitz, 2004). However, it is interesting to note that the desire to remix the album in a more "roots" fashion does not prevent the removal of some of the conversational snippets found on the original album. Surely, they too help construct mythologies of the real? This inconsistency is puzzling, in authorial/remixing terms, as is the claim made by mixing staff who undertook the physical work in John Harris's article (2003):

> Studio employees who had been handed 32 reels of tape [were] told to come up with a new album and then left to get on with it. Much to their amazement when he heard the final version, McCartney requested no changes whatsoever.

This comment suggests that it was the principle rather than the actual mechanics of the remixing process that was important. McCartney seems to have wanted the influence of Spector's authorship diminished in favour of his own but was prepared to defer to others, resulting in an album with a collective sense of authorship rather than a strictly personal view.

Clearly, any tampering with the original works of great auteurs such as the Beatles will result in some opposition, as well as will result in sales both of the new and old versions of tracks. These same factors can also account for the successive remastering jobs that Jimmy Page has carried out on Led Zeppelin tracks. However, where remixing really begins to take on a separate, authored role distinct from the original material is in more technologically determined and less auteur-based forms such as reggae and disco. Much has been written about the mechanics of remixing elsewhere (Burgess, 2013), but my concern, as ever, is with the impact of the process upon notions of authorship.

Among the unwritten rules of remixing are such notions as bring in an outsider to get a fresh input, speed up or slow down the track, make a song more dance-floor friendly, make a dance-floor track more "song-based", make the sound more "alternative", isolate or foreground one element, lengthen/shorten the original track, and/or remove all but the vocals and rebuild. In strict terms, a remix should not add any new elements (although Burgess notes that this is not true in hip hop or many other contemporary recordings [2014]), but this does not appear to be a prerequisite, thus rendering a remix also a rerecording in many cases. Another issue is the notion, previously touched upon, that once recorded music becomes a database of sounds capable of endless manipulation, any notion of an original or even finished track is open to question.

Just as was the case with Berry Gordy seeking to keep his session players anonymous, the industry, albeit with a different imperative, acts to render the remixer even more anonymous than the producer. This may be the result of judging their role to be strictly technological rather than musical/creative, thus rendering them unfit to assume the mantle of author. However, such were the *transformative* possibilities made evident within the remix that this situation began to shift during the 1980s. Such was the power of the remixer that by 1987, Phil Harding and Ian Levine—remixers at PWL (Stock, Aitken and Waterman) productions—could negotiate not only an authorial credit for their work ("Additional Production and Remix by . . ."), but also a royalty, instead of the hitherto customary flat fee. They were thus transformed from unknown piece workers into named composers. As I have attempted to show elsewhere, once you are named and acknowledged, then you assume authored status. This newfound status was partly the consequence of the sheer amount of time and transformative work that remixers were devoting to their art by this period. For Harding:

> It had become common practice by the mid-1980s to replace everything instrumentally on the records we were being asked to remix, keeping only the vocals. This often became a huge job and really, in our view, part of the production process.

(2009: 141)

As a consequence of more critical recognition, the humble remixer gains production status and rewards, with the 1% royalty (which Harding claims became common industry practice) being deducted from the producer's own royalty on all remixed tracks. However, according to Burgess, "established producers will not accept a reduction in their royalty—it has to come out of the artist's share" (2014).

Another means by which we can appreciate the growing authorial status of the remixer is through the development of the remix album whereby a single or, more commonly, a group of remixers are given the creative license to sometimes radically reconfigure an artist's work. This is, in a sense, a modern equivalent of the "Variations" syndrome found within orchestral music. Concurrent with this practice lays the surrendering, or at least partial displacement, of agency and author(ity) that passes from the artist to the remixer, but often to the authorial benefit of both parties. As was noted earlier in the chapter when the role of the producer was being explored, it is the issue of transformation that can often render the degree of change so significant that the notion of the remixer as auteur can be raised. Many examples of remix albums can be noted, but two particularly pertinent to this discussion are *We Are Glitter* (2006) by Goldfrapp (and remixers) and *Lady Gaga: The Remix* (2010).

The former consists of twelve tracks, eleven of them from the duo's previous album *Supernature* (2005). Two tracks have two different remixes. Some remixes are by "acts" (the Shortwave Set, the Flaming Lips) and some by DJs or remixers (Benny Benassi, Ewan Pearson). As previously mentioned, the term remix is actually a misnomer, as most of the tracks also feature "additional programming", "additional production" and even some additional instrumentation on certain tracks. Thus, etymology defeats us, as in effect the tracks are more than simple remixes, but still fall short of the full connotations of rerecording. The degree of transformation from the originals varies, but all are still essentially transformative in ways that conform to the unwritten rules of remix techniques previously mapped out.

On the Stuart Price remix of Lady Gaga's "Paparazzi" (2010), many of the aforementioned techniques apply, but the track is further removed from the original by the transposition of melodic fragments that change the whole mood of the song. This is not achieved by a simple key change in the chorus, as the root key of Ab is utilized in its relative minor form of F minor, allowing the chorus melody to remain the same, but the verse melody is changed so that the initial "comforting" move from G to C (under "We Are the Crowd") becomes the more disturbing A flat to C in the remix, enabled by a change in verse key from C minor to F minor (Turrell, see the acknowledgments). When discussing this remix in class, the few experienced formal musicians (or those lucky few possessing perfect pitch) identified this shift in musicological terms, but the rest of the group still identified the change wrought by the remix, even if their use of language was vaguer ("the mood changes", "it's darker", etc.). The point here is not to differentiate the two types of response, but rather to state that the subtle, yet transformative changes wrought by the remixer are the mark of an auteur and are acknowledged as such. This is aided by other more obvious changes: the tempo is increased from 115 to 125, the song is shortened by nine seconds, drum and percussion sounds are changed and made more prominent by a sparser mix, the synth string progression in the middle eight darkens the mood, and the piano is brought up in the mix. As well, there are doubtless more subtle mix alterations that all but a very few would be able to identify.

Authorship and sampling is a subject that I will return to in a later chapter as a final aside relating to the work of Stuart Price. Under his alias the Thin White Duke, Price remixed Coldplay's "Talk" (2005). The original makes great use of a sample from Kraftwerk's "Computer Love" (1981). On the remix, this sampled element is reduced in presence, as are the Coldplay elements of the song in favour of the remixer's contributions—but all components are still present. Thus, authorship, in terms of degree, allows for the reconfiguration of a new collage. A remix of a sample-based original is a transformation, but not at the cost of effacing previous authored contributions. In this sense, authorship is as much an accretion as an originating act, and this problematizes the hierarchies of originator, interpreter and technologist that I am about to explore.

Below the constructed top-down hierarchy of artist, producer and (now?) remixer, those responsible for remastering would probably be found at the bottom of the pile. I am making this assumption as a result of the role of the remaster being seen as purely technological and thus, in traditional romantic terms, not creative or authorial. However, Toynbee is correct in observing that creativity in pop always has a performative dimension—it is meant for someone else to experience (2000: 58). This leads us to the quixotic work of Evan Eisenberg, who offers a way beyond constructed long-established oppositions. In *The Recording Angel* (1987), Eisenberg turns the relative status between the professional musician and the amateur (i.e., "listener") on its head in a text that jumps between ungrounded postulation, formal musicological analysis and informal field work interviews. He attempts to establish the importance of what he terms the "phonologist" and the status of the recording. Eisenberg argues that the traditional qualitative divide between instruments and phonograms, or players and listeners, must be challenged. In a text that carries strong echoes of Jacques Derrida's challenge to the basis of logocentrism (wherein speech's hegemonic status places it above that of writing, or within Barthes' notion that the reader "writes" texts), Eisenberg maintains that the amateur listener is not passive, but rather creative, interpretive and even the constructor of the musical text:

how can the interpretive musician claim to make music? On the grounds that a moment ago there was empty air and now there is music in it? Then anyone with a phonograph can make the same claim.

(1987: 146)

Of course, this is a radical position and one that dismantles the foundations of Western art aesthetics. Nevertheless, in essence, Eisenberg's views are directly applicable to both the role of the "re-mastering angel" and the subsequent impact upon us all as phonologists.

Genesis 1970–75 (2008)

In a brief analysis, paradoxically for a Genesis box set consisting of seven remastered studio albums (produced by Nick Davis) and six live performance DVDs, this final musical example allows for some of Eisenberg's more fantastic theories to be grounded in empirical listening experiences. This is the third and final box set covering the classic lineup's early studio albums. Because of the age and rudimentary technology originally available, it transforms the material more comprehensively than previously released box sets covering later material. Most would conclude that there are principally two reasons to remaster old material. The first is to "clean up" original analogue tape masters (which thus renders the process distinct from remixing, although there are clearly crossovers between the two processes), and the second imperative is financial. These collectors' items retailed at around £100 when they were released in the UK and have since increased in value (the cheapest second-hand copy I could find on Amazon at the time of publication was £156.14). Leaving aside the monetary implications of the reauthoring process, it has to be said that the critical reception to such releases is extremely diverse—ranging from horrified to ecstatic. This, again, relates to authorship, but as much about the authorship of the phonologist as the remaster (or, in another sense, the searcher and the sought).

What exactly has been done to the original tracks is difficult to quantify because individual listening experiences are just that. But from a personal point of view, the overall impression is of, literally, discovering instrumental and vocal elements that, if present on the originals, remained beneath audibility and thus, empirically, did not exist. What reviewer David Negrin refers to as "lost moments" (2014) are, in addition, moments that were never found in the first place. The process is perhaps most akin to the way that old photographs can now be digitally cleaned to reveal hitherto invisible people. As a result, knowing the originals so intimately, it is hard not to conclude that Eisenberg's notion of the listener making music is not so far off the mark, although this notion is, of course, predicated on the skill of the remastering auteur. This figure, as far from the notion of the romantic creator as is possible to imagine, has *transformed lives*. A technological process assumes the role, through human agency, of great, authored art.

Summary

Burgess, in commenting on the limitless possibilities engendered by DAW production techniques, talks about "micro-vision" (2013: 155), which consists of making tiny, incremental changes to a mix after staring at a screen for days and which hardly anyone will notice. This is one of the crucial issues in exploring the authorship of production. The producer-as-auteur construction (and all of the other production roles investigated in this chapter) gives a name and a personality to a partly technological set of processes that most fans of music don't understand, and many may not particularly care about. This authorial construction, as well as allowing for another marketing dimension (within journals, interviews, documentaries, master-classes and even the establishment of the "celeb"), actually contrives to diminish the more *recognizably* authored work (as a result of having a prior text as comparison) of the humble mixer, remixer or remaster.

When a producer has a name, they are granted assumed authorial status. On an album such as *Fleshtone* (2010) by Kelis, in addition to the customary array of producers associated with the EDM genre, the album credits list the artist as executive producer, as well as two other co-executive producers and two more associate executive producers. What these credits don't tell us is what these weighty roles *actually consist of*. Burgess, after a lifetime as a producer in and researcher of the music industry, is surely correct in concluding that a role such as executive producer makes a situation wherein "day-to-day involvement ranges from non-existent to active monitoring of the project . . . [and] credits activate future work and income by establishing your brand" (2013: 187). Conversely, the unnamed mixer/remixer/remaster has their authorship identified through their work rather than their public visibility and can still obtain the awards and recognition accrued by the creative auteur. Conversely, the executive producer's role "is not Grammy-eligible" (Ibid). Demarcations based on authorial distinctions still remain.

For a final aside relating to the concept of the anonymous auteur "behind the desk", Trevor Horn and friends play live in a manner that returns them to their original beginnings in popular music in a "hobby band" (no criticism intended) called . . . The Producers.

As a response to the rhetorical question "do we hear production?", my empirical response would be that yes, we do, in certain situations. When driving down a motorway listening to music on an MP3 player early in 2014, an album concluded, but for safety reasons, I was unable to scroll to another. Instead, I just listened to the next album on the list. This happened to be a personal compilation of Billy Joel's biggest hits. Perhaps as a result of its direct comparison with the previous album (whose name now escapes me) and perhaps as a consequence of being a relatively detached appreciator of Joel rather than an obsessed fan, I was immediately struck by the clarity and assurance of the production on the several tracks I had transferred from the CD onto the player. Not only was the production technically sound, but each track was produced in a manner that was sympathetic to the particular song or the mood evoked. Thus, the producer (Phil Ramone, for all these examples) on "An Innocent Man" (1983) adds spacious hall echo on both vocals and the snare drum, which complements the "arena ballad" feel of the song. "Uptown Girl" (1983) features a much more cluttered and ambient mix, with banks of multitracked backing vocals having an indistinct feel redolent of 1960s' productions for the likes of the Four Seasons. The song also makes little use of the panned stereo picture to remain close to some aspects of the Spector sound. Most strikingly, on "Still Rock & Roll to Me" (1980), the production has been made to actually function as a homology of the narrative and feel. Lyrically, the song is a dialogue between a performer and a nonperformer and relates to conflicts over how much perceived elements in music and style have changed, or need to change, in order to resonate with new listeners. The production enters into this dialogue by juxtaposing very retro elements, such as the slap-back echo on the vocals, with the "dead" drum and chopped rhythm guitar sounds redolent of the 1980s' zeitgeist. Thus, in both production and narrative terms, the song reinforces the message that things may change, but the underlying message remains the same. The song is not traditional rock'n'roll, but it is *still* rock'n'roll. The production, in emphasizing this point, is clearly making an artistic, as well as a technological, statement.

I will have more to say regarding new technologies functioning as authoring devices in the next chapter, but my final example relating to the question "do we hear production?" again relates to another MP3 player function. As many will have done, I have opted for the menu listing "artists" rather than "albums" on occasion. This can result in a very different listening experience. My player had combined two Nerina Pallot albums (*Fires* [2006] and *Year of the Wolf* [2011]) into one maxi-album, with sequentially two track ones and two track twos, each from a different album. What this results in is a way to more clearly differentiate production. The earlier album is produced mainly by Howard Willing, but with other tracks produced by Wendy Melvoin, Eric Rosse and Pallot herself. The latter album is solely produced by Bernard Butler. In summary, the earlier album has a brighter, more "radio friendly" sheen, whereas the latter is a little more muffled, quieter and includes a more cluttered stereo mix featuring higher levels of guitar distortion. Significantly, *Fires* lists Willing as "recording" all tracks, which may account for the fact that the album's production has a unity despite being produced by several people. The disjunctures in production function both to temper the over-clinical approach of one and the over-muffled approach of the other (of course, such judgments are subjective). Thus, the technology and the listener combine to author a new empirical experience, but one that merely augments the experiences of each album in isolation. What is most interesting is that this hybrid album works very well. Authorship and authoring processes give pleasure in often unexpected and unacknowledged ways.

Acknowledgments

My thanks go to Richard James Burgess for his valuable critical observations made after reading a draft of this chapter. Additionally, I am very grateful to Tony Turrell for his musicological analysis in the "Remix, Remaster" section of this chapter.

Bibliography

Ahonen, Laura (2008) *Constructing Authorship in Popular Music: Artists, Media and Stardom*, Milton Keynes: VDM Verlag.
Anon. (2013) "Metropolis Presents . . . in the Studio with Timbaland", *the Guardian* advertisement, November 8.
Barthes, Roland (1977) "The Death of the Author", in *Image, Music, Text*, London: Fontana, pp 142–148.
Blaine, Hal (2003) *Hal Blaine and the Wrecking Crew*, Alma, Mich.: Rebeats.
Bradby, Barbara (1988) "Do-Talk and Don't-Talk: The Division of the Subject in Girl-Group Music", in Frith, Simon & Andrew Goodwin (eds.) (1990), *On Record: Rock, Pop and the Written Word*, London: Routledge, pp 341–368.
Brown, Mick (2008) *Tearing Down the Wall of Sound: The Rise and Fall of Phil Spector*, London: Bloomsbury.
Burgess, Richard James (2013) *The Art of Music Production: The Theory and Practice*, Fourth Edition, New York: Oxford University Press.
Burgess, Richard James (2014) Personal correspondence, October 5.
Cunningham, Mark (1996) *Good Vibrations*, London: Sanctuary.
Eisenberg, Evan (1987) *The Recording Angel*, London: Picador.
Frith, Simon (2012) "The Place of the Producer in the Discourse of Rock", in Frith, Simon & Simon Zagorski-Thomas (eds.), *The Art of Record Production: An Introductory Reader for a New Academic Field*, Aldershot: Ashgate, pp 207–221.
Frith, Simon & Simon Zagorski-Thomas (eds.) (2012) *The Art of Record Production: An Introductory Reader for a New Academic Field*, Aldershot: Ashgate.
George, Nelson (2003) *Where Did Our Love Go? The Rise and Fall of the Motown Sound*, London: Omnibus.
Harding, Phil (2009) *PWL: From the Factory Floor*, Bury St Edmunds: Wb Publishing.
Harris, John (2003) "The Beatles, *Let it Be . . . Naked*", *the Observer*, 13 November, accessed 17-06-14, http://observer.theguardian.com/omm/10bestcds/story/0,12012, 106287900.hy.

Hurwitz, Matt (2004) "The Naked Truth About the Beatles' *Let it Be . . . Naked*", *Mix Magazine*, 1 January, accessed 18-02-14, http://mixonline.com/recording/interviews/audio-naked-truth-beatles/.

Mayhew, Emma (2004) "Positioning the Producer: Gender Divisions in Creative Labour and Value", in Whiteley, Sheila, Andy Bennett & Stan Hawkins (eds.), *Music Space and Place: Popular Music and Cultural Identity*, Aldershot: Ashgate, pp 149–162.

McIntyre, Phillip (2012) "Rethinking Creativity: Record Production and the Systems Model", in Frith, Simon & Simon Zagorski-Thomas (eds.), *The Art of Record Production: An Introductory Reader for a New Academic Field*, Farnham: Ashgate, pp 149–162.

Moorefield, Virgil (2010) *The Producer as Composer: Shaping the Sounds of Popular Music*, Cambridge, Mass.: MIT Press.

Morris, Pam (ed.) (1994) *The Bakhtin Reader: Selected Writings of Bakhtin, Medvedev and Voloshinov*, London: Edward Arnold.

Negrin, David (ed.) (unknown author) (2014) Review of Genesis 1970–75, *World of Genesis. com*, accessed 3-04-14, http://www.worldofgenesis.com/GenesisAlbumReviews.htm.

Negus, Keith & Michael Pickering (2004) *Creativity, Communication and Cultural Value*, London: Sage.

Sillitoe, Sue (2004) "The Prodigy. Liam Howlett: Recording *Always Outnumbered, Never Outgunned*", *Sound on Sound* magazine interview, October, accessed 9-12-13, http://www.soundonsound.com/sos/Oct04/articles/prodigy.htm.

Thompson, Ben (1998) "Seven Years of Plenty", *Rock's Back Pages*, accessed 19-12-13, http://www.rocksbackpages.com/Library/Article/the-prodigy.

Toynbee, Jason (2000) *Making Popular Music: Musicians, Creativity and Institutions*, London: Arnold.

Warner, Tim (2003) *Pop Music: Technology and Creativity—Trevor Horn and the Digital Revolution*, Aldershot: Ashgate.

Whiteley, Sheila, Andy Bennett & Stan Hawkins (2004) *Music, Space and Place: Popular Music and Cultural Identity*, Aldershot: Ashgate.

Zak, Albin (2001) *The Poetics of Rock: Cutting Tracks, Making Records*, Oakland: University of California Press.

Audio-Visual Sources

Adele (2011) *21*.
Art of Noise (1984) "Close to the Edit".
The Breeders (1993) "SOS".
The Buggles (1979) "Video Killed the Radio Star".
Coldplay (2005) "Talk".
Johnny Cash (1994) *American Recordings*.
Frankie Goes to Hollywood (1983) "Relax".
Genesis (2008) *1970–75*.
Goldfrapp (2005) *Supernature*.
    (2006) *We Are Glitter*.
Billy Joel (1980) "Still Rock & Roll to Me".
    (1983) "An Innocent Man", "Uptown Girl".
Kelis (2010) *Fleshtone*.

Kraftwerk (1981) "Computer Love".

Lady Gaga (2009) *The Fame Monster* (including "Paparazzi").

(2010) *Lady Gaga: The Remix* (including "Paparazzi", Stuart Price Remix).

Last Poet (1970) "Right On".

Led Zeppelin (1969) "Whole Lotta Love".

Malcolm McLaren (1983) *Duck Rock*.

Nerina Pallot (2006) *Fires*.

(2011) *Year of the Wolf*.

Nirvana (1993) "Very Ape".

Johnny Pate (1971) "Shaft in Africa".

Pavloff, Jim (2010) "Making of the Prodigy's 'Voodoo People' in Ableton", 20 January, accessed from YouTube, 3-04-14.

(2012) "Making of the Prodigy's 'Firestarter' in Ableton", 28 December, accessed from YouTube, 3-04-14.

The Prodigy (1991) "Charly".

(1992) *The Prodigy Experience*.

(1994) *Music for the Jilted Generation*, "Voodoo People".

(1996) "Firestarter".

(1997) *The Fat of the Land*, "Breathe".

(2004) *Always Outnumbered, Never Outgunned*.

(2009) *Invaders Must Die*.

Propaganda (1984) "Dr Mabuse" (various mixes).

(1985) *A Secret Wish*.

Scott, Ridley (1982) *Blade Runner*.

Steeleye Span (1973) "Gaudete".

Suckling, Chris (producer) (2014) "The Carol Kaye Story", BBC Radio 2 documentary, broadcast 2 June

6

THE ZEITGEIST AS AUTEUR

Contexts, Scenes, Technologies

In the Introduction to this book, I attempted to provide an overview of some of the major developments in the debates and issues surrounding the authorship question that have taken place over the past few hundred years. In the process, it was argued that authorship in popular music discourse was a relatively overlooked concept. Subsequently, I explored this critical oversight by arguing that authorship is often subsumed beneath signifiers such as "authenticity," "honesty" and "originality", partly as a result of the dominance of essentially romantic paradigms, which can still hold sway in the critical field. In this, the final chapter, I propose that we attempt to bring issues and debates up to date both by widening the focus to include the exploration of scenes, audiences, contexts and technologies, and also by arguing that the critical terrain itself must adapt (yet in some cases has already adapted) to the constant shifts that characterize the world of popular music.

Several books have attempted to articulate the study of popular music and culture with regard to new technological innovations. In 1996, Paul du Gay and others adapted the Sony Walkman to this task in a manner that was both educational and forward-looking in their book *Doing Cultural Studies: The Story of the Sony Walkman*. What is interesting today, when revisiting this book, is to note how rapidly terms age or develop. Mention of cassettes and videos return us effortlessly to the 1990s' zeitgeist as much as talk of the developing internet, then in its relative infancy. More recently, Dylan Jones takes a personal journey through music via the descendant of the Walkman—the iPod (2006). What is remarkable for a book researched only around a decade ago is to notice that this text predates several technological innovations now standard: the tablet, YouTube and the smartphone—all of which have had an impact upon music consumption, and in the case of the smartphone, threaten to resign the iPod and other MP3-type devices to the same cultural backwater as the audio cassette or the Betamax player. In opposition to Jones, both Travis Elborough (2009) and Richard Osborne (2012) have broached the historical development of music formats such as vinyl, cassettes, the twelve-inch single and the LP. They maintain that "outdated" technologies still have their place in the contemporary music scene and are indeed flourishing.

These books provide a much-needed accompaniment to academic texts implicitly dealing with issues of authorship in that they connect the concept to social contexts, lived experiences and the everyday. They indicate how, with a little extrapolation, authorship can be shown to be present in myriad aspects of musicultural life for billions around the globe. The work of Osborne and Jones, in particular, is worthy of deeper scrutiny at this point.

Osborne's history of the analogue record is a fundamentally deconstructive text in that the writer never focuses upon authorship per se, yet in the absences, gaps and contradictions, authorship looms as a chimera or phantom presence. Thus, even in the early days of recorded musical releases, gramophone players and record artwork functioned both as art objects and to publicize named authors. Recorded sound confers authorial "immortality" (Osborne, 2012: 22). The limited duration of discs helps to author songs and their structure as well, and even the subversion of technology (playing a record at the wrong speed, playing it backward or "scratching" it) helps author avant-garde processes. For Osborne, the shellac (later, vinyl) disc triumphs over the cylinder for reasons of quality and wider repertoire, despite the limitation of not being available for self-recording. This indicates the dominance of authorial consumption over creation—a process that shows no sign of abating despite the ease with which digital technologies now allow for the listener to become the (virtual, if not actual) composer.

As the LP form became widely available beginning in the late 1940s, new authoring processes were set in place. The fact that sound quality diminishes toward the centre of the record partially determined song order and thus the phonologist's listening experience (Ibid: 28). The growth of the concept album, which Osborne links to the albums of Frank Sinatra in the late 1950s (Ibid: 98), helps confer fine-art status on a commercial form. Indeed, perhaps it is no accident that the construction of a canon of great, authored works in popular music coincides with the hegemony of the vinyl LP (mid-1950s to early 1980s) (Ibid: 183). It is also significant that most Top 100 lists compiled by journalists or fans also heavily favour the vinyl era.

Particularly outside of the affluent United States, the vinyl single remained hugely important, specifically for youth in the 1950s and 1960s. This has authorial implications not only economically but also in terms of genre. Many groups did not author the A side of a single; however, more self-composition, often in a less "commercial" style, was allowed on the B side (Ibid: 150–159). Even radio reception and programming can be seen to play its part in the authoring process, with both the lack of advertisements on the BBC and the growth of FM formatting allowing for uninterrupted broadcasting of long tracks or even whole albums in the late 1960s (Ibid: 125). The development of the twelve-inch single in the late 1970s allowed for longer, louder, bass-heavy tracks, both affecting the listening experience of the phonologist and helping to facilitate the rise of the DJ-as-auteur. Conversely, at around the same time, the resurgence of interest in the seven-inch single was partly aided by the widespread adoption of the picture sleeve, allowing for the authorship of photographers and designers to become an important component (Ibid: 158, 161–181). Many years later, debates around DJ authorship and the choice of vinyl, CD or laptop still rage (see Attias, Gavanas and Rietveld, 2013).

As a self-confessed "vinyl junkie", Osborne spends little time on alternative formats such as the cassette. However, as well as demonstrating its short-lived period of hegemony (overtaking vinyl sales in 1985 before it was superseded by CDs after a few years), Osborne does indicate one of the cassette's huge advantages: the feasibility of mixtape authoring (Ibid: 82). This capability is subsequently taken much further by technologies such as the MP3 player, which brings us to Jones.

With his background in style and fashion, it is no surprise that Jones spends much time discussing the aesthetical form of the iPod rather than focusing in general on the MP3 player format. It is interesting to note that features such as the virtual wheel, which allows the rapid selection of individual components and was so loved by early adopters, has already been confined to history by the innovation of touch-screen scrolling. In a similar fashion, we must always be wary of assigning too much authorial credit to a piece of equipment that is as much developmental as it is revolutionary. Jones notes the endless possibilities for constructing playlists to suit any occasion (2006: 128), but, of course, as previously stated, this is merely a less time consuming, more comprehensive adoption of the possibilities engendered by earlier innovations: both the cassette recorder and the iPod allow for sequential authoring, with the subsequent empirical impact upon mood and environment. Jones talks of reconfiguring Beatles' albums without the Ringo tracks and that "albums ceased to matter" (Ibid: 18) as a consequence. Many of us were removing "Octopus's Garden" (1970) from our cassette mixes many years ago! But Jones' claim for the death of the album, although too presumptive, does deal with one of the many other features now taken for granted that do indeed possess a more radical potential. The ability to randomly shuffle music, to play a complete collection alphabetically, to play the complete works of an act in any order, to escape the imposed authorship of the album: these all have significant implications for authorship, as my analysis of the Nerina Pallot hybrid album in Chapter Five demonstrated.

For Jones, "this is the first time [he] can remember technology influencing content, or the consumption of content, in such a profound way" (Ibid: 245). The paradox is that such processes merely swap one form of imposed authorship (album track one, track two, etc.) for another, albeit random, imposition, but still one that removes the ability of the listener to exercise authorial agency. Is this why some listeners adore surrendering choice to a digital device while others are deeply disturbed by the concept? However, whatever the individual's take upon an iPod's features, most commentators and users do recognize (or implicitly experience) the positive impact upon a key signifier of the postmodern zeitgeist—eclecticism.

Eclecticism and the Challenge to the Hegemonies of Rock

Partly at the expense of the mythologies of rock, devices such as the iPod encourage at least a questioning of the established models of rock authorship. These were previously touched upon in Chapter Five, but by focusing upon technology and its adoption by audiences and scenes, we can judge just how far romantic models of authorship have been placed under critical scrutiny.

In mapping out the constructed distinctions between high and low art in popular music discourse, academics such as Roy Shuker (2002) and Jason Toynbee (2000) have shown the role that the myths of authorship play in this process. Many date the emergence of a distinction between rock and pop as happening around 1967, with a fragmentation of popular music and its audiences into jealous tribes and factions. Almost all major popular music theorists deal with such bifurcations, which Auslander sums up as:

> The ideological distinction between rock and pop is precisely the distinction between the authentic and the inauthentic, the sincere and the cynical, the genuinely popular and the slickly commercial, the potentially resistant and the necessarily co-opted, art and entertainment.
>
> (2008: 81)

Frith indicates a growing schism between "art rock" and "too direct black soul" (1981: 20–21). This is predicated upon perceived/constructed differences of race, colour, genre and audience expectations and uses. Many commentators concentrate upon the differences between "black" and "white" music, but what is being depicted is at least as much about demarcations of genre as about race or even pigment. These distinctions can still remain; witness the naming of an unashamedly retro music label operating in the US in 2014. It is called, portentously, *Truth and*

Soul, and explicitly rejects most contemporary production practices and digital instrumentation (see Batey, 2014).

Early music-based ethnographers such as Paul Willis (1978) show how subcultural differences in the appropriation and consumption of music among different youth groups in the 1970s are certainly based partly upon race and class, but the respondents also implicitly recognize genre distinctions. The media also played an important part in this bifurcation of music into pop/soul/dance and "serious" rock. However, Simon Jones' later study (1988) detailing the cross-fertilizations between black and white communities in Birmingham show how the passage of time, as well as generic and technological innovations, has the effect of partly dismantling rigid distinctions in musical taste, resulting in fusions and musical eclecticism. This is well summarized by Soul II Soul's Jazzie B: "My generation of West Indian origin is the last of its kind. My children will be almost totally English. We are now living in a multi-racial society . . . black and white grew up together we're compatible" (sic) (cited in Baker, 1989: 64).

It is too easy to generalize the developments in popular music over the past few decades and make overarching statements relating to "the death of rock", "the triumph of dance" or rap as "the new rock'n'roll". What is more accurate is to deal with mutations and shifts that have an impact upon audiences, markets and perceptions of authorship. There is an ebb and flow in the perceived dominance of genres that are only ever partial in their hegemonic impact. Recent decades have witnessed the emergence of genres such as house, techno, grunge, Britpop, gangsta rap, dubstep, and EDM, but it is in the more widespread acceptance of technological processes such as sampling, time-stretching, auto-tuning and the impact of the "virtual" studio and software such as Pro Tools and Logic that we find more comprehensive shifts in attitudes toward authorship, rather than in the more parochial genre-based distinctions of the past. This process has been gradual and incremental. As long ago as 1988, Simon Frith claimed that one of the most significant byproducts of widespread digital technology has been "the systematic dismantling of the belief system that sustained rock'n'roll, the idea that a recognizable person (or group of persons) made a specific noise" (1988: 124). Auslander references Andrew Goodwin's notion of "the normalization of mediatized sound" (2008: 38). Auslander claims that the synthetic "handclaps" found on the Roland TR808, which were originally merely replacements for human sounds, are now seen as the real norm and are automatically deferred to as the default sample. By extension, he rejects "the argument for ontological differences between live and mediatized cultural forms—we must redefine our understandings" (Ibid: 184). Within this scenario, it is increasingly difficult to claim that any primary or original popular music text can be based on the distinctions between so-called "organic" or "synthetic" recordings. The eclecticism engendered by contemporary technologies and values allows for the now-mythical organic autonomous rock group to survive alongside computer-based dance producers and all the authorial shades between these two constructed opposites. All have their place, both in the global market for pop and on the iPod playlist. The proof of authenticity (and, by extension, authorship) offered by both recordings and visual performances are now consigned to the past and the rock(ist) paradigm.

The status of sampling is an object lesson in how attitudes to new authoring processes change over time. In the early 1990s, sampling was one of the hot topics both within the industry and for scholars wrestling with notions of authorship, creativity and aesthetics. In my own postgraduate research on postmodernism's relationship with popular music, I devoted much time to mapping out the differences of opinion prompted by the process. These range from the draconian (Morton, 1988: 3; Ressner, 1990: 103) to the utopian (Toop, 1989: 75; Cutler, 2004: 138–156; see also Ahonen, 2008: 181–197). As is so often the case, Frith is prescient in his conclusion that:

> Most listeners, for example, no longer care that they have no idea what instrument (if any) makes their favourite sound. And the most significant rearguard action against technological change is, as usual being fought by the music business itself.

> (1988: 125)

The use of the word "rearguard" is telling in that Frith implicitly recognizes who is going to win in this battle (rearguards often get overwhelmed or wiped out!), and, of course, it is a battle partly about authorship. Time has proved him right. The industry accommodates innovations by working out new income streams from sampling. It does this via sharing of credits and through one-off payments for use, in Rebecca Leydon's terms, "as a form of corporate buyout in which those with sufficient means simply purchased a set of musical skills that they had not themselves acquired" (cited in Covach and Spicer, 2010: 195). Significantly, even the authorial controversies provoked between "originators" and "plagiarists" seem latterly to have been accommodated (see Barnet and Burriss, 2001: 69–84). I referenced the conflict between the JAMMS and Abba over unauthorized sampling in 1987, which resulted in band members Bill Drummond and Jimmy Cauty symbolically burning all of the offending records (Moy, 1992: 84, 86). By 2005, Abba would be willingly allowing Madonna to sample a significant phrase from "Gimme, Gimme, Gimme (A Man after Midnight)" (1979) within her hit "Hung Up" (2005). In the same year, Coldplay, then becoming known as one of the biggest global rock acts, sampled Kraftwerk's "Computer Love" (1981) to great effect on "Talk" (2005). These examples caused some controversy within their fan bases (see Ahonen, 2008: 190–191), but were generally accepted as a valid authorial device.

In 1990, Simon Reynolds saw the sampling issue as artistically enabling:"What's barely considered is the formal possibilities and aesthetic implications of sampling" (1990: 167). Ultimately, sampling (or later mutations such as "mash-up") is now almost unquestioningly seen as artistically valid (see Gunkel, 2012; Ahonen, 2008: 190). But as with all other forms of creativity, validity does not imply success or quality. There are good and bad original songs, and there are good and bad uses of samples or mash-ups, but as ever, judgment rests on individual taste. New technologies, as Ahonen rightly states, produce "new kinds of evaluative hierarchies" (2008: 196). However, few can dispute that the process is fundamentally about authoring and creation (knowledge, imagination, skill, selection, rejection, combination and practice). Gunkel freely uses terms such as "plundered", "derivative" and "parasitic" (2012: 81) to describe the practices of the mash-up, but in a long conclusion reflecting upon the implications for authorship, he also recognizes that such creative processes "[call] for a reconfiguration of accepted models of textual production and creativity . . . [which] also has a complementary effect on the understanding of reception and consumption" (Ibid: 84, 86). His final observation, despite acknowledging the usefulness of the author function, turns away from concepts of authorial intent and asks us to focus on simply "what has been said, and what we—the reader, listener, viewer, user etc.—do with it" (Ibid: 86).

More recently, technological developments such as the Novation Launchpad allow for the storage of multiple samples, which can then be played/triggered in real time using one or two boards set up in a grid with sixty-four pads on each board. Each pad holds a sample that may be percussive, rhythmic, vocal or instrumental. In filmed performance, the process resembles a kind of "3D" piano set up (for instance, M4SONIC playing "Virus" [2012] on YouTube). This process combines traditional keyboard dexterity and live performance skills with the technological procedures of sampling. It shows that traditional and postmodern authorial processes can work in tandem to the detriment of neither. Established notions of authorship are still problematized by the fact that the viewer is unaware whether the samples are "composed" by the player, but in any case, the traditional playing virtuosity remains unaltered. In actual fact, the creative choices made possible far supersede those made by a standard keyboard player.

Mutations and Glitches

Part of the creative appeal of popular music has always been in its ability to subvert new technologies. This can take the form of scratching vinyl discs, the myriad applications of auto-tuning or the developments of whole musical subgenres based on the "misuse" of rudimentary technology—as was the case with the "chip tune" compositions found within early video game audio capabilities (see Driscoll and Diaz, 2009). As with so many of these innovations, the result has been to widen the field of authorship beyond the formally trained or even the ostensibly musical. Innovations have to be placed in a historical continuum in order to identify how the critical terrain so often struggles to come to terms with the possibilities offered by new technologies. One era's overused gimmick becomes critically recuperated as the next era's marker of the zeitgeist. In 1967, the widespread adoption of phasing, excessive amounts of stereo panning and the utilization of effects such as fuzz-tone were considered unmusical by traditionalists. Furthermore, "overuse did much to effect a musical backlash in the immediate post-psychedelic era, as well as 'trapping' many musicians and groups within certain market expectations" (Borthwick and Moy, 2004: 53–54). Now, broadly speaking, they are merely signifiers of the psychedelic genre that function as one of the authors of an era. Whether such innovations are the result of the audience *demanding*, or merely *accepting*, them is moot (back to notions of the assumed and the assigned), but ultimately beside the point. The end result is that the listening experience is affected and the phonologist is constructing a new authoring episteme as a consequence. The same can be said for the "back to basics" production styles of punk or grunge or the bass-heavy saturation sounds of various dance forms. In a club environment, wide stereo separation is an obstacle to consumption; the sound needs to be consistent regardless of where the listener/ dancer is situated on the dance floor. Again, this musical, production-based and then, ultimately, authorial choice arrives through a combination of technological, genre-based, location and audience/scene imperatives.

Some have viewed a whole decade as a signifier of a sound-based zeitgeist. This is particularly true, with admittedly a considerable degree of critical sleight-of-hand when the mythical 1980s are explored. For Jones, this is summarized as "the time-capsule *clank* [his emphasis] of over-produced synthesised drums . . . every track swathed in atmospheric synthesised swirls, every hook punctuated by piping sampled horns, and every crescendo building on banks of overlaid keyboards" (2006: 104).

Leaving aside any criticism related to the overgeneralized nature of this statement, what is true is that the increasingly synthetic and digital nature of sound production has partly accounted for both the rise to prominence of forms of dance music and the widespread adoption and acceptance of such techniques throughout popular music as a whole. Jones' depiction of the 1970s has rock music as "the standard, the benchmark, the order of the day" (Ibid: 196), which, again, allowing for journalistic laziness, does contain more than an element of truth. In broad terms, the experimentalist baton incrementally passes from rock to dance forms over the past few decades because of the more implicit and wide-ranging links between dance forms and new digital technologies. In the process, romantic or "rockist" values of authorship are problematized. However, as Andrew Hugill rightly notes, "Digital signals an end to the evolutionary line in music in a linear form—the evolution goes off in myriad directions" (2012: 15). There are indeed now many ways to produce music. Folk acts can record using Pro Tools. Neil Young can bemoan, at great length, the poor sample rates of MP3 and digital technologies throughout his autobiography (Young, 2013), and then record an album using rudimentary technology that is then made commercially available on the very same playback formats that he criticizes: "*A Letter Home* was made in a restored 1947 Voice-O-Graph booth . . . the result is muffled, distorted and buried beneath layers of crackle and hiss" (Petridis, 2014). Technologies fragment; processes fragment; values fragment.

It is, however, the perceptions of excessive use of gimmicks that affect the critical climate, as has been the case more recently with the critical backlash against the perceived excesses of auto-tuning, but it should be noted that many of these innovations were, and continue to be, at least partly, the result of random mutations of existing technologies. This process has continued more recently with the development of the term that has become both a noun and an adjective— "glitch"—of which more is discussed below.

For Hugill, "music is a technology-based art form, but its technologies are traditionally seen as something to be mastered in order to produce sounds that seem 'natural'" (2012: 8). This quotation exemplifies the romantic mythologies that existed in the past. Elements of this stance still continue to hold sway, which an exploration of auto-tuning can demonstrate.

From its early adoption as a corrective device for moving off-key vocals to the nearest "correct" pitch, it is true to say that auto-tune's use and the surrounding critical climate—both positive and negative—have proliferated. It is not within the bounds of this chapter to do any more than note this phenomenon. What is more pertinent is to note that according to some prominent inside sources, its use is now very widespread, both within recordings and in live performances. Surprisingly, bearing in mind the myth-assumptions of authenticity attached to genres such as country and middle of the road, it is claimed that the likes of Faith Hill and Shania Twain have adopted (allowed?) their performances to be auto-tuned (Treacy, 2007). Michael McCall has explored the widespread adoption of auto-tune in the country scene and the controversies and different opinions raised (2004). Genres such as hip hop and EDM, always heavily reliant upon new technologies, have generally been more embracing of auto-tune, although this has still not prevented global artists such as Jay-Z from protesting its use, both in print and on record (Jay-Z, "D.O.A [Death of Auto-Tune]", 2009). Several points need to be made: first, that all popular music is mediated and at least partially dependent upon technology; second, that because auto-tuning affects vocals, it is both more noticeable and more controversial, as the voice could be considered a more recognizable indication of personal authorship than an instrument; third, that auto-tune can be considered akin to historical processes such as echo, reverb or automatic double tracking, which are all now widely accepted as valid creative tools; and, last, that there are degrees of auto-tuning that may well render many of its applications as unnoticeable or subliminal to the vast majority of the listening public.

If we take a single musical example, "Green Garden" by Laura Mvula (2012), the controversies and critical sleights-of-hand engendered by auto-tuning and its relationship to authorship can be mapped out. The initial observation relates to vocal grain. Immaterial of whether the artist has been auto-tuned on this track, certain voices, like Mvula's, with little appreciable vibrato and a legato/portamento style, do possess the same smoothness between tones associated with auto-tune. Although it is totally possible to auto-tune live performances, it is *unlikely* that Mvula's singing at the Urban Prom in the Royal Albert Hall on October 8, 2013, was auto-tuned. Why? Because of the romantic paradigms attached to the setting, the history of the Promenade Concerts, and the artist's own classically influenced background. The point is, however, that I simply may be mistaken. Mvula sings three songs, "Sing to the Moon", "Father, Father" and "That's Alright", often accompanied by three backing vocalists. However, for the sake of argument, let us assume that Mvula is not being auto-tuned live. On the studio version of these songs, contributors are credited and instruments listed, but it comes as no surprise that specific effects and technologies are not—this is clearly impractical. This leaves the individual phonologist to judge whether auto-tune has been employed. According to the album credits, almost all of the lead and backing vocals are handled by Mvula, and clearly the singer has been multi-tracked, ADT'd, and various vocal effects have been utilized; however, if auto-tune has been used, it is either unrecognizable to this listener or the degree of use is very small. However, on "Green Garden", certainly, the wordless refrains (sounding like oo-wah-oo) that enter at twenty-five seconds and fifty-two seconds sound auto-tuned, as they are very layered, "robotic" and contain a huge amount of portamento. Auto-tune may well also be employed in the chorus, beginning at 1.27, and also the change section at 2.34, although on both these occasions, the vocals are deeper in the mix, and so the effect is harder to identify.

Live versions of "Green Garden" filmed in either television studios or music venues (dated February 8, June 26, and August 27, 2013; see bibliography) certainly provide further evidence that Mvula is not reliant upon appreciable (if any) amounts of auto-tune, as her vocals include "scat" improvisations and microphone "pops" but are well-pitched and projected. The backing vocals on all three performances sound remarkably similar, leaving us unsure as to whether they have been prerecorded. On the other hand, it may be that the backing vocalists are simply professional, talented and highly consistent. But what is without debate is that the amount of auto-tune is not the same as on the album version. This disparity indicates that perhaps the authorship of the live and the recorded must be seen (or heard) to be different in Mvula's music. Yet again, romantic paradigms of authenticity are merely displaced and not dispensed with by modern technologies of authorship.

How does this brief empirical investigation illuminate the analysis of authorship and technology? The first conclusion must be that all experiences of auto-tuning are partially determined by a range of contextual factors—some of which only expose the inconsistencies of social and individual aesthetics. On Mvula's album, it is clear that the use of auto-tune is not consistent and therefore not *corrective* but rather *creative*. Thus, it is far more than the musical equivalent of a word-processing spell-check function. Evidence suggests that Mvula has a very good voice, well-pitched and with a wide range and a personal, identifiable grain. Auto-tune is employed to add a specific feel to certain multi-tracked vocals, but is often overlaid by other, individual vocal tracks that are clearly not so "treated", if at all. However, this is not to say that the more comprehensive use of this process by other singers or in other genres should be automatically condemned, but rather that this demonstrates differing authoring strategies. But to counter this anything-goes-attitude to technology, it is evident that her undoubted ability, added to the widespread utilization of traditional instruments (for instance, celesta, tubular bells, glockenspiel, flute, clarinet, contrabass, etc.), has influenced this reading, encouraging the adoption of romantic, subjective terms such as "very good", "well-pitched" and "talent". It has shown that a technique such as auto-tune is an authoring process that is still deeply affected by more traditional values relating to human agency and creative choices. In addition, in this technologically sophisticated age, individual judgments are difficult to quantify and corroborate by hard evidence. "Green Garden" was the single that helped launch the artist's career. Was the degree of auto-tune thus a promotional device designed to help ground the otherwise traditional sound of Mvula's album in a more youthful or contemporary terrain?

Authorship and "Failure"

The mutation of terms from the adjectival to those of nouns has recently been demonstrated by "glitch". From an onomatopoeic expression signifying technological error or failure, the word glitch now connects to subgenres of music drawing upon random, chance or deliberate subversions of hardware and software. For Kim Cascone, "glitches, bugs, application errors, system crashes, clipping, aliasing, distortion, quantization noise . . . are the materials composers seek" (cited in Cox and Warner, 2004: 393). The writer makes persuasive claims as to the democratizing "mess around" potential for glitch authorship, that such processes can be seen as the technological equivalent of drugs for creativity (Ibid: 394), and that we are now in the post-revolutionary period of the digital information age. By this, it is suggested that such technologies and their cultural appropriation by creators and consumers are now so embedded in the mainstream that "specific tools themselves have become the message" (Ibid: 393). Thus, notions of an avant-garde versus mainstream binary distinction are effaced or, at least, compressed by the rapid migration of experimental, conceptual techniques into the commercial market. Just as a post-structuralist view posits language itself as an authoring component, so technology can be viewed in the same light. This is a contemporary manifestation of one of popular music's most salient tendencies—for the dismantling of the romantic tropes of authorship in favour of what Brian Eno has termed "scenius". This is the collective authorship of the crowd, scene or mass market. Paradoxically, the failure of romantic authorship is itself manifested through creative "failure", which audiences willingly participate in.

As well as historicizing glitch, particularly in its avant-garde manifestations, Torben Sangild makes important interventions into the authorship debate by posing questions relating to the "irrationality" of computers, which, it is claimed "are interactive and thus not restricted to their 'inner' binary calculations, just as human beings are not just molecules moving in the nervous system" (cited in Washburne and Derno, 2004: 269). Thus, a computer crash or malfunction can be read as akin to a physical or mental breakdown in a human organism. But regardless of whether the glitch takes place in a computer or a human, creativity and authorship can result. This notion of authorship resulting from an interface between irrational agents again asks us, after Rorty (see Chapter Three), to form a new vocabulary (glitch as a positive signifier) in order to deal with new creative possibilities.

Years before the adoption of glitch as a musical signifier, Simon Reynolds was prescient in using the parallel term "noise"—which, of course, has historical links dating back at least to futurism. Originally writing in 1988, Reynolds talks about "the subversive fallacy". He states, "[T]he whole discourse of noise-as-threat is bankrupt . . . forget subversion, the point is self-subversion, overthrowing the power structure in your own head" (cited in Cox and Warner, 2004: 56, 57). Although this quotation is capable of being interpreted as a resigned criticism of the lack of radical potential in art, it can also be read as a celebration of both the radical mainstream (not a contradiction in terms!) and the radical self, made evident by new authoring processes (see also Reynolds, 2007). Of course, as already indicated, we have had noisy interventions into mass culture for many years, but recent possibilities, what Cascone terms "the tendrils of digital technology [offered by] a cultural feedback loop in the circuit of the internet" (cited in Cox and Warner, 2004: 393, 397), mean that these glitch interventions are now globally disseminated, often by those with no formal musical or creative skills. How do we measure their cultural acceptance? By adopting, in part, the evidence of sales figures and the audiences for live demonstrations of glitch. As well as deconstructing the binary of avant-garde versus mainstream, artists as diverse as Aphex Twin, Björk, Skrillex and Kanye West show that within different scenes and musical genres, adoptions of glitch (to whatever degree they are employed) are now collectively experienced as valid authoring processes.

A critical tendency has been to favour or highlight the more challenging uses of glitch by experimental or lo-fi artists, but as is ever the case within the field of popular music, the real impact comes when such techniques filter into the mainstream. For Eliot Bates, "in multi-million dollar studios pops, hisses, clicks, and record noise are now routinely added to 'dirty up' otherwise pristine digital recordings" (cited in Washburne and Derno, 2004: 289). An artist with the stature and longevity of Björk, in collaboration with others, can exercise a broad critical acceptance of the authoring dimensions of glitch and also demonstrate something of the breadth of possibilities. These can consist of the marriage of string sections and harsh techno timbres on albums such as *Homogenic* (1997), including compressing vocals to an extreme degree resulting in oppressive harmonics on "Pluto", constructing a skeletal rhythm track from what sounds like computer workings or sampled shuffled cards on "Cocoon" (from *Vespertine*, 2001), or fashioning verbal utterances into percussive beats on *Volta* (2007). In terms of affect, Björk's uses of glitch are broad, ranging from the disturbing and intrusive to the ethereal, sensual and ambient.

Tribute Acts and the "Performative Audience"

A major critical intervention within the field of popular music discourse was made in 2006 by Shane Homan and others in the reader *Access All Eras: Tribute Bands and Global Pop Culture*. This wide-ranging text explored various aspects of the recent tribute act phenomenon and also the impact of such upon fans and audiences. In his introduction, Homan rightly notes how tribute acts had hitherto been seen as the "invisible other . . . that does not correlate with institutionalized (and idealized) discourses that present . . . a package of 'authentic' virtues: self-directed, original and independent of industry standardization" (2006: 3). This does not prevent owners of image rights and authored logos from exerting authority over some aspects of a tribute act. Homan notes the problems that the Bootleg Beatles faced when promoting their concerts using copyrighted typefaces (Ibid: 42). Such instances often fail to acknowledge that tribute acts have been shown to make a positive impact upon the sales of the originals. Elsewhere, other contributors establish connections between the tribute act and postmodern tropes such as simulation, hyper-reality, nostalgia and the disruption of linear time and history. At this point, we might again note the disruption of the linear chronotope already mentioned when exploring "retro" artists in Chapter One. Tribute bands have the ability to reproduce studio-based albums with accuracy that was not possible when the original works were written and recorded. Thus, Beatles' tribute acts can cover post–1966 originals in a manner not conceivable during the original band's career. Paradoxically, the bounds of technical authorship stretch as linear time compresses into a hyper-real continuous present within the tribute act milieu.

Industry and demographic shifts promoting back catalogue over new releases, the proliferation of "gold" networks and the retro nature of television, and stage and screen (notions of "the specular hierarchy"; see Moy, 2000) have all had an impact upon audiences, values and modes of consumption. What is evident throughout the research is that, in many circumstances, audiences are seeking (and constructing) far more than just a mere copy or an imitation. They are experiencing and contributing to an authored experience.

Perhaps more important for the purposes of the present argument are the ethnographic findings based on the audiences for tribute acts. Interviews indicate a wide range of responses ranging from the simplistic (notions of a good night out, including elements of humour and irony on behalf of both fans and performers) to the more complex, with extremely knowledgeable audiences seeking a completist experience wherein acts are expected to replicate even the most minute aspects of an originator's oeuvre. Andy Bennett comments that "the replication and reproduction of objects and images is increasingly taken for granted and largely perceived as 'normal'" (2006: 21). This postmodern attitude can be reinforced by noting the fundamental paradox at the heart of the tribute act scene—that audiences watching cover acts mainly seek a form of *authenticity through ostension*. Therefore, while it is clearly important for the tribute act to sound like the originator, it is equally or perhaps more important that there is a visual resemblance. I remember my disappointment when attending a gig by a Doors tribute act, Riders on the Storm, in the 1990s. The music was a close approximation, as was the image projected by the Jim Morrison simulacrum. But the other members of the band looked nothing like Densmore, Kreiger and Manzarek. In this situation, a sense of irony was not enough to overcome a doubtless unrealistic expectation on my part.

My final observation on the importance of the specular results of the authorship of such acts rises from the fact that while many films of tribute band concerts are commercially available, there are few, if any, music-only discs released by the same performers. Author image, or an approximation of it, clearly wins out over any attempts to produce or market a musical simulacrum in this case.

Clearly, this brief investigation exemplifies an overall audience aesthetics based upon a fragmented, dis-unified sense of authenticity, a belief in fakes, a love of the genuine imitation. Ultimately, paraphrasing Judith Butler's notion of performativity gives us an expression of authorship within the tribute act that extends the performativity of the acts to that of the audience—a performative audience, one willingly participating and reveling in the contradictions inherent within this very popular dimension in popular music. Finally, for the contemporary audience, it matters little whether the response to a tribute act is ironic or romantic; the response is contingent upon sets of specific circumstances rather than reflective of some core value relating to authorship.

A Brief Word on Genre, Etymology and Interpretability

Following the examples of fields such as literary analysis and film studies, many popular music theorists have more recently concerned themselves with notions of genre (Borthwick and Moy, 2004; Fabbri, 1982a; 1982b; Holt, 2007; Negus and Pickering, 2004: 68–90). I do not have the space to do anymore than make a small offering to this area by exploring how etymology and genre allows for contributors to the *contexts* of popular music (journalists, the industry and audiences) to make important contributions to authoring processes.

An important early intervention into the genre debate in popular music came from Franco Fabbri (1982a; 1982b). At around the same time that organizations such as IASPM (International Association for the Study of Popular Music) began to make a valuable contribution to this new field of scholarly study, Fabbri's work broke new ground and has been much-referenced in the ensuing years. Fabbri draws upon the work of semiologists/linguists such as Umberto Eco and Roman Jakobson, and after Eco, he sees the genre question as a discussion about "cultural units of meaning . . . a genre is culturally defined as, in some way distinctive" before going on to argue that genre construction is about negotiation across cultures, languages and time (Fabbri, 1982b: 134). For Fabbri, genre must be about social construction in order to transcend notions of mere style. Its social nature and the challenge posed to hierarchies are valuable in that they bring us to the issue of social authorship. Thus, he states:

> A genre which amalgamates complicated relations between composers, performers, audiences, critics and organizers, each with their own particular rules, may be no more worthy of attention and analysis than a genre based on arbitrary agreement between twelve journalists and a record producer.
>
> (1982a: 54)

Fabbri sees the study of musical genre as being important, first, to overcome an aesthetics that sees works as existing outside of time and culture and, second, to overcome the more sociological methodologies of music, which ignore the semiological nature of genre and texts. His construction of genre analysis is then one that is socially amorphous and nonspecific: "a dynamic relation between expression and content" (1982b: 136). It is also one that recognizes the importance of nonformalized empirical analysis as a way beyond traditional musicology's concern with notation because "a record buying adolescent of today has clearer ideas on musical genres than the majority of musicologists" (1982a: 55). This is a radical position, but may actually be a little conservative. Many children can differenti-ate and identify musical genres many years before they reach puberty. In addi-tion, with the possibilities now given by contemporary digital technologies, many children are now not only identifying genres, but also composing within their constructed, fluid boundaries and disseminating their work globally.

Fabbri's concluding point is that "genres, therefore, can help us to understand musical events, but, above all, they permit us to speak of them" (1982b: 142). This last phrase resonates with the Wittgensteinian notion of thought being con-structed via language systems. As semioticians have argued, we only fully concep-tualize and imagine the signified objective of "tree" once we have the symbolic signifier of "tree" within a language. Furthermore, language and etymology are the most effective ways to socially communicate our understanding of "tree-ness". Genre, as a linguistic categorizing system, "ensures the interpretability of the text" (Feuer, 1987: 119). Moreover, it constructs social authorship, encouraging demar-cations, distinctions and taste communities. Without etymologies of genre, it is very difficult to express taste. Taste itself is predicated upon genre distinctions, although, as has been argued, such distinctions are fluid.

Whereas overarching meta-genres such as rock or pop transcend historical epochs, others such as progressive rock or Britpop do not. Such genres (or sub-genres) are intrinsically tied to an era, a mode of production, a zeitgeist and a set of social circumstances that effectively ensure their demise or, at least, mutation into other forms. Genres have a degree of elasticity, but there invariably comes a point when they split under the pressure of some force or another—be it musical, technological, commercial or social (Borthwick and Moy, 2004: 3).

Within popular music, in broad terms, it has not been the primary authors (writers, players, producers) who have constructed etymologies of genre, but rather the secondary social authors—the journalists, the marketers, the scenes, the individual fans. Indeed, when questioned about their relationship to a genre or movement, most musicians actively distance themselves from any such member-ship. This perhaps signals a romantic self-perception relating to a sense of artistic autonomy from the machinations of the industry and a wish to appear unique. Nevertheless, it is patently obvious that the commercial world is built upon genre distinctions, categories, or what Negus and Pickering refer to as "conventions" (2004: 68). Without a means to categorize music, it is all just noise, and unauthored noise at that. Genres exist to help differentiate styles and taste communities, or to connect the one to the other more effectively. What is significant is that as the audience for popular music has fragmented, so have the number of generic terms. Broad distinctions such as soul, jazz, pop and reggae now function as umbrella terms or meta-genres. Journalists create new terms to encourage the belief in constant mutation and innovation. Audiences create new terms to signify creative agency or the power of the "tribe". Terms may be onomatopoeic (cha-cha-cha, wobble, grunge, ska), geographical (UK garage, Belgian new beat, Detroit techno), metonymic (drum and bass), locational (disco, house, pub rock, stadium rock), symbolically positive (new age, soul, world), symbolically negative (punk, crunk) or physiological (trance, rave, dream house), etc.

Etymologies of Acts: The Ian Anderson Brand

Among the first acts of authorship for any musician is the question of the performing name. No nomenclature is *natural*; even the choice by a performer to retain a birth name is an authoring act connoting notions of the real, the down to earth, the authentic. It is significant that certain genres promoting myths of authenticity (country, folk, blues, etc.) place much greater store on birth names for performers than genres more concerned with the construction of identity, with countering so-called "mainstream values", or in exposing myths of realism (dance genres, DJ music, rap, etc.). In terms of collective names, there are certain ironic examples. Flowers of Romance, Pink Fairies, 10,000 Maniacs and Violent Femmes expose the distance between the denoted and the connoted. But most collective names suggest a unified choice of authoring has been made; in other words, the denoted and the connoted are closely aligned. Megadeth, the Pale Fountains, Daisy Chainsaw and Metallica sound how the names suggest they should. Equally, artwork, album titles and even literary fonts are all similarly authored to present a collective identity allowing for effective marketing and tribal identity.

A glimpse back over the years focusing upon Ian Anderson, front man, main author and leader of Jethro Tull, sheds light on the naming process and its connotations for authorship. Jethro Tull was founded in 1967 and finally ended as a recording and touring entity in 2011. The band grew out of other outfits, and it has always been claimed, not least by Anderson himself, that their booking agency named the band (that of an eighteenth-century agricultural innovator) after several other names had been used to help gain bookings (Anderson, 2014; Graff, 2014). It just happened that Jethro Tull was the name being adopted at the time of the band's critical breakthrough, so it stuck. Such is Anderson's centrality to the band that, for many, he *was* the band, with some fans in America assuming that Jethro Tull was Anderson's real name: "After years of being addressed by fans as 'Jethro' or even 'Mr. Tull' I have learned to accept and smile at the reflection of my alter ego" (Anderson, 2014). This band achieved global success, particularly in the 1970s and 1980s, despite line-ups proving relatively unstable. At the core remained Anderson, accompanied for many years by guitarist Martin Barre. Many other players worked with Anderson for extended periods, but certainly for most fans, the only indispensable element was Anderson—a clear demonstration of auteur theory. According to an unnamed source, after the album *Stormwatch* (1979), Anderson was left with just Barre in the band after a number of departures.

Anderson wanted the next project to be a solo album and drew largely upon guest musicians. However, his label pressured him into releasing it under the Jethro Tull name, presumably for commercial reasons to cash in on the prominence of the band over Anderson's own name. It was released with the name *A*, paradoxically, as the master tapes for his mooted solo album were marked as such, standing for Anderson (anon, 2014a). The album had a more contemporary, synthetic feel compared to former albums and was not received well by fans.

From 1982, the band resumed their more folk-based path, and Anderson's first true solo album, *Walk into Light*, was released in 1983. This was again a far more programmed and electronic album than Tull's sound but could now be judged in its own terms as part of the Ian Anderson brand-name oeuvre. From this point, several more Jethro Tull albums were released to varying degrees of success and acclaim, ending with *The Jethro Tull Christmas Album* in 2003. More Ian Anderson solo albums were released in the period from 1995 to 2014. Typically, Anderson's solo work was more acoustic, instrumental, made greater use of various flutes and showed a growing interest in "world music". In comparison, Tull albums were heavier and rockier, culminating in their unlikely award for Best Hard Rock/Metal Performance Vocal or Instrumental at the Grammy Awards in 1988 (Ibid: 2014). However, by the time of the release of *Homo Erraticus* in 2014, there was little difference between Anderson's solo music and that of later period Jethro Tull. In 2012, a follow-up to 1972's *Thick as a Brick* was released, but as an Anderson solo album. Both this work and 2014's *Homo Erraticus* allowed Anderson to write under the nom de plume Gerald Bostock, a fictional character who has aged since 1972 and in 2014 "chronicles the weird imaginings of one Ernest T. Paritt" (Anderson, 2014).

Anderson's last two solo albums have proven his most successful, in terms of chart positions, reaching the top 20 in both the UK and Germany. What this chronology indicates is the gradual shift in brand-selling power from the title Jethro Tull to that of Ian Anderson. Jethro Tull had more authorial etymological status than Ian Anderson in 1983, but now the position is reversed, especially with Tull no longer releasing new material. In view of Anderson's long-standing business nous and the fact that his work is copyrighted and published under the heading "The Ian Anderson Group of Companies", it seems naïve not to judge the replacement of the Jethro Tull name with Anderson's own as a shrewd commercial move. In Anderson's words, "It's a body of work I rather think is now kind of historical, since the weight of it lies back in the 70s and 80s in terms of volume. And I rather think it's nice to kind of leave that as legacy" (cited in Graff, 2014). Thus, the legacy recordings will continue to sell as back catalogue while newer material is freed from the connotations of the name—despite the huge musical connections between Anderson and his retired band. This example indicates both the ability of the market to absorb changes of nomenclature and also reflects the decline in the band-name-as-brand in recent years. A more detailed analysis of one historically specific genre will indicate how deeply the symbolism of etymological authorship runs in popular music in what might be termed the "post-rock era".

Etymology and Dance Music

Following the emergence of what became known as "acid house" (essentially an authorial misnomer, in some senses) in the UK around 1987 to 1988, dance music underwent one of its periods of high-profile mainstream success in Europe. Various terms cover the genres that emerged (*were named*) in the period around 1988 to 1992, among them were acid house, techno, hardcore, rave or, more simply, dance. Until members of the industry managed to recuperate author figures and images with the promotion of both Britpop and grunge in the early 1990s, dance music in this period was relatively faceless, being built upon both the figure of the DJ and the loosely defined collective. In terms of the latter, the etymologies associated with such outfits—Nomad, Orbital, Plutonic, Sunsonic, Xpansions, Isotonik, Energise, Altern-8, Technotronic, Digital Orgasm, N-Joi—reflect both this amorphous, nonspecific identity and also the connoted feelings of communal bliss associated with drugs such as MDMA, or ecstasy (see Redhead, 1990).

Most of the above-named acts had short-lived success, but the dance scene did give rise to the more durable career paths of DJs such as Danny Rampling, Paul Oakenfold and Carl Cox. In addition to the many DJs retaining their own birth names, numerous others adopted stage names, allowing them to assume authorial personae and, in some cases, genuine author images. Names would include John Pleased Wimmin, 2 Many DJs, Skrillex, Dangermau5, etc. What is perhaps more interesting is the phenomenon whereby a DJ changes names to suit different styles of release. Straw notes that Norman (born Quentin) Cook became

> Pizzaman when making techno-house (and) Fatboy Slim when releasing big-beat records . . . By changing names as he shifts genres . . . Cook . . . refuses to build the obvious points of continuity between these different practices, to let each new style add to the asset value of his name over time. In other periods, or in other styles of music, this would be commercially foolhardy, but in the field of contemporary dance music it is strategically appropriate.
>
> (cited in Horner and Swiss, 2000: 207)

Since 2000, Cook's performing names have proliferated, with Martin James (2002) noting the following additions to his catalogue of author names: Brighton Port Authority, Mighty Dub Katz and Beats International. It should be noted that some of these names consisted of Cook working in a collective manner with others. In addition, and very much going against received wisdom that suggests that author names need to be stable in order to market and promote their product, Cook has achieved great commercial success: first, as a relatively low-image author; second, as an author often constructing his music on the basis of numerous elements sampled from other authors; and, third, while operating under a wide variety of monikers.

More recently, Stuart Price has trodden a similar path to Cook, albeit with an even greater variety of names and associated styles. Price is also known as Les Rhythmes Digitales, Zoot Woman, Paper Faces, Man With Guitar, Thin White Duke, Jacques Lu Cont, SDP, Pour Hoomme, Tracques and Crystal Pepsi (anon, 2014b). Again, some of these names are collective projects, and despite being principally known as an electronic writer and producer, Price also works within the rock terrain and has produced both dance, electronic and rock/pop acts. As his biography notes, many name choices have an ironic, punning or mischievous edge, with Price assuming the role of a French musician/DJ during a period of success for the likes of Air and Daft Punk.

As with Cook, this bewildering number of author names has not prevented Price from gaining great commercial success in a variety of roles. Perhaps the speed of communication made possible by the internet and globalized media allows for far greater flexibility and mutability in authorial etymology.

Summary

In the early 1990s, Keith Negus's research into the workings of A&R departments in major record companies showed how the "organic", gigging rock band was prioritized and valued over the dance or rap act (1992). Not only are these distinctions at least partly effaced in the modern music scene, but also the whole infrastructure of record labels, A&R departments, the music press, record retailers, etc., has been totally reconfigured. Top-down hierarchies based upon traditional working and marketing practices have been mainly replaced by what we might term a more rhizomatic approach. In a sense, this is the manifestation of the most recent tendencies found in Jacques Attali's historical overview of the political economy of music, what he termed "composition" (1985). Although originally written in 1977, the author seems to preface many of the democratizing possibilities made manifest by the digital world of communication. Certainly, the World Wide Web was aptly named in terms of the ways in which musical ideas are now diffused. Many theorists have articulated these developments in great detail, and it is only necessary to note the implications for authorship at this juncture. What I have termed the "hegemonies of rock" have been challenged by new technologies, the partial displacement of the band as the prime authoring unit in popular music, and the widespread acceptance of newer models of authorship, composition and dissemination. But as is so often the case, this has not resulted in the replacement of one paradigm with another, but merely within a rich proliferation and fragmentation that the essentially eclectic nature of popular music has countenanced.

Ahonen has already broached the burgeoning critical field of online fan-based critical communities at some length (2008), and as the technologies improve, social media will continue to have an impact upon authorship debates. As the hard-copy world of traditional music journalism continues to decline, in terms of both volume sales and influence, online communities increasingly map out the critical terrain. For Ahonen, "online discussion forums and other web communities provide interesting material that can serve as new points of departure for future studies on music authorship" (2008: 198). As one small, concluding example demonstrates, online comments and critical dialogue can often descend into mere vitriol, but even this aspect can still be viewed as engaging, albeit on a superficial level with authorship issues. If we explore the online comments provoked by the release of a new album by Swedish group Opeth, ostensibly trivial posts actually tap into far more profound aesthetical debates.

Opeth is an interesting case study, as a result of the band's longevity and its musical eclecticism. In addition to producing music (at various points) that spans the metal-based (sub)genres of death metal, prog metal, jazz metal and progressive rock, the band also includes the auteur figure Mikael Åkerfeldt—the only constant musician and the principal songwriter, vocalist, lyricist and guitarist. As well as noting that fans of metal-based music are particularly committed and passionate about their chosen genre, online comments continually centre on discussions of and assumptions/mythologies connected to authorship. They exemplify the startlingly individual nature of authorship debates, wherein an album that moves too far away from the authorial template can be castigated by one fan and lauded by another. This relates to how far any act is able to diverge from its assumed, authored path. For some fans, the band can do whatever they like, in terms of music style, but for others, these musical shifts result in comments that suggest that the music no longer represents the values contained within the author name Opeth. Equally, for some, Åkerfeldt essentially *is* the band and can take it in whatever direction he chooses, whereas for others, his dictatorial authorship has resulted in the ruination of the act's critical legacy. For some, the band's direction on *Pale Communion* (2014) has become too "proggy", and they bemoan the lack of "death growl" vocals found on earlier, heavier albums such as *Watershed* (2008), whereas others find the new direction to be a positive dimension. Regardless of the aggression implicit in online comments, this critical inter-fan intensity again signals the fundamental and ongoing significance of the authorship debate. Many fans feel that they have a proprietorial and authoritative connection to the band; they *own* the music. As I stated in the Introduction, *authorship really matters.*

Bibliography

Ahonen, Laura (2008) *Constructing Authorship in Popular Music: Artists, Media and Stardom*, Milton Keynes: VDM Verlag.

Anderson, Ian (2014) Sleeve notes accompanying *Homo Erraticus*.

Anon. (2014a) "Jethro Tull (band)", accessed 22 July, http://en.wikipedia.org/wiki/Jethro-Tull-band.

Anon. (2014b) "Stuart Price", accessed 15 July, http://en.wikipedia.org/wiki/Stuart-Price.

Attali, Jacques (1985) *Noise: the Political Economy of Music*, Minneapolis: University of Minnesota Press.

Attias, Bernardo, Anna Gavanas & Hillegonda Rietveld (2013) *DJ Culture in the Mix: Power, Technology and Social Change in Electronic Dance Music*, London: Bloomsbury.

Auslander, Philip (2008) *Liveness: Performance in a Mediatized Culture*, London: Routledge.

Baker, Lindsay (1989) "Funki Like a Dread", *the Face*, April, pp 60–64.

Barnet, Richard & Larry Burriss (2001) *Controversies of the Music Industry*, Westport: Greenwood Press.

Bates, Eliot (2004) "Glitches, Bugs and Hisses: The Degeneration of Musical Recordings and the Contemporary Musical Work", in Washburne, Chris, & Maiken Derno (eds.), *Bad Music, the Music We Love to Hate*, New York: Routledge, pp 275–293.

Batey, Angus (2014) "Back to the Future", *Guardian Film & Music Guide*, 29 May, pp 6–7.

Bennett, Andy (2006) "Even Better than the Real Thing? Understanding the Tribute Band Phenomenon", in Homan, Shane, et al. (eds.), *Access All Eras: Tribute Bands and Global Pop Culture*, pp 19–31.

Borthwick, Stuart & Ron Moy (2004) *Popular Music Genres: An Introduction*, Edinburgh: Edinburgh University Press.

Cascone, Kim (2004) "The Aesthetics of Failure: 'Post-Digital' Tendencies in Contemporary Computer Music", in Cox, Christoph & Daniel Warner (eds.), *Audio Culture: Readings in Modern Music*, New York: Continuum, pp 392–398.

Cutler, Chris (2004) "Plunderphonia", in Cox, Christoph & Daniel Warner (eds.), *Audio Culture: Readings in Modern Music*, New York: Continuum, pp 138–156.

Driscoll, Kevin & Joshua Diaz (2009) "Endless Loop: A Brief History of Chiptunes", *Transformative Works and Cultures, Vol. 2*, accessed 14-05-14, http://journal.transformativeworks.org/index.php/twc/rt/printerFriendly/96/94.

Elborough, Travis (2009) *The Vinyl Countdown: The Album from LP to iPod and Back Again*, Berkeley: Soft Skull.

Fabbri, Franco (1982a) "A Theory of Musical Genres: Two Applications", in Horn, David & Philip Tagg (eds.), *Popular Music Perspectives: Papers from the First International Conference on Popular Music Research*, Exeter: IASPM, pp 52–81.

Fabbri, Franco (1982b) "What Kind of Music?", in Horn, David & Richard Middleton (eds.), *Popular Music 2: Theory and Method*, Cambridge: Cambridge University Press, pp 131–143.

Feuer, Jane (1987) "Genre Study and Television", in Allen, Robert (ed.), *Channels of Discourse: Television and Contemporary Criticism*, London: Routledge, pp 113–133.

Frith, Simon (1981) *Sound Effects*, New York: Pantheon.

Frith, Simon (1988) "Video Pop: Picking up the Pieces", in Frith, Simon (ed.), *Facing the Music*, New York: Pantheon.

du Gay, Paul et al. (1996) *Doing Cultural Studies: The Story of the Sony Walkman*, London: Sage.

Graff, Gary (2014) "Ian Anderson Releases New Solo Album, Talks 'End' of Jethro Tull", *Billboard*, 14 April, accessed 22-07-14,http://www.billboard.com/articles/news/6052275/ian-anderson-solo-album-homo-erra.

Gunkel, David (2012) "What Does It Matter Who Is Speaking? Authorship, Authority and the Mashup", *Popular Music and Society*, 35(1), pp 71–91.

Holt, Fabian (2007) *Genre in Popular Music*, Chicago: University of Chicago Press.

Homan, Shane (ed.) (2006) *Access All Eras: Tribute Bands and Global Pop Culture*, Berkshire, Open University Press.

Horn, David & Richard Middleton (eds.) (1982) *Popular Music 2: Theory and Method*, Cambridge: Cambridge University Press.

Horn, David & Philip Tagg (eds.) (1982) *Popular Music Perspectives: Papers From the First International Conference on Popular Music Research*, Exeter: IASPM.

Horner, Bruce & Thomas Swiss (eds.) (2000) *Key Terms in Popular Music and Culture*, Oxford: Blackwell.

Hugill, Andrew (2012) *The Digital Musician*, London: Routledge.

James, Martin (2002) *Fatboy Slim: Funk Soul Brother*, London: Sanctuary.

Jones, Dylan (2006) *iPod, Therefore I Am*, London: Phoenix.

Jones, Simon (1988) *Black Culture, White Youth: Reggae Tradition from Jamaica to UK*, London: Palgrave Macmillan.

Leydon, Rebecca (2010) "Recombinant Style Topics: The Past and Future of Sampling", in Covach, John & Mark Spicer (eds.), *Sounding Out Pop*, Ann Arbor: University of Michigan Press, pp 193–213.

McCall, Michael (2004) "Pro-Tools", *Nashville Scene*, accessed 20-05-14, http://www.nashvillescene.com/nashville/pro-tools/Content?oid=1190101.

Morton, John (1988) "Editorial", *Musician* Magazine, March, p 3.

Moy, Ron (1992) *Dirty Notes: Making Links between Popular Music and a Postmodern Aesthetics*, unpublished PhD thesis, Liverpool: University of Liverpool, July.

Moy, Ron (2000) *An Analysis of the Position and Status of Sound Ratio in Contemporary Society*, Lampeter: Edwin Mellen Press.

Negus, Keith (1992) *Producing Pop: Culture and Conflict in the Popular Music Industry*, London: Edward Arnold.

Negus, Keith & Michael Pickering (2004) *Creativity, Communication and Cultural Value*, London: Sage.

Osborne, Richard (2012) *Vinyl: A History of the Analogue Record*, Farnham: Ashgate.

Petridis, Alexis (2014) "Neil Young: *A Letter Home* review—a Gloriously Gloomy Album of Lo-Fi Covers", *the Guardian*, 22 May, accessed 4-06-14, www.theguardian.com/music/2014/may/22/neil-young-a-letter-home-review.

Redhead, Steve (1990) *The End of the Century Party: Youth and Pop Towards 2000*, Manchester: Manchester University Press.

Ressner, Jay (1990) "Sampling Amok", *Rolling Stone*, June, pp 103–105.

Reynolds, Simon (1990) *Blissed Out: The Raptures of Rock*, London: Serpent's Tail.

Reynolds, Simon (2004) "Noise", in Cox, Christoph & Daniel Warner (eds.), *Audio Culture: Readings in Modern Music*, New York: Continuum, pp 55–58.

Reynolds, Simon (2007) *Bring the Noise: 20 Years of Writing about Hip Rock and Hip-Hop*, London: Faber & Faber.

Sangild, Torben (2004) "Glitch: The Beauty of Malfunction", in Washburne, Christopher & Maiken Derno, *Bad Music: The Music We Love to Hate*, London: Routledge, pp 257–276.

Shuker, Roy (2002) *Key Concepts in Popular Music*, London: Routledge.

Straw, Will (2000) "Authorship", in Horner, Bruce & Thomas Swiss (eds.) (2000), *Key Terms in Popular Music and Culture*, Oxford: Blackwell, pp 199–208.

Toop, David (1989) "Noise in the New Age", *the Face*, July, pp 72–76.

Toynbee, Jason (2000) *Making Popular Music: Musicians, Creativity and Institutions*, London: Bloomsbury.

Treacy, Christopher (2007) "Pitch Adjusting Software Brings Studio Tricks", *the Boston Herald*, 19 February, p 32.

Willis, Paul (1978) *Profane Culture*, London: Routledge.

Young, Neil (2013) *Waging Heavy Peace*, London: Penguin.

Audio-Visual Sources

Abba (1979) "Gimme! Gimme! Gimme! (A Man after Midnight)".

Ian Anderson (1983) *Walk into Light*.

    (2012) *Thick as a Brick 2*.

    (2014) *Homo Erraticus*.

Björk (1997) *Homogenic*, "Pluto".

    (2001) "Cocoon".

    (2007) *Volta*.

Coldplay (2005) "Talk".

Jay-Z (2009) "D.O.A. (Death of Auto-Tune)".

Jethro Tull (1972) *Thick as a Brick*.

    (1979) *Stormwatch*.

    (1980) *A*.

    (1987) *Crest of a Knave*.

    (2003) *The Jethro Tull Christmas Album*.

Kraftwerk (1981) "Computer Love".

Laura Mvula (2012) *Sing to the Moon*, "Father, Father", "Green Garden", "That's Alright".

    (2013) Versions of "Green Garden" from the Graham Norton Show (February 8), the Bowery Ballroom (June 26) and the Hype Hotel (August 8), accessed from You-Tube, 20-5-14.

M4SONIC (2012) "Virus", accessed from YouTube, 20-5-14. My thanks to Chris Cawthorne for making me aware of this clip.

Madonna (2005) "Hung Up".

Opeth (2008) *Watershed*.

    (2014) *Pale Communion*.

Neil Young (2014) *A Letter Home*.

CODA

The Searcher and the Sought

In this summary of both the process and findings of my research, I am initially returning to Garber's quotation that prefaced the Introduction (2008: 28). She suggests that in looking for an author, we actually reveal more about ourselves than about our quarry. Thus, an exploration of authorship becomes a metaphor or a displacement activity for an investigation of the self. This being the case—and it is a position I also hold—what can be said about the process that illuminates this self-exploration? More importantly, how might this impact the exploration of others who may be undergoing research into the same topic or in popular music more generally. Initially, I beg the reader's indulgence in delving back into personal history in the hope that broader conclusions can be drawn.

At some point in the mid-1970s, having seen and enjoyed the film *Taxi Driver* (Scorsese, 1976), I was having a discussion with a friend about whether we should go and see another film by the same director, *Mean Streets* (Scorsese, 1973). This film predated *Taxi Driver* but was being rereleased in the wake of that film's critical and commercial impact. My vague memory suggests that my friend indicated that we should see *Mean Streets* because it was another Scorsese film, to which my reply was to the effect that surely it was a Robert De Niro film. This difference in apportioning authorship goes right to the core of debates on the topic within popular music studies. All we have to do is consider how films and music albums differ in terms of how they are referenced; the film by the name of the director and the album via the name of the performing act. But that is a side issue. At the time, I was responding in an unscholarly manner, yet unwittingly railing against the canonization process that results in a hierarchy of aesthetics underpinning an Establishment view of art, culture and creativity. Clearly, this is an example of naïveté and even ignorance stumbling upon and provoking a profound, philosophical debate.

A few years down the line, as a still-untutored autodidact attending art house films at the *National Film Theatre* in London, my critical stance would have doubtless changed. The cult of the auteur was deeply inscribed as I sought out films from the oeuvre of Ingmar Bergman, Fritz Lang and Douglas Sirk, to name but a few. As a long-standing lover of history, biography would have held great sway as I searched for stylistic continuities and connections with the lives of the directors as a means of arriving at a deeper understanding of the auteur's work. Strong elements of this aesthetics remain with me to this day. It is important to maintain that newer ways of thinking do not wholly displace older ways, but merely problematize them. For the last few years, I have been exploring the novels of a now-forgotten writer active and very popular between the 1920s and 1950s—Francis Brett Young. I was made aware of this writer by another "hero" of mine, the comedian and author Stewart Lee. In his book (2010), Lee recounts his pleasurable experiences reading Young's novels set in the border area known historically as Mercia. The authority of Lee (I admire his work and so I *trust* him) added to my preexistent love of the English/Welsh Marches and encouraged me to explore the work of another author and now hero. To date, I have read over twenty of his books. I willingly make biographical connections between Brett Young's life and his work, finding pleasure in this traditional form of literary analysis yet knowing that I am also mythologizing both the man and the oeuvre. So, old critical methods are problematized but still willingly and self-consciously adopted.

Mythology, post-structuralism, deconstruction, hegemony, postmodernism—all of these weighty concepts deeply affected me during my belated years of scholarship and still inform the way I think and write. Of all the schools of criticism investigated during undergraduate and postgraduate studies, it was postmodernism that seemed particularly to strike a chord with me. It seemed a playful and entertaining way to account for the theoretical contradictions, inconsistencies and fragmentations that all of us wrestle with. It also moved beyond the dogmas of established critical schools. Of course, it was flawed, but it gave its acolytes the thrill of having your critical cake and eating it. Postmodernism was mischievous. When others criticized it for being trivial, ironic, shallow, lacking an ideological credo, and being reactionary and nostalgic, the postmodernist's response could most fittingly be "yeah, so?" It was all of these things, but it was also capable of engendering radical ideas, being challenging, multiplying ways of seeing and being self-aware in the process. Thus, it allows for the self-conscious construction of hero figures but never allows us to forget the mythologizing processes at work. Conversely, it allows us to forward the construction of the listener-figure as authorial. At a stroke, it is canonical, anti-canonical and deconstructive of the discourses surrounding canonization.

When Jean-François Lyotard (1984) talked about incredulity toward meta-narratives, he encouraged skepticism toward belief systems and belief itself. I believe (!) this further encourages an interest in bricolage, pluralism and interdisciplinarity that breaks down rigid distinctions of race, class, genre and ethnicity. In my postgraduate thesis, this encouraged me to construct a postmodern aesthetics that moved beyond the binaries of pop versus rock, black versus white, art versus commerce, technology versus creativity, authentic versus inauthentic, listener versus creator. Looking back at this work, I now realize that much of what I was actually dealing with was implicitly about theories, concepts and roles within the world of authorship. Authorship can itself be viewed as a meta-narrative, and in some manifestations, it is a restrictive and damaging one. Ahonen states, "The celebration of auteurism thus works as another means of legitimating the generally shared assumptions as to what kinds of music *should be valued more highly than others* (my emphasis)" (2008: 101). In simple terms, my issue lies not with an individual's choice of what to like or dislike, but rather within the myths of what one *should* like, which takes away autonomy and free will, leaving us the victim of hegemonic forces.

The Author and Epistemology: Where Does Meaning Reside?

In common with Eisenberg's construction of the phonologist (1987) and post-structuralism's construction of the reader as author, prominent scholars in the field of popular music studies have adopted a similar epistemological rationale. For Frith, "listening itself is a performance: to understand how musical pleasure, meaning, and evaluation work, we have to understand how, as listeners we perform the music for ourselves" (1998b: 203–204). Moore asks, "To what extent does the sound that the musician makes belong to that musician? . . . Can this be determined from within the text itself?" Before he adds, "Meaning is not embedded in the music listened to, but is discovered in the act of listening" (2012: 261, 265). How, then, does the "active listener" approach authorship and epistemology in an empirical sense?

In his close reading of what he terms the textural shape of music in the "soundbox" (Ibid: 30–44), Moore suggests that listening experiences are contingent upon factors of technology, space and place. To these we might add the contextual factors of time and background knowledge. Most of us will doubtless have had the experience of hearing a musical element for the first time despite already listening to a particular piece hundreds of times. This leads us all to such existential questions as "If I didn't hear it, was it always there?" Of course, once heard, this musical fragment will always register in future encounters by very virtue of the fact that it seemed to appear at a specific moment rather than having an immanent presence. It is thus noticed more—it can never be "written out" of the experience. Therefore, accumulated musical knowledge is not only incremental but also random or chaotic.

It has been difficult during the course of this research not to become a little obsessed with the topic, seeing the concept of authorship raised in some unlikely ways and through some unlikely means. The occurrence of listening to David Bowie's "Space Oddity" (1969) via a car sound system with one faulty stereo channel made me question how far we can take the issue of authorship and epistemology. I had long been aware of the prevalence of the main and harmony vocal line on this song, aided by the wide stereo separation that was such a feature of this era, but to have the main vocal line mostly erased by a faulty piece of equipment brought the distinction into much sharper emphasis. In the process, my empirical experience of the song was transformed. But can this random experience really count as one of authoring on the part of the active listener? A response to this question is dependent upon many factors, but, yet again, questions of authorship *speak us*. Posing the question is perhaps more important than any answers provoked by such circumstances. Authorship always asks questions of us.

To this listening experience must be added issues relating to the individual assumption of where meaning resides: is it within the lyrics, vocal expressions, image, music, arrangement, production or a combination of all of these elements? Lastly, how does biography intrude upon epistemology? How do we answer the conundrum posed by Moore: "To what extent does the sound that the musician makes belong to that musician" (2012: 261)?

Case Study: Joni Mitchell "Little Green" (1971)

I would first have become aware of Joni Mitchell when her single "Big Yellow Taxi" was a UK hit in 1970. I cannot recollect the first time I heard an album by Mitchell, or even which album it was, but probably it was *Blue* (1971). I certainly recall hearing tracks from the album in a "head shop" in Newquay in 1973 and thus would have become familiar with the track "Little Green". The singer-songwriter genre has always placed great store upon the centrality of lyrics, often in a confessional/autobiographical register. And, certainly, at around this time, I could probably have recited complete song lyrics, even complete album lyrics from the likes of Cat Stevens and Elton John. However, the question of whether lyrics hold the key to unlocking meaning is problematic. In his essay "Why Do Songs Have Words?" (1988a: 105–128, originally written in 1980), Frith notes how content analysis can shift, historically and in terms of disciplinarity, from lyrics to music, context, marketing techniques and industry considerations. Certainly, any of us who have taught in the field soon learn that some students will focus upon lyrical content as an epistemological source far more than others. What this preamble is trying to establish is that the search for meaning is diffuse and contingent upon many factors. Doubtless, in my youth, I would have subscribed to the notion that meaning resides within language, and having no recourse to understand the language of production, music or the culture industry, the language of words would have been my repository of comprehension. But even this connection between words and meaning has no absolute unity.

Despite working on the premise that, in the past, words equaled meaning for me, it transpires that I never actually *understood* "Little Green", but this is not to say that no pleasure was derived from it. Other Mitchell songs were understood, lyrically, but this one was not. Again, memory does not permit me to recall when I was told what "Little Green" was "really about", but it may have been on reading Brian Hinton's biography published in 2000. This example of rock journalism follows the familiar pattern of seeking epistemological closure through two principal sources: lyrical analysis and biographical observations from both the artist and others with some connection. Hinton's initial observation is intriguing, as he describes the song as "almost impenetrable, although obviously about Joni's lost daughter" (2000: 129). Elsewhere in the book, Mitchell's early pregnancy, resulting in her giving up the child for adoption, is noted (Ibid: 12). Strangely, Mitchell and her daughter were reunited after many decades in a similar fashion to that of Hinton reuniting me with the "true" meaning of the song. I cannot quote these lyrics in any detail, without obtaining permission from the owners of the copyright—another authorial dimension worthy of consideration! Of course, once you read the lyric in light of this biographical information, it all becomes obvious, or at least most of the lyrical content fits into the artist's life narrative. But again, this begs the question that I posed earlier, if you do not notice an element within a recording, was it always there? It depends on how we approach epistemology. One point that cannot be overlooked is that it is no longer possible ever to read "Little Green" in former terms once we are made aware of the biographical narrative. One can choose to discount or overlook this data, in what has been termed an *oppositional reading*, but its presence in the interpretive memory cannot be denied. Another question posed is to reflect upon another semiotic phrase—an *aberrant decoding*. Is the interpreter, when not privileged to the "full story" behind the song, wrong in terms of constructing the incorrect or incomplete meaning, or even in constructing no meaning at all? Can sonic pleasure ever be constructed without an epistemological linguistic or biographical foundation?

A way beyond such impasses may lie, yet again, in the concept of the chronotope. This will allow for a constructed individual interpretation that is always in a state of flux, contingent upon myriad contributory factors (time, place and context). It will allow for any fresh biographical evidence to be added and incorporated into a multilayered reading that does not deny or efface earlier stages in the search for, or indeed *denial* of, understanding that a more ontological, sensual or visceral connection may have engendered. The authorship of the artist or the biographer thus becomes part of the sequential authorship of the reader. "Little Green" can be seen to offer levels of interpretation that are not the *property* of any party.

It now seems clear to me that many elements of postmodernism's fractured and inconsistent world view chime with the anti-canonical, fragmented view of authorship that I have been attempting to expound in this book. In answer to the question of how this research has changed me, I would say, in essence, not much. However, it has given me reasons for why and how, in underlying ways, I have remained the same person. I reflect back upon the teenager reading compositional credits on album sleeves and labels, who even then, in an unscholarly fashion, was fascinated by the fact that Deep Purple and Black Sabbath would credit all compositions on early albums collectively (for instance, *Deep Purple in Rock* [1970] and *Master of Reality* [1971]) while other bands would not. What did this mean and what did this signal? In terms of Black Sabbath, the group credit was a symbol of the band's collectivism. It actually glossed over the fact that most of their lyrics were written by the bassist and that the lead vocalist contributed hardly any words until their fifth album (see Osborne and Rosen, 2001). But the band actively chose to be represented as a compositional unit. As is ever the case, this additional information forces a reappraisal of the authorship question.

Time has given me a referent—authorship—through which to answer questions that reveal the critical self. In echoes of pianist Glenn Gould's retirement from live performance, I gave up attending concerts many years ago, due in part to issues with amplification and sound quality, but also as a result of the phonologist in me not wishing to share my authoring experience with others. On my own, listening to recordings on headphones, I could *become* the band or the performer and *write* the text. In a live setting, I found this impossible. With the technology of the CD or iPod, I could write my version of the album and sequence the songs, whereas in the live venue, I could not "fast forward" through less-favored pieces. In short, my authoring processes were compromised by the concert experience. As a listener, I had the control/plaisir to create my own jouissance!

In my obsession with some of the more esoteric manifestations of authorship (accreditation, age, etymology), I am very aware of the more obvious elements that have been overlooked in this study. Even within this partial reading of authorship issues and roles, I can also identify those facets of my character that rail against the hegemonies of stardom, honours and awards, even if I never fully escape (or desire to escape) the pull of hero-worship: in summary, *authority*, as much as authorship, has been put under scrutiny. I agree with Ahonen that "the author remains" (2008: 203), and there are many sound, justifiable commercial and aesthetical reasons for this. Authorship and the author figure serve many personal, social and capitalist needs. But this important figure is a social construct. If we grant the author auteur status, then this should be the result of active, self-conscious individual strategies, not through an unquestioning acceptance of hegemony and hierarchy.

What aspects of authorship have I overlooked? In particular, aspects of fandom, video mediation, performance, new technologies, the concept of genius and the role of the DJ have not been given much space. Some of these aspects have already been engaged with by other scholars, whose work this book is indebted to. All I can conclude is that there is still much work to be done in the area of popular music authorship, and this book can only offer a small contribution. As is invariably the case, the more you research a topic, the more you realize how much still needs to be done.

The Future for Authorship in Popular Music

It is always tempting for us to look into the future as well as reflecting upon the past. However, this practice is full of pitfalls. In absolutist terms, claims of the death of the author have the same dubious status as those that have circulated in pop journalism relating to the death of the single, the death of the album, the death of the band or the death of the well-crafted song. Particularly, during assumed periods of great change, the temptation is to adopt a year zero approach to future developments. In the early 1990s, many would claim that a sea change was taking place in pop, mindful of the rise of dance culture and the status of the DJ. Nelson George entitled a book *The Death of Rhythm and Blues* (1988) in which he bemoaned the decline of traditional songwriting. He was premature. Rhythm and blues did not die, it evolved, and the charts continue to be full of traditionally crafted pop songs now constructed via new, virtual technologies. The old meets the new; the one does not replace the other. For Garrett, "if the pop hero is no more, perhaps that's because the pop group is fading fast. The old group idea . . . is being replaced by new, more flexible collectives" (1991: 51). Subsequent events have only supported the *partial* displacement of the band by individual DJs, rappers and those looser collectives Garrett indicated. But the band still survives and thrives. Whenever the Rolling Stones embark on a world tour, they are guaranteed sell-out crowds and gross figures at least the equal of any other act. Similarly, traditional bands such as U2 and Coldplay remain hugely popular. Most recently, One Direction have topped the US album charts with their first three albums—the first British/Irish act to do so (Ellis-Petersen, 2014b: 11). Of course, the industry calls them a "boy band" to reflect the assumed lower authorial status of an act that is principally a vocal group, but the five members still work together as part of a musical unit; their authorship is merely manifested differently to more so-called "organic" outfits. It is doubtless that the "rockist" world would prefer them to all pick up guitars, but different audiences and markets exhibit different authorial values, and these only proliferate over time. Authorship values stand today in disunity and flux.

The single track survives but increasingly as a download or a streamed product rather than in some concrete form. The album form has similarly partially mutated into a playlist, but to suggest that this indicates its "death knell" (Ellis-Petersen, 2014a: 13) is shortsighted. As with the issue of the band's status, these are evolutionary, not revolutionary, changes. The world of popular music offers endless possibilities for mutability, and the concept of authorship mutates alongside such changes. But new developments are incremental and supplementary; old ways and old values survive in tandem. Furthermore, we must not fall into the trap of assuming that these changes are solely driven by youth or new technologies. Physical sales of music will survive. Despite the huge impact of computer-based gaming, live human interaction via fantasy board games featuring dice and scale models such as *World of Warcraft* and *Warhammer 40,000* continue to flourish (see elementgames.co.uk). The old thrives alongside the new. How do most physical gamers learn about painting and building their models? They learn partly via physical interaction, partly from print sources and partly online. This seems to me a metaphor for how people learn about and consume popular music in the contemporary age.

The future for authorship in popular music will witness a further fragmentation and challenging of traditional, hierarchical, hegemonic values. According to Ahonen, "one might also venture to say that the author's role, as a uniting factor, has become even more essential in the era of fragmented (post-) authorship, when various authorial constructions are struggling to coexist" (2008: 203).

Popular music is a chaotic enterprise often working within rigid structures, stereotypes and assumptions. Within its bounds lie the implicit contradictions of authorship. The form has never been just about notions of the romantic, individual author, but neither is it solely about collective authorship, and we must continue to be wary about pronouncements that do not recognize the possibility for future authorial shifts.

In 2004, Negus and Pickering sought to challenge romantic notions of individual expression by forwarding the concept of collective authorship, and in general terms, they were right to do so. However, they substantiated their position by arguing that an individual cannot create and exhibit a film. Subsequent history, new technologies and the possibilities of the internet have proven them wrong. Few foresaw the transformations wrought in authorship by the iPad, the tablet or the smartphone app. The firmament can only change in the light of new technologies, which are difficult to imagine. Much the same applies to developing fields of popular music creation, production and distribution. All distinctions and binary divides are rendered unstable. As Ahonen concludes, "the boundaries that once separated the role of musical author from that of the listener, or the professional music maker from the amateur, are becoming more and more indistinct" (2008: 201).

Authorship issues allow for the construction of a micro-politics, in my case encouraging an aging cynic disillusioned with conventional politics and the power of hegemonic forces to access a degree of idealism: in this book, my opinions on authorship doubtless account for the strong representation of female auteurs and of various ethnicities. Their inclusion transcends notions of mere political correctness by demonstrating how gendered struggles with authorship provide both empirical victories against hegemonic forces and the potential for further advances. When we combine the study of authorship with the experience of consuming popular music, our responses give us all the potential for a sharp insight into our own values, prejudices, connections with the transcendent and hopes for a future fairer world.

Bibliography

Ahonen, Laura (2008) *Constructing Authorship in Popular Music: Artists, Media and Stardom*, Milton Keynes: VDM Verlag.

Eisenberg, Evan (1987) *The Recording Angel*, London: Picador.

Ellis-Petersen, Hannah (2014a) "Playlist Sounds Death Knell of the Album Despite Fight Back by Musicians and Fans", *the Guardian*, 30 July, p 13.

Ellis-Petersen, Hannah (2014b) "Right Direction: Boy Band's Sales Triumph", *the Guardian*, 2 August, p 11.

Frith, Simon (1988) "Why Do Songs Have Words?" in *Music for Pleasure: Essays in the Sociology of Pop*, Cambridge: Polity.

Frith, Simon (1998a) *Performing Rites: On the Value of Popular Music*, Oxford: Oxford University Press.

Garber, Marjorie (2008) *Profiling Shakespeare*, Abingdon: Routledge.

Garrett, Sheryl (1991b) "Posse Power", *the Face*, March, pp 42–53.

George, Nelson (1988) *The Death of Rhythm and Blues*, London: Omnibus.

Hinton, Brian (2000) *Joni Mitchell: Both Sides Now—the Biography*, London: Sanctuary.

Lee, Stewart (2010) *How I Escaped My Certain Fate: The Life and Deaths of a Stand-Up Comedian*, London: Faber & Faber.

Lyotard, Jean-François (1984) *The Postmodern Condition*, Manchester: Manchester University Press.

Moore, Allan (2012) *Song Means: Analysing and Interpreting Recorded Popular Song*, Farnham: Ashgate.

Negus, Keith & Michael Pickering (2004) *Creativity, Communication and Cultural Value*, London: Sage.

Osborne, Ozzy & Steven Rosen (2001) *Black Sabbath*, London, Sanctuary.

Audio-Visual Sources

Black Sabbath (1971) *Master of Reality*.
David Bowie (1969) "Space Oddity".
Deep Purple (1970) *Deep Purple in Rock*.
Elementgames.co.uk.
Joni Mitchell (1970) "Big Yellow Taxi".
    (1971) *Blue*, "Little Green".

INDEX